INTERCOLONIAL ASPECTS OF AMERICAN CULTURE ON THE EVE OF THE REVOLUTION

INTERCOLONIAL ASPECTS OF AMERICAN CULTURE ON THE EVE OF THE REVOLUTION

With Special Reference to the Northern Towns

BY

MICHAEL KRAUS

OCTAGON BOOKS

A DIVISION OF FARRAR, STRAUS AND GIROUX

New York   1972

Copyright 1928, by Michael Kraus

Reprinted 1964
by special arrangement with Michael Kraus

Second Octagon printing 1972

OCTAGON BOOKS
A DIVISION OF FARRAR, STRAUS & GIROUX, INC.
19 Union Square West
New York, N.Y. 10003

LIBRARY OF CONGRESS CATALOG CARD NUMBER: 64-24838

ISBN 0-374-94636-1

Printed in U.S.A. by
NOBLE OFFSET PRINTERS, INC.
NEW YORK, N.Y. 10003

To
MY SISTER

PREFACE

A New York merchant, Gerard Beekman, when writing to his brother in May, 1767, of the great difficulty he had in collecting some debts from Connecticut customers, added that he saw " no prospect of getting anything from the best of them out of that dam'd country." The attitude that is indicated in these expressive words has undoubtedly influenced subsequent historical treatment of this period; it is taken for granted that mutual antagonism prevailed, or that the colonies were practically strangers, with few elements of unity.

Beekman's thought and language were echoed many times in the nineteenth century when the middle western farmers resented eastern domination; both thought and language are still very much alive. Yet, the recognition of such sectional hostility blinds no one to the essentially national character of the territory included in these United States. Of course no one would claim the existence of anything like a genuine national spirit in the colonies, but to overlook the factors that were promoting such a feeling and to exaggerate instead the forces separating them, hardly prepares us for the events of 1765 and later. Certainly mutual hostilities existed, which I have hardly thought it necessary to note; nearly every book on colonial American history mentions them. I have preferred, rather, to confine my attention to those elements which fostered intercolonial communication, and to trace the growing consciousness of a common destiny. I have not exhausted the field by any means; not only is the treatment restricted to a certain territory but my sources of information are as well. Much material, especially in collections outside of New York, remains unused and the subject still invites consideration.

I have contracted many debts in the course of this work. Prof. Nelson P. Mead and Mr. Oscar Janowsky of the department of history, Mr. Ernest Nagel in the department of philosophy of the College of the City of New York, and Prof. Bernard Faÿ of the University of Clermont-Ferrand, France, read parts of the manuscript; to the staffs of the local libraries, especially that of the New York Historical Society, and for various favors rendered by Prof. Dixon Ryan Fox of Columbia University, I am very grateful. My greatest debt is to Prof. Evarts B. Greene, in whose seminar I began my graduate studies including this one, and whose kind but effective criticisms throughout its entire preparation have given this effort whatever value it may have. Its mistakes are my own.

MICHAEL KRAUS

COLLEGE OF THE CITY OF NEW YORK.

TABLE OF CONTENTS

INTRODUCTION

A well known caricature of Lord Byron shaking the dust of England off his clothes is somewhat suggestive of an older style of American historiography. Under the influence of the Revolutionary heritage an author was, perhaps, wont to take especial pride in pointing out that the colonies grew up in a new environment, depending on their own resources seemingly apart from the rest of the world.

Time and a better historical perspective have served to draw a truer picture of colonial conditions, emphasizing the position of the American colonies in the scheme of the British empire. The work of a number of scholars in the past thirty years has made plain the relations of the colonies to England and the rest of the empire, in what was essentially, from the ministerial point of view, a great commercial organization. Yet despite this recent emphasis on eighteenth-century imperial relations, other phases of English contact with her American colonies are still very much in the shadow or buried away in obscure articles and little known studies. While we know now a great deal about political relations and commercial regulations, we know much less about the communication of political ideas or actual commercial relations. For example, not a great deal has been done to show the volume of trade with the colonies, its composition, how it was carried, the trade routes and the means and methods of payment. These are all important as shedding much light on many of the political questions that arose between 1760 and 1775 and the alignment of certain classes in their attempted settlement, both in England and the colonies.

Another aspect of much importance is the relation of the educated classes in the colonies to those in England, and those curious about historical parallels will be interested in comparing the relationship between England and the continent in the Tudor and Stuart periods, and that of the American colonies with Europe in the eighteenth century. French culture was the standard of respectability and furnished the models upon which English genius exercised itself, or, if Italian influences are traceable, they usually made themselves felt through French channels. So too, in the eighteenth century the rich fruits of European civilization were carried to America and there were some who cultivated a taste for them. The people of greatest social and commercial influence in the colonies were those who likewise maintained direct or indirect contact with the culture of Europe. Before and after the formation of the higher institutions of learning in the middle colonies and in New England, many students went abroad to study law or medicine, and also to travel on the continent. This method of securing a professional education was continued for many years. The scientific relations were not inconsiderable, the names that come to mind most readily being those of Cadwallader Colden of New York, Benjamin Franklin and John Bartram of Pennsylvania, John Mitchell of Virginia, Peter Collinson in England, Gronovius at Leyden and Linnaeus at Upsala, Sweden.

The influence of the older English universities in the curricula of the youthful colonial institutions was marked; it is well to remember the large number of colonials in the seventeenth century who held Cambridge or Oxford degrees. Much more is the impress noticeable in the character of the literary fare, especially towards the middle of the eighteenth century. The influence of Addison and Pope is evidenced in almost every newspaper and in most of the magazines that struggled through a brief existence. About the same time Milton comes into a more general recognition, and in the dramatic presentations that become fairly familiar after the mid-century, Shakespeare secures a wider audience and the plays of the Restoration period elicit much applause. Music which had been closely connected with religion finds secular expression in the work of James Lyon and Francis Hopkinson, while European music is comparatively well known, a favorite musician being Handel. Colonial art, especially the painting of portraits and miniatures had, of course, a direct European tradition and the relations between both sections of the world were very intimate; Benjamin West who located in England was an effective intermediate agent. Architecture took its cue from James Gibbs' " Rules for Drawing in Architecture ", and in the furnishing of the wealthier homes of the colonists would be found the latest in English furniture, some of which was manufactured in the colonies. The English coffee-house and clubs of merchants and professional organizations of doctors and lawyers had their counterparts in the new world, and the freedom of conversation and behavior of the former can be matched in the latter.

Notwithstanding such influences working toward the secularization of colonial life, the religious spirit was still very powerful. The established moulds being unresponsive to the changing conditions, a vast number of people found emotional expression in that tremendous phenomenon known as " The Great Awakening," observable in England and America, while the Continent itself was not free from religious changes. This great convulsion, for such it was, had important effects on the subsequent history of the colonies, influencing the founding of schools and lessening to a considerable degree the predominant position of the established classes throughout the colonial governments. A period marked by the intensification of religious life in certain classes saw also the spread of skeptical and deistic ideas.

The above mentioned characteristics of colonial civilization have been cataloged with a definite purpose. It has been seen that studies have been made portraying the international relations (especially political) of the colonies, but comparatively little has been done to place them in the general stream of European civilization, for assuredly they belong therein. Without such an approach one cannot understand the life of the seaboard cities, e. g., Boston, New York, Philadelphia and Charlestown, South Carolina. The vogue of electrical experimentation for the dilettante and for the specialist, so fashionable in Europe, found its echo in America where the choice spirits corresponded with one another and founded a philosophical society as an intellectual clearing house. The reigning political philosophy of the day, that of Locke, had its students in America, where in nearly every representative library could be found a copy of the " Two Treatises on Civil Government ".

And yet, while pointing out the imperial relations of the colonies and the general international character of colonial civilization, writers have perhaps in their reaction to the Bancroft style of historiography stressed too lightly the independent growth of the colonies and their relations with one another. Even a careful scholar like Carl Becker was led to write "The only bond of union between the colonies was the British government; and the people of the various colonies had usually but little intercourse with one another". Such an interpretation hardly does justice to many influences, subtle or obvious, which were creating for the colonists a common fund of experiences. It is true that a large proportion of the commerce was with colonies not on the North American mainland, yet a respectable amount was transacted among the continental group; and what is also significant the cessation of the Seven Years' War left the interior open to trade and land speculation which further rooted the seaboard interest in America. The intercolonial religious organizations tended to exert centripetal forces. The intercolonial relations respecting the Indians and plans for union and defense introduced leading individuals in the colonies to one another. The erection of the colleges in the middle colonies and in Rhode Island brought together students from every part of America, a fact not without significance for a more tolerant understanding. These unifying factors are to be kept in mind to understand what has seemed to many students the spontaneous gathering of the colonists in 1765, and the cooperation subsequently of widely scattered groups, in favor of or against a continued political association with Great Britain.

This study is concerned with the diffusion of certain aspects of civilization in a limited area and in a specified period, as a contribution to an enlarged picture of the background of the American Revolution. Boston, New York and Philadelphia were the most important northern colonial cities and because of their influence on American life merit considerable attention. Other cities, notably Charlestown, South Carolina, played large parts in colonial life but it was deemed best to confine the investigation to the northern area. The attempt is beset with many difficulties; most prominently, is one studying people or only a class of people? The articulate group leaves literary remains, the inarticulate leaves merely remains. Only slightly true today, when almost any one who is literate can leave his imprint, it was too true of the eighteenth century, where granting your literacy, you had few opportunities to express it. So that we may frankly admit that most of the following discussion is restricted to a fraction of the population, with allusions to the other fraction. But it is easy to plead that throughout history a small part of mankind has left its impress on the larger part. And eighteenth-century America proved no exception.

CHAPTER I

Intercolonial Business and Business Men

The first New Englanders had hardly become acquainted with their immediate surroundings when economic opportunities to the west and south were thrust upon them. Thus early they came into contact with the Dutch of New York who were equally acquisitive, and with the planting of William Penn's colony a new source of competition and profit arose. Exceedingly thin were these ties among the colonies that huddled close to the Atlantic seaboard in the seventeenth century, but the following years were witness to a steadily increasing intercolonial trade which fashioned new bonds through the widening avenues of communication.

There is no unanimous agreement about the condition of colonial roads generally, but a comparison of the better highways with similarly classed English thoroughfares indicates the latter were of no higher standard.

In my Journey to London, [wrote an irate correspondent to the Gentlemen's Magazine in 1747] I travel'd from Harborough to Northampton, and well was it that I was in a light Berlin, [coach] and six good horses, or I might have overlaid in that turnpike road. But for fear of life and limb, I walk'd several miles on foot, and met 20 waggons tearing their goods to pieces.

A few years earlier an English traveler in Boston had written that despite the lack of turnpikes the roads were " exceeding good in summer" and added, with a keen remembrance of his native conditions, "it is safe travelling night or day, for they have no highway robbers to interrupt them." [1] Although opinions differ about details, it is reasonably certain that for the most part the roads connecting the larger colonial cities were in fair shape, and within a radius of about thirty or forty miles of these cities, they were usually in an excellent state. The rapid settlement of the areas between Boston and Philadelphia made it imperative that proper highways be laid out. Copley, the Boston painter, who made the trip from his home town to New York in 1771 wrote, " you scarcely lose sight of an house." [2] The evidence of letters, newspapers, legislative enactments and plans for improvements reveals much traveling over the roads connecting the more important places in each colony. The almanacs printed the routes and distances between the principal towns, and before the mid-century the first American guide book had appeared. It included with other information, the road running from Boston to Jamestown, Virginia, a number of branches from this highway and the distances between the more important centers. [3]

From the leading urban areas branched out a system of roads, more numerous near the center of activity, and at the outskirts thinning out to three or four well-traveled highways. Beginning with a local area one can trace the process of expansion which demanded more and more extensive programs of transportation.

Increased travel necessitated building a free bridge over the Harlem River to supplant the toll bridge on the road to

[1] Quoted in Ralph Straus, *Carriages and Coaches: Their History and Their Evolution* (London, 1912), p. 176; M. A. Willard, *Roads of England in the Eighteenth Century* (MS. thesis, Columbia Univ.), Bennett, " MS. History of New England, 1740," *Mass. Hist. Soc. Proc.,* vol. v, p. 125.

[2] *Copley-Pelham Letters, Mass. Hist. Soc. Coll.,* 1914, p. 179.

[3] J. T. Adams, *Provincial Society* (*A History of American Life,* vol. iii, N. Y., 1927), p. 257.

Boston.[1] That transit difficulties have long plagued New York is confirmed by demands for relief from crowded conditions on the ferry to Brooklyn. A suggestion that another line be added referred to the "Beneficial Effects from a Division of Interests in the Ferrys of the Town of Boston, and City of Philadelphia, where Passengers are treated with an obliging Attention and wait but a few minutes for their Transportation."[2] About the same time improved conditions of ferriage across the Hudson River facilitated transportation over an important link in the route between New York and Philadelphia.[3]

More ambitious undertakings were under way to better the channels of communication. New Jersey appointed commissions to run out straight public roads binding New York and Philadelphia. In this internal development policy Lord Stirling, an eighteenth-century captain of industry, played an important role, for he was instrumental in opening up roads making the way safer and shorter between the two cities. His plans for improved water transportation suggested that the Delaware river be rendered navigable upwards from Trenton, so giving "an easy conveyance to . . . . (the) natural mart Philadelphia."[4] Throughout the century acts of the various legislatures attempted to keep pace with the growing needs.

By 1760 there were several well-defined arteries of land travel connecting the larger towns. A traveler leaving Boston might choose one of four ways to reach New Haven whence a road to New York led along the Sound. Travel-

[1] *N. Y. Post-Boy,* Nov. 20, 1758, in I. N. P. Stokes, *The Iconography of Manhattan Island* (N. Y., 1915-1926), vol. iv, p. 702; cited hereafter as " Stokes ".

[2] Stokes, vol. iv, p. 846.

[3] *H. C. Westervelt, Ferries Out of New York,* no. 15.

[4] *N. Y. Mercury,* Dec. 18, 1766, Jan. 26, 1767, Stokes, vol. iv, p. 770; *Stirling Papers,* Jan. 7, 1768.

ers often took a sloop from Newport or New London which carried them to Sterling or Oyster Bay, Long Island, and then followed an easy trip to New York.[1]   There were several routes between the latter city and Philadelphia all of which seem to have been frequently used.[2]

The usual modes of private land travel were by carriages or on horseback.   The former were coming into more general use with the increase of wealth which encouraged traveling for recreation, and by 1753 Massachusetts had about seven pleasure carriages to every thousand persons. An Englishman in Boston thought the city outdid London in the luxuriousness of its private travel facilities, and some of its choice conveyances were exported to other colonial cities.   Actual count soon revealed New York even more self-indulgent in this regard.   Sometimes individuals hired out their private carriages or invited others to join them on a journey,[3] but these vehicles in the main were for the comparatively wealthy; the large majority traveled astride the horse.   So common was this means of conveyance that it was necessary to have horse-blocks in front of nearly all houses.[4]   The comparative figures are illuminating.   At a horse race on Hempstead Plains, Long Island, over seventy chaises and chairs were visible, while it was estimated that

[1] C. M. Andrews, *Colonial Folkways: A Chronicle* (New Haven, 1919), p. 215, *et seq.*

[2] W. H. Benedict, "Travel Across New Jersey in the Eighteenth Century and Later", *Proc. of N. J. Hist. Soc.,* new ser., vol. vii, p. 99.

[3] A. M. Earle, *Stage-Coach and Tavern Days* (N. Y., 1900), p. 227; G. W. W. Houghton, *Coaches in Colonial New York* (N. Y., 1890); Bennett, "MS. History of New England," *loc. cit.,* p. 124; Cornelius Van Horne advertises "three good riding chairs from Boston", *N. Y. Post-Boy,* May 25, 1747, Stokes, vol. iv, p. 603; Edward Willett advertises use of curricle and pair of horses for "any gentleman going to Boston", *N. Y. Post-Boy,* Aug. 30, 1756; Robert Bell in *Boston Gaz. or Country Journal,* Aug. 27, 1770, invites company to N. Y. or Phila.

[4] A. M. Earle, *Home Life in Colonial Days* (N. Y., 1899), p. 335.

more than one thousand horses brought the less well-to-do spectators.[1]

From early days in the eighteenth century there were public transportation agencies serving a restricted area, e. g., Boston to Providence. For some years one man had a monopoly on hauling freight over part of the road between New York and Philadelphia. Before the middle of the century the demand was sufficient to warrant the establishment of regular routes covering a much larger territory. A wagon was to go once a week from Burlington to Amboy Ferry which was part of the New York-Amboy-Burlington-Philadelphia route, run in opposition to the Philadelphia-Trenton route. In a short time improvements made the service more rapid and competition soon arrived in the person of Joseph Borden, a boom-town promoter who attempted to build up Borden's Town as a way station in opposition to Trenton.[2]

Thus far the various stages in the journey between the two largest cities in the middle colonies were made under separate managements. By 1750 Daniel O'Brien was ready to connect the various links and convey his patrons and their merchandise all the way under a single management. His advertisement claimed an easier and shorter trip,[3] and despite other competitors who immediately came into the field, O'Brien prospered and added another stage boat to his transportation line.[4] In 1764, what was probably the first through stage was put into operation between New York and Philadelphia, making the trip in three

[1] N. Y. Weekly Post-Boy, June 4, 1750.

[2] Benedict, loc. cit., pp. 97, 100-104.

[3] N. Y. Post-Boy, Oct. 22, 1750, March 25, 1751; Stokes, vol. iv, 623.

[4] N. Y. Post-Boy, Aug. 12, 1751, April 22, 1754; Stokes, pp. 629, 648; Post-Boy, May 28, 1753; ibid., p. 638; Post-Boy, June 4, 1753, ibid.; for O'Brien see Post-Boy, Oct. 30, 1752; Sept. 24, 1753; Feb. 23, 1756, ibid., pp. 635, 636, 679.

days until further economies cut it down to two. Princeton was the half-way station where passengers and freight were exchanged. The passengers who paid twenty shillings each " may now go from New York to Philadelphia, and back again in five Days, and remain in Philadelphia two Nights and one Day to do their business in." [1]

These "flying machines" were now forced to meet the offer of Abraham Skillman's "New Flying Machine," to go directly to Philadelphia in two days with a load limited to eight passengers. They met the challenge by reducing the elapsed time to a day and a half which evidently proved too speedy, for the old schedule of two days was soon restored. Three trips a week in summer and two a week in winter were promised. Mercereau's stage permitted each passenger fourteen pounds of baggage, but made a distinction between those inside and those outside the coach. [2] By the end of the colonial period there seems to have been a sufficiency of transit facilities in the middle colonies to meet a steadily increasing demand.

Between New York and Boston there was not so much travel for either pleasure or business as between New York and Philadelphia, but several years before the Revolution there was enough to cause the institution of a stage service which was to leave each terminus once a fortnight. Advertised as a four-day trip, it usually took longer. [3] The more important method of transport, especially of merchandise, between cities along the seaboard, was by water. This coastal

---

[1] Sovereign Sybrandt, *N. Y. Mercury*, Oct. 1, 1764, Stokes, pp. 743, 775; John Barnhill and John Mercereau, *Post-Boy*, May 28, 1767, *ibid.*, p. 775.

[2] Skillman, *N. Y. Mercury*, April 22, 1771; Mercereau, *ibid.*, Jan. 3, 1774, Stokes, pp. 819, 844; Benedict, *loc. cit.*, pp. 109-114.

[3] *Historical Magazine*, ser. i, vol. ii, p. 298; Quincy's description of trip in Earle, *Home Life in Colonial days,* 346; Brown's stage started Sept. 7, 1772 from Boston, left once in fourteen days, S. A. Drake, *Old Boston Taverns and Tavern Clubs* (Boston, 1917), p. 68.

trade, grown to such proportions that regular packets were scheduled to run between the larger towns, was carried mainly in sloops, although schooners and shallops also found many cargoes.   In 1762, the first regular transportation service through Long Island Sound was opened with two sloops plying between Newport and New York.[1]   In the entry-book at Boston about half the vessels appear several times in the course of the year, indicating a certain regularity in sailing dates.[2]   Salem and Philadelphia were joined at times by vessels that sailed back and forth.[3]   Several years before the first American land travel-guide appeared, " The New England Coasting Pilot from Sandy-Point of New York unto Cape Canso in Nova Scotia " was advertised to lighten the worries of navigators in a well ploughed sea.   The ever increasing sea travel and commerce called for improved docking facilities and lighthouses as safeguards against hazards.[4]

Over the roads connecting the widely strung settlements rode the post, which struggled for many years before it attained any semblance of regularity.   The postal system was not really established until William III granted a patent to Thomas Neale, although years before Governors Lovelace and Dongan in New York had agitated for such an establishment.   They suggested a service binding all the colonies, and through Dongan's energy it was partially suc-

---

[1] *N. Y. Gazette* (Weyman), Sept. 13, 1762, Stokes, pp. 726-27.

[2] S. E. Morison, " Commerce of Boston on Eve of the Revolution," *Am. Antiq. Soc. Proc.*, April 1922 (1773).

[3] "A List of Vessels Insured by Timothy Orne, etc., Dec., 1757-Dec. 1758 ", *Essex Inst. Hist. Coll.*, vol. xxxi, pp. 88-95; " Timothy Orne, Jr., 1740-58 ", vol. xxxvii, pp. 77-80.

[4] Captain Cyprian Southack in *Boston News-Letter*, May 19/26, 1718, in G. F. Dow, *The Arts & Crafts in New England, 1704-1775* (Topsfield, Mass., 1927) ; Bradford's *N. Y. Gaz.*, July 1, 1734, Stokes, p. 536.

cessful.[1] Up to 1691 when Neale secured his patent, the
action of individual colonies determined what progress might
be effected in the creation of such a system.   The monopoly
granted to Neale for twenty years empowered him to establish
service between Massachusetts, Pennsylvania and New York,
and to open post-offices in the chief places.   Andrew Hamilton, the deputy-postmaster, shrewdly arranged with the
several provincial legislatures to fix charges for the service
which ran over a line of posts extending from Portsmouth,
New Hampshire to Philadelphia; the mails were carried over
it weekly each way, but a deficit early hindered its development.[2]

When Neale's patent was about to expire, a Parliament
act of 1710 consolidated the system throughout the British
dominions under the supreme control of the postmaster-general in England.   The offices at Boston, Philadelphia and
New York, hitherto independent of one another were brought
together in the general system with headquarters in the last
named.   The rates, payable by the addressee, were graduated
according to distance and weight, four pence for a sixty
mile carriage and six pence for a hundred miles.   The post
left every Friday from Philadelphia and arrived in New
York the next night; left for Boston Monday morning and
exchanged bags with the rider from that city at Saybrook
on Thursday, but it was difficult to maintain this schedule
despite earnest efforts.[3]

With the choice of Franklin as postmaster-general the
service experienced a general shaking-up.   A long tour of

[1] *N. Y. Col. Doc.*, vol. iii, pp. 349, 356; W. Smith, " The Colonial Post-
office ", *Amer. Hist. Rev.*, vol. xxi.

[2] Smith, *loc. cit.*, pp. 262-67; W. E. Rich, *History of the United States
Post Office to Year 1829* (*Harv. Economic Studies*, vol. 27, Cambridge,
1924), pp. 12-17.

[3] William Smith, *The History of the Post Office in British North
America 1639-1870* (Cambridge, 1920), pp. 18-21; Rich, pp. 25-28.

inspection resulted in "new and shorter routes"; milestones on the principal roads were to guide the traveler as well as the post. By day and night riding it was expected that a letter and reply between New York and Philadelphia could be sent within two days; between Boston and Philadelphia "in six days instead of the three weeks then required." Although this arrangement was not immediately effective, Franklin did make the whole organization more useful.[1]

The needs of business and other correspondence were demanding greater attention. " At the end of 1756 one hundred and fifty letters were advertised as held at the New York office, three years later the number unclaimed in Philadelphia was over five hundred." Even more significant for intercolonial ties were the results that followed the general lowering of rates suggested by Franklin. Instituted in 1765, the " lowered rates did not at all lessen the revenue of the office, the increase in correspondence serving to offset the lower return per unit." [2]

Through these multiplying avenues of communication the urge of gain led to many contacts throughout the colonies. The Indian trade, land speculation, the traveling peddler. shipbuilding and other interests reveal at times severe competition or common understandings across colonial boundaries. The commercial bonds between New York and Philadelphia were closer than either had with Boston, but in an indirect way they maintained close connections with the New England metropolis through Newport.[3] The merchants of New Haven conducted a large intercolonial business; it was reported in 1760 that they were £20,000

[1] Rich, *op. cit.*, pp. 29-36; *N. Y. Mercury,* Jan. 2, 1764, Stokes, p. 739.

[2] Postmaster Alex. Colden acknowledges needs of trade, Stokes, p. 664; Adams, *op. cit.*, p. 302, quoting *N. Y. Gaz.*, Jan. 3, 1757, *Pa. Gaz.*, Jan. 3, 1760; Rich, *op. cit.*, pp. 38-41.

[3] *N. Y. Gazette and Weekly Mercury* (Gaine), 1773, a few issues missing. At N. Y., 55 ships entered in from R. I.; 34 out to R. I.

in debt to New Yorkers.[1]   Young Jews from other cities
were frequently in Boston for their employers; in fact
there was a very well developed consciousness of mutual
business interests among colonial Jews, many of whom
were among the mercantile aristocracy.[2]   Merchants very
early began to tap more distant markets where they maintained selling agencies, whose wares were advertised in
the local papers.   The intimate relations, business and social,
that existed between New York and Philadelphia in the
1760's, may be seen in the "Letter Book" of John Van
Cortlandt.   Like other representatives of "big business," he
had agents located in the most advantageous places to which
he might send his sugar.   When his Virginia representative
became incapacitated, merchants from both cities recommended another individual for the post.   The trade with his
Philadelphia correspondent, with whom Van Cortlandt exchanged visits for business and recreation, totaled over
£1000 in two years.[3]   Goods were sold on credit, and bills
of exchange were utilized to settle the balances.   An example
of these financial arrangements is a draft of £400 sterling by
Richard Vichors of Boston on Hugh Wallace of New York,
the latter to pay Mr. Nathaniel Holmes in Philadelphia.[4]
The growing interprovincial commerce set schoolmasters
and text-book writers to working out arithmetical short-cuts

[1] F. B. Dexter, ed., *Extracts from the Itineraries and Correspondence
of Ezra Stiles* (New Haven, 1916), p. 83.

[2] L. M. Friedman, "Early Jewish Residents in Mass.," *Amer. Jew.
Hist. Soc. Publica.*, vol. xxiii; Leon Hühner, "Jews of New England",
ibid., vol. xi.

[3] John Van Cortlandt, *Letter Book*, 1762-1769; John Van Cortlandt,
Ledger, 1770-1772, p. 79, 141.

[4] *Record Book of James Emott, Attorney and Notary Public, N. Y. C.*,
June 23, 1766.   Philadelphia was practically the single source that pro-
vided all the colonial paper currency.   L. H. Weeks, *A History of Paper
Manufacturing in the United States* (N. Y., 1916), p. 14.

to convert any sum of " New York Currency or the Currency of any other Colony into Sterling." [1]

This intercolonial trade which included many articles but was especially heavy in fish, flour, provisions and lumber, involved in some instances simple barter, and sharp competition was a conspicuous feature of eighteenth-century American commerce. Philadelphia starch was frequently sent to New York and found a demand in Massachusetts also.[2] The Pennsylvania capital imported fish and peltries from New England and Nova Scotia, usually for reexportation, and in exchange, large quantities of salt, imported into Philadelphia duty-free, were returned.[3] Charlestown, South Carolina, shipped large quantities of rice to the northern ports which sent back flour, sugar and manufactured iron products.[4] By the middle of the century, Boston was regularly importing breadstuffs from New York, Philadelphia and Baltimore. The dependence of Boston on the middle colonies is strikingly revealed in a request to Governor Morris of Pennsylvania to lift an embargo. "As provisions are much wanted in this Town, and as supplies are withheld from us by the restraint laid on the exportation of Flour from Philadelphia, . . . be pleased to permit (the) Vessels . . . . loaded with Flour . . . . to depart . . . . for this Port." [5] The keen rivalry

[1] Hugh Hughes, ad't 1772, in R. F. Seybolt, "Evening Schools of Colonial New York City", *N. Y. State Local History Leaflets*, p. 649; reprint fifteenth annual rep. of State department of education.

[2] V. S. Clark, *History of Manufactures in the United States 1607-1860* (Washington, 1916), pp. 113-114.

[3] M. A. Hanna, *Trade of the Delaware District Before the Revolution, Smith College Studies in History*, vol. ii, 4, pp. 257-262 and note 91; in one quarter 100,000 hhds of salt were sent from Phila. to Boston.

[4] Edward McCrady, *The History of South Carolina Under the Royal Government* (N. Y., 1899), p. 390, note 1; Pelatiah Webster's "Journal," *South. Hist. Assn. Pub.*, vol. v, p. 2.

[5] Selectmen of Boston to Gov. Morris, July 29, 1756, *Penn. Archives, 1748-1756*, p. 708.

between the two leading cities of the middle colonies in the marketing of this and other products, is clearly indicated in an appeal from the New York merchants that they be informed as soon as the embargo is lifted, so that "they may Start upon an equal footing."[1] From early days New York kept a close watch on the Philadelphia flour and lumber situation, and when the latter's products were preferred, the former set up more rigid standards for the preparation of these products for sale. She had to, for Pennsylvania flour had invaded the home market. A writer discussing frauds in local manufacture claimed New Yorkers bought only enough to last them till a vessel came from Philadelphia with a supply of the better sort.[2] Rum and molasses from New England helped to keep the financial balance; fatted cattle were driven to the New York market and sometimes as far as Phila- delphia. Wool, hops, barley and shoes, frequently in large quantities, shipped southward were straining the insufficient docking space.[3]

New England also paid for her imports by the services of her boats that sailed up and down the coast. "The Number of Vessels engaged in this business is surprisingly great" wrote the Boston port collector.[1] Many of her bottoms were bought by merchants in other colonial cities. In fact there seem to have been frequent intercolonial sales in ships.[6]

[1] *Penn. Archives, 1748-1756*, p. 702, Archibald Kennedy to Gov. Morris, July 15, 1756.

[2] J. A. Stevens, Jr., ed., *Colonial Records of the New York Chamber of Commerce, 1768-1784* (N. Y., 1867), pp. 30, 57-58, 110-111; *N. Y. Post-Boy*, Oct. 22, 1750, Stokes, 623.

[3] P. W. Bidwell and J. I. Falconer, *History of Agriculture in the North-ern United States* (Washington, 1925), pp. 142-143; Boston coastwise exports 1767, included 11,000 pairs of shoes, most of which went to Phila- delphia and New York, Morison, *loc. cit.,* p. 44; for docks, Stokes, pp. 762, 769.

[4] Report of 1768, reprinted in *Mass. Hist. Soc. Proc.,* vol. 58, p. 423.

[5] "Ship Registers, Port of Phila., 1740-1772," *Pa. Mag. of Hist. and Biog.,* vols. xxiv-xxvii, xxviii.

On one occasion four large ships were put on the market by a Bostonian; if not sold, they were to be loaded with freight by his New York correspondent.[1] The advertisement of the sale of a captured Indiaman's cargo at Louisburg drew prospective buyers from the middle colonies.[2] Insurance on vessels from Newport was usually covered by New York underwriters who pooled their resources.[3] New York and Philadelphia were competitors in the field of insurance too. C. J. Shippen wrote to his father he was pricing New York premiums; "when I get an answer, I shall either insure there or here immediately."[4] New York merchants also were not loath to take better terms, if offered, in Philadelphia. Sometimes New York offered advantages which vessels bound from Boston or Philadelphia shared with local residents. On the other hand the brothers Bache, located in Philadelphia and New York, cooperated in underwriting vessels and cargoes.[5]

The colonial whale fishery brought ships from many of the ports together, the large majority from Massachusetts with scattering contributions from Rhode Island, Connecticut and New York. Throughout the century New York made spasmodic efforts to share more extensively in this enterprise, but with ill success.[6] The competition for the valu-

[1] Lewis Deblois to Dirck Brinckerhoff, May 26, 1766, *Dirck Brinckerhoff Papers*, 1765-1768.

[2] Lewis Morris to Commodore Warren, Aug. 27, 1745, *N. J. Hist. Soc. Coll.*, vol. iv, pp. 260-261.

[3] W. B. Weeden, *Am. Antiq. Soc. Proc.*, n. s., vol. v, p. 118; letter Feb. 2, 1760, *Commerce of Rhode Island, Mass. Hist. Soc. Coll.*, ser. 7, vol. ix, pp. 79-80.

[4] Thomas Balch. ed., *Letters and Papers Relating Chiefly to the Provincial History of Pennsylvania (Shippen Papers)*, (Phila., 1855), p. 185; Sept 17, 1760.

[5] "David Franks as Insurance Broker," *Am. Jew. Hist. Soc. Pub.*, vol. xxvi, pp. 268-270; *Wm. Walton's Book of Insurances*, Jan. 1773; Stevens, *op. cit.*, biographical sketches, pp. 41-44.

[6] W. S. Tower, *A History of the American Whale Fishery (Pub. of*

able oil led to the formation in 1761 of a trust, the "United Company of Spermaceti Candlers," with headquarters in Rhode Island.[1] An elaborate program, to which the participants adhered for over a year, provided for the complete regulation of the industry in New England through the fixing of prices. If the whalers, many of whom hailed from Nantucket, continued to demand high prices, the associated merchants agreed

to fit out at least Twelve vessels upon our joint Concern to be employed in the . . . fishery, each manufacturer . . . to furnish and receive an equal proportion in and from said vessells and we also agree to add to the number of these Vessells from time to time as many more as may then appear most proper.

Not content with these monopolistic restrictions, the group further pledged itself "by all fair and honourable means" to prevent any newcomer from setting up a plant in New England. When this agreement expired in 1763 a more inclusive one, taking all America for its province, was negotiated to extend for a year. It named the individuals from whom spermaceti would be bought, and all that was carried into any colonial port was to be considered common stock divisible proportionately among the signatories; e.g., the Philadelphians were to get seven barrels of every hundred brought in. Continuing the policy laid down in the previous plan, but on a grander scale, this group instructed its factors to give it "the most Early Notice of any attempt to set up any other Spermaceti Works Because the Present Manufacturers are More than Sufficient to Manufacture All that is Ever caught in America." It was an industry that required a comparatively large capital outlay, and on various

Univ. of Penn., Ser. in Pol. Economy and Public Law, no. 20, Phila. 1907), p. 37; *Holt's N. Y. Journal,* April 21, 1768; *Gaine's N. Y. Gaz.,* June 5, 1775, "United Whaling Company".

[1] *Commerce of Rhode Island, loc. cit.,* pp. 88-100 (1761-1763).

occasions cooperative manufacture of spermaceti candles was the practise.   Peter R. Livingston of New York and Robert Jenkins of Rhode Island were in partnership, while the bitter rivalry between William Rotch of Nantucket and the wealthy John Hancock led to an unsuccessful attempt to compose their differences and jointly control the oil trade.[1]

There was intercolonial business cooperation in other enterprises also.   Philadelphia and New York merchants owned ships together; they sold tea and coffee in partnership. Two New Yorkers combined to ship 100 hhds of flaxseed from Philadelphia, for it was cheaper than sending it from their own port.[2]   A Hartford doctor carried on the business of an apothecary and grocer with capital furnished by his partner, a fellow practitioner in Boston.[3]   The large scale of manufacture in the 1760's is revealed in the really tremendous undertaking of Peter Hasenclever.   He came to New York from England and had hundreds of Germans with their wives and children brought over to assist in opening iron works.   By the end of 1766 he had four furnaces and seven forges in New York and New Jersey, a pot and pearl-ash manufactory on the Mohawk River, all of which meant building miles of roads.   While his company did not permanently prosper, it indicates how business energy roaming far afield was leaping over colonial barriers.[4]   The Stirling works in New York with an annual production of about fifteen hundred tons of pig worked into bar iron, were

[1] *Ibid.*, pp. 137-139; A. E. Brown, *John Hancock His Book* (Boston, 1898) pp. 64-66.

[2] " Ship Registers ", *loc. cit.*, vol. v, pp. 24, 25; Uriah Woolman, *Day Book,* 1764-1773, Phila., e. g., entry Dec. 28, 1764; Gerard Beekman's *Letter Book,* Dec. 29, 1757; letter to Capt. James Miller, Feb. 1752.

[3] G. W. Russell, *Early Medicine and Early Medical Men in Connecticut* (*Proc. of Conn. Med. Soc.*, New Haven, 1892), p. 83.

[4] Henry A. Homes, *Notice of Peter Hasenclever* (Albany Institute, 1874).

widely known, and the early manufacturers in Massachusetts and Pennsylvania depended on bog ores from East New Jersey.[1] The pig iron shipped to Massachusetts was cast into pots and kettles or made into nails and implements, some of which were reshipped to the central and southern colonies. To Philadelphia were returned scythes made from bar iron shipped to New England. Salem scythes were advertised as superior to other makes in New York which, with Boston, furnished a ready market for Pennsylvania stoves.[2]

Provincial enterprise brought New York and Philadelphia in competition for the Lisbon trade; the West Indies and Central America brought colonial ships into keen rivalry. The merchants were very well informed about prices over wide areas and picked the highest markets for their goods, but often made mistakes because quotations changed rapidly. A low market in New York drove its merchants to sell in Philadelphia but usually with the same ill success, showing how quickly the nerve centers of business were already reacting to each other.[3]

Busy as the merchants were in the buying and selling of goods, they were not too busy to overlook the large field for investment in real estate speculation. In this sphere of money-making and empire building, boundary lines were easily erased, and colonials everywhere competed or joined hands in what was probably the most important of American enterprises. Many of the colonies were interested, for

[1] J. B. Pearse, *A Concise History of the Iron Manufacture of the American Colonies* (Phila., 1876), pp. 47-53; *Stirling Papers,* July 24, 1767, Nov. 18, 1773, Dec. 1, Dec. 10; Henry Lloyd in Boston sold Stirling's iron, also Phila. bar iron, " ads " in *Boston Eve. Post,* Dec. 13, 1773, June 20, 1774.

[2] Clark, *op. cit.,* p. 114 and note 10, p. 115; *N. Y. Post-Boy,* May 28, 1744, Boston axes, Nov. 26, Pa. fire places, Sept. 8, 1746; J. L. Bishop, *A History of American Manufactures* (Phila., 1866), vol. i, p. 487, note 3; *Boston Gaz. and Country Journal,* Nov. 13, 1769, fire places.

[3] Gerard Beekman, *Letter Book,* April 2, 1754, Nov. 5, 1764.

example, in land sales promoted by William Alexander, "Earl of Stirling," an active native capitalist; Franklin was requested to encourage the efforts in England.[1] The Susquehanna Company, formed in Connecticut for the development of Pennsylvania lands claimed by the former colony, had a membership of eight hundred and fifty.[2]

The rapidly accumulating mass of free capital eagerly sought profits in lands to be settled, and with the treaty of Paris (1763) a vast area for investment was thrown open. "Immigration and the natural increase of population were counted on to double and triple land values frequently," writes Volwiler. Sometimes a decline in urban real estate enhanced the attractiveness of rural scenery. A note came from Philadelphia that an " Abundance of People is Dayly Moveing into the Country from this Town which makes house Rent fall here Prodigiously and a Number now Empty." [3] Virginia planters, New Englanders, Pennsylvanians and a few New Yorkers were the leaders who, by individual operations or in " numerous land companies," found new wealth and planned new colonies. There were few prominent men who were not participating. The " Indiana Company," formed to secure a land grant, included many from Pennsylvania and New Jersey. From New York, Moses Franks was despatched to present a memorial for a similar grant. So powerful was the speculative urge, it is confidently asserted, that " during the years 1769-1773 many Americans manifested as much interest in the developments associated with Vandalia (Grand Ohio Company) as in the

---

[1] Benjamin Franklin, *Calendar of Papers, American Philosophical Society* (1906-08), vol. ii, p. 135, June 30, 1772; *Stirling Papers*, Oct. 23, 1769.

[2] L. H. Gipson, *Jared Ingersoll, a Study of American Loyalism* (*Yale Hist. Pub., Miscellany*, vol. viii, New Haven, 1920), 317.

[3] Richard Stevens to Walter Rutherford, Dec. 12, 1765, *Rutherford Papers*, box 4.

Townshend Acts or the Boston Massacre."[1]   Probably the
most important single individual who was active for years in
these enterprises was George Croghan.   New York, Albany,
Philadelphia, Lancaster and Burlington all lent him the
necessary capital, and the extent of his undertakings may be
seen in the sale of three-fifths of his 250,000 acres in New
York, when adversity came in 1770.[2]   In Vermont and New
Hampshire, speculators from New York and New England
sought golden fruits.[3]   A like desire drew Philip Schuyler to
Detroit with a proposed settlement of Germans or Jews,
to be mixed with Anglo-Saxons to guard against "detached
settlements."[4]

The captains of finance in those days talked as easily
about planting new settlements as their modern successors do
about putting up new buildings.   Abraham Lott wrote to
John Wendell in Boston that he had interested others in New
York in the proposition to plant a township on the Connecticut River.   Wendell was to get the settlers; "If you know
of another good and Valuable township I can find friends
that will take it."[5]   New Yorkers however, did not need to
go beyond their own province to seek real estate investment.
The activities of James Duane, one of the largest speculators,
indicate the attractiveness of these ventures nearer home.

[1] A. T. Volwiler, *George Croghan and the Westward Movement*
(Cleveland, 1926), 273; C. W. Alvord, *The Mississippi Valley in British
Politics* (Cleveland, 1917), vol. i, pp. 77-103.

[2] Volwiler, pp. 281-284; the Coldens, Gov. William Franklin, Michael
Gratz and the Whartons were purchasers; James Duane in New York was
asked to sell 20,000 acres of this land for the Whartons, Galloway and
others; March 18, 1775, *Duane Papers*.

[3] "N. Y. Land Grants in Vermont," *Vermont Hist. Soc. Coll.*, vol. i,
pp. 153-155; *New Hampshire, Provincial, State and Town Papers*, vol.
xxvi; pp. 22-23, 372, 459, 679.

[4] *Schuyler Papers*, from Thomas Brand, London, March 10, 1763.

[5] *Wendell Family Papers*, April 7, 1770; Wendell had real estate in
N. Y. City, July 10, Aug. 23, 1765; letters from Richard Morris, 1770.

Modern methods were already old in the 1760's. To his Schenectady agent, Duane sent a number of prospective buyers. In an interesting letter naming these individuals, the New Yorker spoke the prologue to the American real estate drama of the twentieth century. He wrote, "The first has purchased, the rest intend to take a view first, and if they like the land to settle also." Duane added that since " they are a set who have connections in Philadelphia and can be serviceable to me," they should be shown around carefully till they get what they want.[1] Philadelphia was very much interested in New York lands. Part of Croghan's holdings went to Michael Gratz who was planning to bring over colonists to develop it. A pamphlet appeared in Philadelphia especially addressed to immigrants lately arrived, or on the way, recommending central New York as a place for settlement. The influence of Sir William Johnson with the Indians was counted upon to facilitate the settlement of a tract of land in upper New York, in which Joseph Reed, a prominent lawyer in the middle colonies, was interested.[2]

The call of God and the call of gain could both be heard, for two of Philadelphia's leading clergymen joined in this great American game.[3] Inter-city real-estate operations were not rare as in the case of a Quaker city speculator who bought some lots in a new German village established near Boston. James Parker, the New York printer, owned a lot near Yale College bought from Franklin, which Jared Ingersoll, a New Haven lawyer, was requested to rent out.

[1] *Duane Papers,* to Isaac Vrooman, May 15, 1765; also Dec. 24, 1765.

[2] W. V. Byars, " The Gratz Papers," *Amer. Jew. Hist. Soc. Pub.,* vol. 23; Charles Evans, *American Bibliography* (Chicago, 1903-25), no. 12574, cited hereafter as " Evans "; *Reed Papers,* Stephen Sayre to Reed, Sept. 3, 1766.

[3] H. W. Smith, *Life and Correspondence of the Rev. William Smith* (Phila., 1879), vol. i, pp. 391, 392.

Philadelphia attorneys advertised the sale of 3000 acres in West New Jersey belonging to a Massachusetts client.[1]

The interior provided opportunities in trade as well as land. All the seaboard colonies were tied more closely to the American scene by the operations of merchants in near and remote sections of the back country. New York and Philadelphia at first had most of the trade of the northern district, the former getting the best of furs, while the latter dealt mostly in deer leather. Boston rum played its part in Philadelphia efforts to get the Indian trade which centered in Albany, where local traders strongly opposed the representatives from the three leading coastal cities.[2]

By the mid-century and even earlier, organizations among merchants testify to their acute class consciousness and recognition of mutual interests. A short-lived "New London Society united for Trade and Commerce" had been formed in Connecticut about 1731, with the support of the most prominent men in the colony. The "New York Mercury" advertised,

For the Encouragement of Ship-Carpenters, able Seamen, and Labourers, in the Country, and the neighbouring Provinces, to repair to the City of New York; the Merchants of this City have agreed to give to the Ship-Carpenters 8*s.* per day; able Seamen 5*s.* and Labourers 4*s.* . . . and no other or greater Wages whatsoever. And all Persons liking the above Proposals, may be certain of constant Employment.[3]

[1] A. B. Faust, *The German Element in the United States* (Boston, 1909), vol. i, p. 261; *Ingersoll Letters*, Feb. 19, 1767, *New Haven Colony Hist. Soc.*, vol. ix; *American Weekly Mercury*, July 1-8, 1742, *N. J. Archives*, ser. I, vol. xii, pp. 132-133.

[2] C. W. Alvord and C. E. Carter, ed., *Illinois Hist. Coll.*, vol. xvi, *Trade and Politics, 1767-1769*, pp. 25, 606, *passim;* C. H. McIlwain, ed., *An Abridgement of the Indian Affairs . . . of New York from the year 1678 to the year 1751 by Peter Wraxall* (*Harv. Hist. Studies*, vol. xxi), pp. lxxxiii-lxxxiv.

[3] F B. Dexter, *Yale Biographies and Annals 1701-45* (N. Y., 1885-1912),

The most powerful group in the colonies was the Chamber of Commerce, founded in New York in 1768, which included all the important merchants.   Its committees settled disputes between native merchants and those from other cities; its power and connections were strikingly exhibited when, by ordering two thousand barrels of flour in Philadelphia, it forced the local bakers, bolters and sellers of flour to retract their demands.   Within six years, Charlestown, South Carolina, whose influential merchant class was well aware of New York affairs, also had a chamber of commerce.[1]

And while economics was emphasizing the artificiality of provincial boundaries for those with a large stake in society, what of those whose share was smaller?   "The itinerant peddler, shoemaker, candle dipper and other petty tradesmen or artificers who made their way from neighborhood to neighborhood weaving from the news and gossip of one and another a web of common thoughts and knowledge" were factors of real value in assisting the growth of common interests and an interchange of ideas.[2]   Fluctuating fortunes drove workmen from place to place to seek the most advantageous employment.   The modern note was creeping into domestic life through the migration of John Elliott who " hangs House & Cabin Bells etc." [3]   The traveling bookseller, like Robert Bell of Philadelphia whose peregrinations covered many colonies, brought profit to himself and pleasure to his patrons with news of a larger world.

pp. 204-05; Aug. 7, 1758; N. Y. merchants agreed to refuse acceptance of English copper half-pence, following the example of Boston and Phila.; counterfeit half-pence caused great confusion in commercial circles; *N. Y. Post-Boy,* Sept. 10, 1750, Dec. 3, 1753, Stokes, 621.

[1] *Chamber of Commerce Records,* pp. 53-54, pp. 21-23; McCrady, *op. cit.,* p. 540.

[2] Adams, *Provincial Society,* pp. 258-259.

[3] Richardson Wright, *Hawkers and Walkers in Early America* (Phila., 1927), p. 108; from Phila., in *N. Y. Post-Boy,* Aug. 16, 1756, Stokes, 682.

The development of established industries and the settlement of others in new homes were due largely to the migratory worker or capitalist. The wool manufacture in later colonial times was heavily indebted to the services of the itinerant weaver. Henry Whiteman, who had served an apprenticeship with Casper Wister, a "Brass Button-Maker in Philadelphia," opened up the same business in New York.[1] Boston owed the local introduction of the silkworm to Philadelphia, which also sent an energetic individual to organize the manufacture of glass. A silk dyer from the same city opened a shop in his new Boston home.[2] Philadelphia was the most important colonial paper market for many years, supplying a steady demand from Boston and other sections; but New England won a partial economic independence through the efforts of Richard Clarke, formerly of New York, who accelerated the development of Massachusetts paper mills.[3]

It is not to be expected that lesser units in colonial economic life should be organized as well as their brethren of the larger portion, although theirs was not a still, small voice. Trade organizations for mutual benefit seem to have been in existence in New York in the 1760's.[4] The guild organizations of shoemakers in Philadelphia and Boston enabled them to guard their respective interests.[5] The

[1] A. H. Cole, *The American Wool Manufacture* (Cambridge, 1926), vol. i, pp. 15-16; *N. Y. Post-Boy*, Sept. 17, 1750, Stokes, 622.

[2] *N. Y. Gazette*, Jan. 14, 1751, *Devoe's Index;* F. W. Hunter, *Stiegel Glass* (Boston, 1914), pp. 144-145; *Boston Rec. Com. Rep., Selectmen's Minutes, 1764-1768,* June 17, 1767.

[3] E. g., adv't in *Boston Evening Post,* Oct. 15, 1770; Weeks, *op. cit.,* pp. 23, 24; Goold, "Early Paper Mills in New England", *New Eng. Hist. and Geneal. Reg.,* vol. 29, p. 158.

[4] Stokes, broadside, p. 773.

[5] B. E. Hazard, *The Organization of the Boot and Shoe Industry in Massachusetts before 1875* (*Harvard Econ. Studies,* vol. xxiii, Cambridge, 1921), p. 10.

New York coopers early sought protection against neighboring colonies by having duties levied on empty casks "to discourage their importation." The house carpenters, bricklayers and others in the same city appealed for relief against the unfair competition of those from other provinces who came to New York in the summer, and in the fall "Returned again to their familys without paying any Taxes or assessments." Petitioners for lower prices to be established on the "Necessaries of Life" quoted the more advantageous situation of neighboring provinces in this regard, and secured remedial legislation.[1]

The influence of these economic contacts increased with the passage of years.

The intercolonial trade, [writes Adams,] with respect to the number of vessels employed, seems to have kept pace with the growth of that with the West Indies and the Old World. Indeed, between 1705 and 1732, the number of vessels entering Boston from other continental ports showed an increase of two hundred and thirty one percent, whereas that of vessels from overseas was only two hundred and twenty one percent. This intercolonial trade must have been of very considerable importance both from the standpoint of trade profits and from that of increasing the acquaintance of one colony with another.

In 1732 eighty-seven vessels from North Carolina docked at Boston and twelve at New York.[2] The extent of this growing trade with reference to specific ports may be measured by the mounting totals of shipping entries. In 1730 at New York, three vessels entered in from Philadelphia and the same number cleared out; seventeen from Rhode Island, twelve to the same place. Forty years

---

[1] J. R. Commons and associates, *History of Labour in the United States* (N. Y., 1918), vol. i, p. 41; *N. Y. Pos-Boy*, Aug. 24, 1769, April 2, 1747, Stokes, pp. 797-98, 602, 737.

[2] Adams, *op. cit.*, pp. 228, 207.

later, twenty-two entered in from the Pennsylvania capital, sixteen out and twenty-three cleared for departure. From Rhode Island, fifty-five entered in, thirty-four out and forty-nine cleared; the trade with the Carolinas likewise showed tremendous increases.[1] To protect this commerce, more mariner's charts were published after the mid-century, and even very detailed maps like that of the coast of North and South Carolina, began to appear for the benefit of Boston traders.[2]

With the changing years came changing fortunes, unfavorable in New England, favorable in the middle colonies. Wages in New York were usually higher than in New England. About the middle of the century, Boston began to grow conscious of its loss in trade, and primacy in some industries had already shifted to other centers. Despite the closeness with which the distillers guarded their business secrets, many still houses and sugar houses too had been set up in New York and Philadelphia. "In every branch of commerce save the coasting trade," Morison asserts, Boston was "decidedly inferior to Philadelphia and distinctly so to New York" in the closing years of the colonial period.[3]

Throughout the correspondence of professional and commercial classes is perceivable a thread of mutual business interests.[4] Sometimes the thread became knotted in the

[1] Dec. 4, 1730, Stokes, p. 518; Gaine's *N. Y. Gazette and Weekly Mercury*, 1773, three issues missing. Entries for Boston in latter period are untrustworthy; successful efforts to escape customs regulations render suspicious Boston port returns.

[2] G. F. Dow, *op. cit.*, pp. 29-31.

[3] Clark, *op. cit.*, p. 156; reduced trade suggested lower assessments, petitions in *Boston Town Records, 1742-1757*; distillers' secrets, *Colden Papers* (N. Y., 1917-23), March 11, 1727/28, April 22, 1728; Morison, *loc. cit.*, p. 50.

[4] E. g., *Forman Papers*, N. Y. and N. J.; *Gates Papers*, N. Y. and Phila.; *J. T. Kempe Papers*, N. Y. and Phila.

chaos of competition, but the more alert minds were usually ready to unravel the difficulties. In this story of economic competition and cooperation is the necessary background for the organizations of merchants and mechanics which played so large a part in the Revolutionary controversies.[1]

[1] For these organizations see the thorough work of A. M. Schlesinger, *The Colonial Merchants and the American Revolution 1763-1776* (*Col. Studies in Hist., Economics and Public Law*, N. Y., 1917).

CHAPTER II

Social Contacts

The growing volume of business and social correspondence which interlaced a vibrant colonial life was the result of more numerous contacts. With an expanding energy, while secure in their seaboard homes, colonists looked unafraid over vast inland areas which invited settlement and exploitation. In the process of carving out this new empire, politics and a lack of sufficient native capital forced a combination of resources attended with constant intercommunication. But provincial existence was not entirely a matter of land, fish, furs and lumber; abundant evidence remains of personal relations that were not writ in water.

Boston, New York and Philadelphia in the middle of the eighteenth century were predominantly English in atmosphere, Boston most decidedly so; the other two cities with fairly large proportions of Dutch, German and French, were less homogeneous. It is important to note the dispersion of these people, especially the English stock, because it is possible to trace many relationships among them, even though settled in widely separated localities. Then too, this kinship is suggestive of many cooperative undertakings.

A Massachusetts traveler who belonged to one of the earlier families could make a trip through Connecticut, across Long Island to New Jersey, and thence to Philadelphia, and meet a number of kinsmen, closely or distantly related. Samuel Curwen of Salem, made such a trip and was surprised at the number he found with Curwen blood in their veins.[1] The Piersons, originally of Long Island, were found in

[1] "Journal of a Journey from Salem to Philadelphia in 1755," *Essex Inst. Hist. Coll.,* vol. 52, pp. 76-83.

Massachusetts and New Jersey. Long Island folk were kept in touch with their relatives on the Raritan by a stage that ran twice a week from New York, through Brooklyn and thence through New Jersey to Philadelphia.[1] Samuel Ward of Philadelphia was related to the Wards of New York and Connecticut; President Aaron Burr of the New Jersey College, was a member of this family group. When Mr. and Mrs. John Bayard of Philadelphia made a tour in 1759 they were the guests of Col. William Bayard in New York and of Balthazar Bayard in Boston. New York and Philadelphia were, to a considerable degree, joined by blood ties in New Jersey whose inhabitants contracted many marriages with those in the aforementioned cities.[2] The Fayerweathers of Boston were related to the neighboring Shippens and maintained a correspondence with the Philadelphia branch of the latter group, which in turn had formed local ties with the aristocratic Plumleys.[3] The prominent Wendells of New York were related to the Quincys, Sewalls, Hancocks and other well known Massachusetts families. Benjamin Smith, a leader in political and mercantile affairs in South Carolina, belonged to the same family as Abigail Smith, the wife of John Adams. From the Continental Congress, Adams wrote to his wife that Stephen Collins, a transplanted native of New England with Boston relatives, was a gracious host, his "house is open to every New England man."[4]

[1] W. S. Pelletreau and J. H. Brown, *American Families of Historic Lineage* (N. Y., 1913), vol. i, pp. 10-30; *N. J. Hist. Soc. Proc.*, 1924, p. 112.

[2] G. K. Ward, *Andrew Warde and His Descendants* (N. Y., 1910-11); J. G Wilson, "Col. John Bayard and the Bayard Family of America", *N. Y. Genea. and Biog. Rec.*, vol. xvi, pp. 54-55; "Marriage Records", 1665-1800, *N. J. Archives*, ser. i, vol. v, p. 22.

[3] Balch, *Shippen Papers*, pp. xvi, xxv, xxviii.

[4] S. V. Talcott, *Genealogical Notes of New York and New England*

There was direct intermarriage of increasing proportions between New York and Philadelphia. Deborah Morris of Philadelphia married John Franklin of New York; Richard Willing of the Pennsylvania metropolis, was mated with Margaret Kortwright. The DeLanceys of New York intermarried with the Allens of Philadelphia, both distinguished families, and the Lawrences in these two cities were similarly connected with the famous Lewis Morris clan.[1] There were fewer family ties of this nature between Boston and New York than between the latter and Philadelphia, but several links were formed including a bond between the Apthorp and Bayard groups. William Ball, a leading Mason in Philadelphia, married a niece of the noted Rev. Dr. Mather Byles of Boston.[2]

The Jews and the Quakers were kept in touch with their respective coreligionists throughout the colonies by ties of kinship and belief. Pennsylvania was a sort of "mother colony for the Germans who settled in other parts of North America." The newly established town of Waldoboro in Maine, was strengthened by the importation of some twenty or thirty German families from Philadelphia. Many individuals scattered throughout the colonies, serving their indentures, had been assigned to their new homes from a common port of entry, Philadelphia.[3] Graduates

Families (Albany, 1883), pp. 383, 386, 393; Barrett Wendell, " Catherine Wendell, a Gentlewoman of Boston ", *Amer. Antiq. Soc. Proc.*, vol. xxix, 242-293; McCrady, *op. cit.*, 406-407; C. F. Adams, *The Works of John Adams* (Boston, 1850-56), vol. ii, p. 361 and note.

[1] J. W. Jordan, *Colonial Families of Philadelphia* (N. Y., 1911), vol. i, pp. 55, 125, 164; C. P. Keith, *The Provincial Councillors of Pennsylvania and Descendants* (Phila., 1883), pp. 154, 431-33.

[2] John Wentworth, *The Wentworth Genealogy* (Boston, 1878), vol. i, p. 520 note; N. S. Barratt and J. F. Sachse, *Freemasonry in Pennsylvania* (Phila., 1908-09), vol. i, p. 136, note 10.

[3] C. A. Herrick, *White Servitude in Pennsylvania* (Phila., 1926), p. 181; Faust, *op. cit.*, vol. i, pp. 251-53; *Pa. German Soc. Proc.*, vol. 16, "Records of Indentures ", Phila., 1771-73.

of Yale, originally resident in Connecticut, settled in the province of New York, especially in its leading city. Many had removed to Massachusetts, but as the century rolled along New York began to replace her New England rival as the scene of greater opportunities. A number of Princeton students sought fields beyond the horizon that limited their native outlook, and its alumni were scattered throughout the colonies, especially in the South. In his travels through Maine and New Hampshire, John Adams sometimes ran across college classmates.[1] Printers and preachers were often connected by family alliances with more than one locality; in a few instances merchants were similarly united.[2] Probably more detailed studies would show a large number of such relationships among the colonial aristocracy.

These associations, beginning largely in blood and belief, were fostered in many ways. Increasing travel for health, pleasure and business was effective in this service, and incidentally broadened the provincial horizon. Capt. John Montresor from New York went to drink the waters at Shrewsbury and the Yellow Springs near Philadelphia. A New York paper announced that Dr. Joseph Warren of Boston was on his way to the Stafford Springs in Connecticut, to examine the mineral water. Of this health resort, where people from many colonies congregated and which John Adams visited, he wrote in retrospection that it was "then in as much vogue as any mineral springs have been in since." [3] Douglass of Boston, wrote Colden that a friendly colleague was traveling through the country for enjoyment and health,

---

[1] S. D. Alexander, *Princeton College During the Eighteenth Century* (N. Y., 1872) ; Adams, *Works,* vol. ii, pp. 240-44.

[2] *Supra,* chap. i; *infra,* chaps. iii, iv.

[3] "Journals of Capt. John Montresor," *N. Y. Hist. Soc. Coll.,* 1881, p. 324; *N. Y. Gaz.,* Aug. 18, 1766 (Weyman), *Devoe's Index; Works,* vol. ii, p. 277, 264 note.

and intended to stop over with the New Yorker.[1]   Theophylact Bache from New York wrote Mrs. Deborah Franklin that Mr. and Mrs. Richard Bache would return home as soon as their friends allowed.   Perhaps the impatience of Benjamin's wife was somewhat allayed by the box of lobsters and a barrel of nuts that were forwarded.   Parker also sent lobsters; Nantucket, where as the phrase goes. Franklin's " keel was laid," sent him the renowned cod.[2] Jared Ingersoll of Connecticut was on friendly terms with Bache and Franklin.   Richard Bache from Philadelphia asked Cornelius Duane to take care of a friend visiting New York for the first time.[3]   To his father-in-law, Robert Livingston, James Duane wrote, " A circumstance that will be pleasing to you is currently reported . . . . that Temple of Boston, the new Surveyor Gen'l of the customs has lately wrote one of his friends, that he intends to return to that city by the way of New York."

Lord Stirling, who lived in New York and New Jersey had many friends in Philadelphia, and among his correspondents were Robert Morris, Governor William Franklin of New Jersey and Philip Livingston Jr., all conspicuous personages. Stirling was accustomed also to give letters of introduction for people intending to visit England, a practise that the better known Franklin frequently emulated.   William Allen of Philadelphia, wrote a letter of introduction for Philip Livingston of New York to General Robert Monckton, stating that their sons had been law students together at the Temple in London, were very friendly and " we have had frequently a mutual intercourse both here and at New York."[4]   John

---

[1] *Colden Papers,* vol. ii, pp. 204-05.

[2] *Cal. of Papers,* vol. v, pp. 203, 202.

[3] *Ingersoll Letters, loc. cit.,* pp. 252, 274-75; *Duane Papers,* July 12, 1761.

[4] *Ibid.,* box 8 (1) April 21, 1761; *Stirling Papers,* Dec. 16, 1767; Chalmers, *Papers Relating to Phila.,* vol. ii, Sept. 26, 1764.

Winthrop, the Harvard professor and Livingston were correspondents; so too, John Morgan, the Philadelphia doctor, and Henry Pelham, a Boston artist.[1]

Ties formed in undergraduate days were continued after college commencements. When William Livingston moved from New York, he was induced to settle in Elizabethtown, New Jersey because of the nearness of two former schoolmates at Yale. One of them, William P. Smith, insisted that another fellow student, Jared Ingersoll, stop over when on his travels and signed himself " an old chum who frequently recollects with pleasure the many agreeable social hours spent with you at alma mater." Ezra Stiles kept in frequent touch with his classmates from Yale who, though scattered through the colonies in after years, sometimes found their way to his door in Newport or entertained him on his travels.[2] Thus through the mail and through personal meetings the great distances that separated the colonials, physically and mentally, were gradually being narrowed.

The similarity in colonial recreations assisted the development of a common outlook. The taverns, where the community commonly gathered, were the centers of social life, and had various amusements more or less alike in different localities. These meeting places, which were the local reading rooms, subscribed to the papers of other cities, and in general performed a valuable service in affording direct contact with visitors who brought news of distant places. Some

---

[1] Stokes, p. 643; C. M. Andrews, *Guide to the Materials for American History to 1783 in the Public Record Office of Great Britain* (Wash., 1912-14), pp. 119-20.

[2] W. J. Mills, ed., William Paterson, *Glimpses of Colonial Society and Life at Princeton* (Phila., 1903); Theodore Sedgwick, *Memoir of the Life of W. Livingston* (N. Y., 1833), p. 157; Gipson, *Jared Ingersoll*, pp. 37-38; F. B. Dexter, ed., *The Literary Diary of Ezra Stiles* (N. Y., 1901), p. 207, note 2, *passim; Mass. Hist. Soc. Proc.*, ser. 2, vol. vii, p. 339, *et seq.*

of these inns became the regular rendezvous for travelers from a particular section; the "Horse and Cart" in New York was a favorite resort, it seems, of New Englanders.[1] Drinking, gaming, billiards, dances and lectures, even in supposedly staid Boston, interrupted the humdrum of existence. The taverns usually housed traveling exhibitions of models of foreign scenic wonders, and animal shows with a touch of P. T. Barnum were not unknown.[2]   An ingenious mechanism, the "Microcosm, or the World in Miniature," which had been on exhibition in Philadelphia, was brought to New York. Microcosms, musical clocks and like diversions were known to all the cities.[3]

There were clubs where many hours were whiled away and much strong liquid consumed. These clubs, as J. T. Adams has said, "were focal points for the creating and sharpening of a common consciousness and a new social organ for the formation of common views." A "Convivial Club" of professional gentlemen in New York counted among its members John Bard, the physician, and Cadwallader Colden; there were occasions when Franklin joined in the conviviality.[4]   Dr. Alexander Hamilton, the genial Maryland traveler, supped with the "Hungarian Club" in New York. "To drink stoutly . . . . is the readiest way for a stranger to recommend himself, and a set among them are very fond of making a stranger drunk."[5]   The social

[1] J. A. Stevens, Jr., "Old New York Taverns," *Harper's*, May, 1890, pp. 852-53; W. H. Bayles, *Old Taverns of New York* (N. Y., 1915), p. 118.

[2] R. E. Painter, "Tavern Amusements in Eighteenth Century America," *Americana*, vol. xi, pp. 92-115; "Peep Show Prints", *N. Y. P. L., Bulletin*, June, 1921, p. 364; G. C. D. Odell, *Annals of the New York Stage* (N. Y., 1927), vol. i, pp. 10, 18-19.

[3] Stokes, p. 678; Odell, vol. i, p. 72.

[4] *Provincial Society*, p. 262; *Westervelt MS.*, p. 49, "Social Clubs", 1750.

[5] A. B. Hart, ed., *Hamilton's Itinerarium* (St. Louis, 1907), pp. 49, 106.

circles of Penn's colony, which in ever-widening circumferences were including more individuals were, perhaps, the choicest in English America. One of the liveliest spirits in the Annapolis "Tuesday Club" was Jonas Green, printer of the "Maryland Gazette," whose profession had carried him from his Boston home through the colonies southward.[1]

The lighter aspects of group life in New England have been overshadowed by an attention to the more sombre elements in the Puritan tradition, while the greater emphasis placed by most historians upon these recreational activities in the middle and southern colonies has further served to prevent a just appraisal of the like in the north. A year before the outbreak of the Revolution, New York and Philadelphia sold a new publication, " Maxims for Playing Whist," but two years earlier, Boston had given evidence of an equal devotion to "Lady Luck." "The passing of Puritanism," Professor Morison reflects, "may be tested by the fact that Boston imported [over 6000] packs of playing cards in 1772, more than any other districts save New York and Maryland." [2]

Capt. Francis Goelet, a New York merchant, was on a voyage when a storm forced him to ride to safety in Boston harbor. He disembarked and entered upon a lengthy holiday in this haven of refuge where the Wendells were among his friends, with whom he joined in "turtle frolics," much like those he had enjoyed in his own town.[3] Goelet dined with Edmund Quincy whose daughters played on the harpsichord, and he found time for additional music, as his memoir records that he attended a concert, evidently a

[1] W. B. Norris, *Annapolis: Its Colonial and Naval Story* (N. Y., 1925), pp. 63-64.

[2] Evans, 13433; Morison, *loc. cit.*, p. 35.

[3] "Journal of Capt. Francis Goelet," *New Eng. Hist. and Genea. Reg.*, vol. 24, pp. 52-54.

membership affair, where he heard a small organ, a base
violin, "one German flute and 4 small violins." In calmer
days tea had satisfied uses other than those dearer to the
hearts of political radicals. John Penn wrote from Boston
to Willing in Philadelphia, "I have promis'd to drink tea
with your old flame this afternoon. . . . We are to be enter-
tain'd tomorrow night with a Concert & a ball." [1]   Dr.
Hamilton reported that the Puritan metropolis had

an abundance of men of learning and parts so that one is at no
loss for agreeable conversation, nor for any set of company he
pleases. Assemblies of the gayer sort are frequent here; the
gentlemen and ladies meeting almost every week at concerts of
musick and balls. I was present at two or three such, and saw
as fine a ring of ladies, as good dancing, and heard musick as
elegant as I had been witness to anywhere.

So insistent was the demand of Terpsichore in some places,
that dancing masters made arrangements to take care of
those whose business occupied them during the day; the
cultivation of the eighteenth-century " Science of Defence,"
the sword, also engaged many instructors. [2]

The larger American municipalities were becoming used
to performances of the best music of the time by orchestras
large enough to play overtures and symphonies. By 1740,
there were weekly concerts throughout the year in Philadelphia and probably in New York, supported by the subscriptions of the same exclusive circles that attended the
dancing assemblies. Certainly by 1762, there were weekly
concerts in the last named city. [3]   Men like John McLean

[1] T. W. Balch, *Willing Letters and Papers* (Phila., 1922), pp. 17-18.

[2] *Itinerarium*, pp. 178-179; *Pa. Packet*, Sept. 13, 1773, supplement;
N. Y. Journal, Nov. 1, 1770; *Boston Gaz. and Country Journal*, Feb. 25,
1771.

[3] O. G. Sonneck, *Early Opera in America* (N. Y., 1915), p. 24; Odell,
vol. i, p. 25; *N. Y. Mercury*, Nov. 8, *Devoe's Index*.

traveled from city to city giving concerts and instruction. To enliven a Princeton commencement, a band of music from Philadelphia was imported, while the celebrated St. Cecilia Society of Charlestown, S. C., went even further afield to advertise in New York for musicians to be hired by yearly contract.[1]

Similarly operas and dramatic productions were fairly common throughout the colonies, except in New England, where the opposition to the theatre was very strong. Even there however, in Portsmouth, New Hampshire, prominent individuals prompted by a New York actor had filed an unsuccessful petition to open a play-house.[2] One of the earliest performances in New York which attracted the attention of Boston, was called the "Recruiting Officer," given at the New Theatre. The "Punch's opera, Bateman or the Unhappy Marriage," played in Philadelphia and New York, was a puppet show. It was evidently still attracting attention some time later.[3] In February 1750, Thomas Kean's theatrical company which played in Philadelphia arrived in New York, where they gave the tragedy of Richard III and a benefit performance for the Charity Free School. New York was interested in Philadelphia theatrical events, for it chronicled the opening of a new theatre in that city,[4] but some months previously a local news item of greater importance noted that the Hallam Company had arrived from London. The season lasted from September

[1] Sonneck, *Early Concert Life in America* (Leipzig, 1907), pp. 75, 171; J. R. Williams, ed., Philip Vickers Fithian, *Journal and Letters* (Princeton, 1900), p. 43; *N. Y. Gaz. or Weekly Mercury*, Sept. 16, 1771.

[2] *New Hampshire Hist. Soc. Coll.*, vol. v, pp. 247-48 (1762); Quakers and Baptists in Phila. opposed the theatre.

[3] *N. E. and Boston Gaz.*, Jan. 1, 1733, Devoe; *N. Y. Post-Boy*, Aug. 31, 1747; Esther Singleton, *Social New York under the Georges* (N. Y., 1902), p. 316.

[4] G. O. Seilhamer, *History of the American Theatre* (Phila., 1888-91), vol. i, pp. 5-6; Stokes, 618; *N. Y. Gaz.*, April 29, June 24, 1754, Devoe.

1753 to March 1754, and strangely enough, for an age thought of as exceptionally pious, Congreve's Restoration dramas were the most successful. "Love for Love," played in New York again in 1925, was well known; Shakespeare, too, had many productions. While the company was in New York, Hallam went to Philadelphia to prepare the ground. In the latter city the season lasted from April to June 1754, and many of the plays given in New York were repeated in Philadelphia. The company was in New York again some years later with certificates testifying to its good character, for in those days actors were sometimes classed with vagabonds.[1]   Both Kean and Hallam programmed operas in New York, and a "gorgeous presentation" of "Cymon" was announced in terms indicative of a close affinity between eighteenth and twentieth century impresarios. It was said during its run at Philadelphia, that several Londoners who saw it compared it favorably with English productions.[2]   In Boston and Newport, the spirit of the law was evaded by having a single individual impersonate all the characters of a play or by taking extracts from operas and dramas, and calling the performance a "Vocal entertainment" or a series of "Moral Dialogues." [3]

The theatre was put on a firmer footing with the arrival of David Douglass. Not to be outdone by Hallam in appealing to popular favor, he also gave a benefit performance for the Charity School in New York. Some three years earlier Douglass had played "Hamlet" for the first time in Philadelphia. Here in 1766, he built America's first permanent theatre where his troupe, known now as "The American Company," performed. Douglass built theatres

---

[1] Seilhamer, pp. 44-79; N. Y. Gaz., Oct. 16, 1758, Devoe.

[2] N. Y. Mercury, May 31, 1773, Stokes, p. 838.

[3] Boston Gaz. or Country Journal, March 19, 1770, May 14; Odell, vol. i, p. 81.

later, in New York and elsewhere, and his efforts in conjunction with those of other players were as a link joining together many budding intercolonial theatrical interests. His New York John Street Theatre held the same influential position possessed by the Southwark Theatre in Philadelphia, and the two cities shared many of his performances. The seasons of 1769-1770 and 1772-1773 in Philadelphia were very successful, and so quickly had Douglass gained the public favor that for the first time a clergyman, the Anglican Myles Cooper of King's College, in a prologue to a benefit performance in New York, openly sanctioned theatre-going, which was generally condemned by the Calvinistic clergy.[1]

Other forms of entertainment were the common heritage of innumerable colonists. Horse racing and exhibitions of horsemanship attracted great crowds of devotees, and interest was not purely local. At a race on Hempstead Plains, Long Island, an audience of over one thousand was estimated, and these events frequently drew spectators from distant cities.[2]   Horsemen throughout the colonies competed with one another for superiority in turf contests, and although Maryland, Philadelphia and New York were especially active, opportunities were also provided for matches between the remarkably fast Narragansett pacer of Rhode Island and the blooded horses of Virginia. James DeLancey with his "Sultana" and "Wildair," was a well known figure in other provinces; he and Lewis Morris Jr. had the best stables in New York.[3]   They followed the races

---

[1] April 26, May 3, 1762, *N. Y. Hist. Soc. Coll.*, 1870, pp. 182-183; Seilhamer, pp. 92, 157, 196, 212, 241, 248, 269, 316, 323-324.

[2] *N. Y. Weekly Post-Boy*, June 4, 1750; Mr. Faulk performed on a horse in N. Y. and Phila., *N. Y. Gaz. and Weekly Mercury*, Nov. 18, 1771.

[3] F. B. Culver, *Blooded Horses of Colonial Days* (Baltimore, 1922), pp. 73-76, 143-151; J. A. Stevens, " Colonial Rivalry on the Turf ", *Rider ; Driver*, Feb. 18, 1892.

at Philadelphia when " Salem " beat " Briton ".   Lovers of
the turf in all the provinces were notified that the gentlemen
of Philadelphia had raised a purse to be run for.[1]   " Lath,"
DeLancey's prize horse, won the Jockey Club purse at
Philadelphia in 1769, a victory repeated the next year, and
once again some time later by " Sultana."   In different ways
intercolonial aspects of the racing game may be noted.
James Rivington of New York and Lord Stirling were
members of the Jockey Club.   Horses were bred and sent
to other colonies, especially from the famous New York
stables, and the "sport of kings" was given a decided impetus
in Philadelphia on the assembling of the Continental Congress.   A less popular sport was cock fighting which sometimes provided intercity matches.[2]

The satisfaction of the sporting instinct in lotteries resulted in many interprovincial contacts.   This game of
chance was a favorite form of gambling in which all classes
of colonial society participated, and news of lotteries traveled
up and down the seaboard.   They were devised to promote
all sorts of enterprises from building colleges to building
roads, and it was customary for organizers of lotteries to
offer their tickets for sale in all the principal colonial cities.
Franklin managed one in Philadelphia to raise money to
finish the steeple of Christ Church and purchase a set of
bells; tickets were available in New York and Boston.
When the Presbyterian Church of Philadelphia held a lottery, tickets were sold in New York.[3]   By 1761, lotteries
in Philadelphia had so increased that the country was flooded

---

[1] *N. Y. Gaz. or Weekly Post-Boy*, April 18, 1765; *Pa. Journal*, June 19,
1766, *N. J. Archives*, ser. i, vol. xxv, pp. 146-148.

[2] *Stirling Papers*, Jan. 7, 1767; *Rider; Driver*, March 11, 1893, March 25,
April 8; "Diary of Jacob Hiltzheimer", *Pa. Mag. of Hist. and Biog.*,
vol. xvi, pp. 95-98; "Diary of James Allen", *ibid.*, vol. ix, p. 180.

[3] A. F. Ross, *The History of Lotteries in New York* (N. Y., 1906?),
pp. 20-22; Thomas Dering, *Journal*, Boston, N. E., p. 26, Feb. 19, 1753.

with tickets, and an act of the next year prevented unauthorized holdings which, however, did not check the introduction of foreign tickets into this fertile territory.[1]

More important as agents in promoting intercolonial good will and producing an atmosphere common to distantly separated groups, were the fraternal societies. Organized for social and mutually beneficial purposes, they have long existed in America. Masonic lodges were actively functioning as early as 1730 in Philadelphia and Boston, and perhaps in other cities as well. Three years later, Henry Price was made "Provincial Grand Master" of New England and the other colonies, an item of interest to Boston and Philadelphia newspapers.[2] A "Grand Lodge" was formed by Price at Boston, to which Philadelphia applied in order that its organization might be constituted regularly. Franklin, well known to Price, played an important part in the Masonic movement, and was the leader of the fraternity in Pennsylvania by reason of appointment by the Boston lodge.[3] A Capt. Richard Riggs was appointed New York Grand Master. Theatre parties are an old custom, for it is recorded that the New York Masons once bought out the house for a performance by the Hallam Company.[4] From the parent society in Boston at least forty lodges had sprung by 1750, whose rolls included the leading colonists in mercantile, military and civil walks of life. It was not unusual for members of the fraternity to attend one another's meetings when passing from city to city so that "a Mason travel-

---

[1] A. E. Martin, "Lotteries in Pa. prior to 1833," *Pa. Mag. of Hist. and Biog.,* vol. xlvii, pp. 313-319.

[2] M. M. Johnson, *The Beginnings of Freemasonry in America* (N. Y., 1924), pp. 58, 79.

[3] J. F. Sachse, *Benjamin Franklin as a Free Mason* (Phila., 1906), pp. 39, 42.

[4] O. H. Lang, *History of Freemasonry in the State of New York* (N. Y., 1922), p. 12; *N. Y. Mercury,* Dec. 3, 1753, in *N. Y. Hist. Soc. Coll.,* 1870, pp. 165, 166.

ing through America instead of being a lonely stranger would have found himself among an organized band of his brothers " in nearly every town.[1] An important personage was Moses Michael Hays, appointed Deputy Inspector General for North America, who visited Philadelphia, New York, Newport and Boston in the performance of his duties. Franklin attended Boston meetings, so did Capt. Goelet during his stay there. Non-residents were sometimes elected to local groups; migrants changed memberships. A Capt. Edward Clarke of New York was elected to the Boston lodge; Henry Dawkins, a New York engraver, on his re-moval to Philadelphia joined the local lodge. The news-papers in the various cities reprinted each other's Masonic items and there is evidence of a fairly constant intercolonial fraternal interest.[2]

A more restricted influence was exerted by societies repre-senting emigrant groups anxious to keep alive sentimental recollections of native homes, and to assist one another in time of need. The Society of the Sons of St. George was located in Philadelphia and New York, but the former branch had honorary members in Boston as well as in the city of its sister organization. The New York society had social relations with other groups, St. David's, St. Andrew's and St. Patrick's. St. Andrew's had branches in Charles-town, Philadelphia and New York whither Dr. Adam Thom-son, a noted physician, had carried the constitution of the Pennsylvania group to furnish the model for the newly organized body of Scotsmen.[3] Philip Livingston of New

[1] Adams, op. cit., p. 263.

[2] S. Oppenheim, " Jews and Masonry Before 1800," Amer. Jew. Hist. Soc. Pub., vols. xix, xiii, p. 95; Johnson, op. cit., pp. 381-383, 175-185; N. S. Barratt and J. F. Sachse, op. cit. p. 46, note 1.

[3] T. C. Knauff, A History of the Society of the Sons of St. George . . . at Philadelphia (Phila., 1923), pp. 196, 210, 223, 240; G. A. Morri-son, History of Saint Andrew's Society of the State of New York (N. Y., 1906), pp. 7, 8.

York, was an honorary member of the Quaker city branch. Adherents of St. Patrick were to be found in Boston, New York and Philadelphia. The earliest American St. Patrick's celebration was held, appropriately enough, in view of its later development, in the first named. In New York City celebrations are recorded as early as 1762, but the probabilities are that, privately, the Saint was commemorated much earlier. Soldiers in the city formed the "Friendly Brothers of St. Patrick" (1769), and two years later a similar society was instituted at Philadelphia. The latter brotherhood which had among its honorary members William Hicks and James Searle, former New Yorkers who became prominent citizens in their adopted homes, included also the name of General Henry Knox, who was attached to the Boston society as well.[1]

Marine societies, whose efforts were mostly directed toward helping distressed captains and their families, date from this period. The leading colonial ports established these organizations almost simultaneously since their advantages were rapidly made known by the ships which sailed in and out of provincial harbors. Boston had one at the turn of the half century; New York's, still in existence, was incorporated in 1769. Within two years the Pennsylvania assembly incorporated a society whose object was " to provide a fund for the care and maintenance of aged and distressed pilots and masters of vessels." Salem, Newburyport and Marblehead had such societies before 1773.[2]

[1] J. D. Crimmins, *St. Patrick's Day: Its Celebration in New York and Other American Places*, 1737-1845 (N. Y., 1902), pp. 15, 25, 27, 215-216, 332, 372, 424.

[2] A. M. Davis, " Colonial Corporations," *Col. Soc. of Mass., Trans.*, vol. i, pp. 211, 212; *N. Y. Gaz. and Weekly Mercury*, Nov. 13, 1769; *The Marine Society of the City of New York* (N. Y., 1925), pp. 5-6; W. C. Heffner, *History of Poor Relief Legislation in Pennsylvania* (Cleona, Pa. 1913), pp. 87-88; *Statutes at Large of Pa.*, vol. vii, pp. 341-350, Feb. 24, 1770; W. H. Bailey and O. O. Jones, *History of the Marine Society of Newburyport, Mass.*, (Newburyport, 1906), pp. 313-314.

Humanitarian feelings also found expression in other ways, and often cut across provincial lines. A Charitable Irish Society in Boston (1737) at first permitted only the admission of Protestants, but it was not long before Catholics were likewise welcomed. Robert Auchmuty, of a family well known in New York too, was a president of the Boston society.[1] Jacob Wendell of an intercolonial family contributed some money to enable poor people of Boston to be employed in linen manufactures;[2] similar societies were founded in other colonies. The Rev. Dr. Auchmuty of Trinity Church, New York, President Myles Cooper of King's College and Provost William Smith of the College of Philadelphia, drew up a scheme for insurance on the lives of Anglican clergymen in New York, Pennsylvania and New Jersey. A corporation for the relief of widows and children of clergymen was established, which held meetings in New York and Philadelphia, attended by civil as well as by religious authorities. By 1770 charters had been secured in Pennsylvania and in New York through the good offices of Colden.[3] The Rev. Richard Peters of Philadelphia and well known in other colonies, was elected president; there were treasurers for New York, New Jersey and Pennsylvania, who collected a goodly sum in a short time.[4] At a meeting held for the benefit of the

[1] *Charitable Irish Society of Boston* (Boston, 1876), pp. 21-23 and note; Crimmins, *op. cit.*, pp. 331-332.

[2] " Early Charitable Organizations of Boston," *New Eng. Hist. and Genea. Reg.*, vol. xliv, pp. 102-103; W. R. Bagnall, *The Textile Industries of the United States* (Cambridge, 1893), vol. i, pp. 35, 50-51.

[3] J. W. Wallace, *A Century of Beneficence, 1769-1869. Historical Sketch of the Corporation for the Relief of the Widows and Children of Clergymen in the Communion of the Protestant Episcopal Church in Pennsylvania* (Phila., 1870) ; *Colden Papers*, vol. vii, Oct. 10, 1769.

[4] Morgan Dix, *A History of the Parish of Trinity Church in New York* (N. Y., 1898-1906), vol. i, pp. 337-338.

corporation in New York, twenty eight ministers from various colonies attended, and were entertained by one of the first performances of Handel's "Messiah" in America. Three years later in New York most of the Anglican ministers in the three middle colonies attended an anniversary meeting at which the Rev. Dr. Peters preached. At both functions the relief society collected considerable funds which were increased by Dr. Ogilvie, a prominent citizen who willed £100 to the corporation.[1] The Presbyterians, the Congregationalists and the members of the Dutch Reformed Church also had organizations to relieve the widows and children of clergymen.[2] These corporate enterprises have had a lusty progeny, whose present-day activities reach into many bypaths only dimly suggested by their eighteenth-century forerunners.

A feeling of community was quickened on the occasion of Boston's disastrous fire in 1760. Governor Pownall of Massachusetts wrote to Lieutenant Governor DeLancey, and it was ordered that the Assembly be asked for a grant to the sufferers and that collections be made for their relief. On June 10 the New York legislature voted £2500 to the victims of the fire in which two hundred families were made homeless. In large measure this money came from citizens of New York City "and is an early indication of the broadly benevolent spirit shown in later years under similar circumstances." Charles W. Apthorp, a well known merchant, donated £100 to the Boston sufferers. While noting the ordinary kindly thoughts that motivate people under such conditions, the New York legislature remarked on the special consideration to be shown in view of the fact that they

---

[1] *N. Y. Journal or Gen'l Advertiser*, Sept. 27, 1770, Oct. 4, Oct. 7, 1773; Rivington's *N. Y. Gaz.*, Dec. 29, 1774, in *N. Y. Hist. Soc. Coll.*, 1870, pp. 208, 236, 258-59.

[2] J. S. Davis, *Essays in the Earlier History of American Corporations* (*Harv. Eco. Studies,* 16, Cambridge, 1917), vol. i, p. 81.

were "our own Countreymen and members of the same Polity." The response to Boston's plight was widespread; collections were taken up in Virginia, Maryland, Pennsylvania, New Hampshire and Rhode Island. Twenty years earlier, in a similar situation, Massachusetts had come to the aid of Charlestown, S. C., by ordering a collection to be made in all the local provincial parishes.[1]

The intercolonial life of the spirit was to be nourished in other ways. Proposals were made for the formation of an American society based on English and Scottish models to promote religious knowledge among the poor in the colonies; books were to be loaned by the society. Requests for information were to be directed to Noel and Hazard, booksellers in New York, and to William and Thomas Bradford, printers in Philadelphia. Elias Boudinot of Elizabethtown, later to be the first president of the American Bible Society, was also connected with the earlier organization.[2] Intercolonial efforts assisted the desire of Eleazar Wheelock to develop his Indian Charity School. Dennys DeBerdt, a merchant known along the seaboard used his influence in the principal cities to further Wheelock's plans.[3] From the Quaker city, Anthony Benezet, a lovely soul, wrote a long letter to Sir Jeffrey Amherst who was in New York preparing for a campaign against the Indians. Benezet urged moderation to prevent the spilling of blood, a quixotic but attractive appeal.[4]

A realization of the common humanity of negroes and whites was early in evidence. The work carried on among

---

[1] Stokes, p. 712; *N. Y. Col. Doc.*, vol. vii, p. 429; *Col. Laws of N. Y.*, vol. iv, p. 454; *N. Y. Gaz. and Post-Boy*, Nov. 27, 1760; *Boston Gaz. and Country Journal*, April 28, 1760; *Itineraries and Corr. of Ezra Stiles*, pp. 120-125.

[2] *Pa. Packet*, Aug. 9, 1773.

[3] "Letters of Dennys DeBerdt," *Col. Soc. of Mass., Trans.*, vol. 13.

[4] Roberts Vaux, *Memoirs of Anthony Benezet* (Phila., 1817), pp. 77-86.

the negroes, by the Society for Propagating the Gospel in Foreign Parts, was of marked value in all the colonies, more particularly in New York and Philadelphia. The Rev. Dr. Cutler admitted negro slaves to his church in Boston, and the Rev. Samuel Auchmuty, transplanted to New York, was appointed catechist to the negroes there. The "Associates of Dr. Bray" opened a school for the colored folk in Philadelphia, and Benezet taught them freely in an institution established by the Friends. Franklin recommended that others be built in Williamsburg and in Newport, Rhode Island; he suggested to the Rev. Henry Barclay of Trinity Church, New York, that Dr. Samuel Johnson of King's College and Auchmuty be appointed to take care of the local school whose enrolment in 1760 showed thirty names.[1]

The anti-slavery movement in colonial times was prompted by several factors, fear of uprisings, the economic argument stressing the inefficiency of slaves, and what may be termed the humanitarian ideal. The "Selling of Joseph," by Chief Justice Sewall of Massachusetts, was a significant tract against the slave trade and slavery itself, although it did not distinctly propose its abolition. Plans were on foot to legislate against the institution in Boston, the very year Sewall wrote. Some years later the economic argument was used as an attack.[2] This Massachusetts sentiment had its reflection in Philadelphia, where John Hepburn in "The American Defense of the Christian Golden Rule" quoted Cotton Mather and made use of Sewall's reprint of the

[1] C. E. Pierre, "The Work of the S. P. G. among the Negroes in the Colonies", *Journal of Negro History*, vol. i, pp. 349-360; J. P. Wickersham, *History of Education in Pennsylvania* (Lancaster, 1886), p. 216; W. W. Kemp, *The Support of Schools in Colonial New York by the S. P. G. F. P.* (N. Y., 1913; *Contributions to Ed., Teachers College, Col. Univ.*, no. 56), pp. 252-257; *N. Y. Mercury*, Aug. 4, 1760.

[2] Albert Mathews, "Early Protests against Slavery," *Col. Soc. of Mass., Trans.*, vol. viii, p. 288.

"Athenian Oracle". Benjamin Lay, who wrote "All Slave Keepers Apostates," quoted Sewall's "Selling of Joseph". Franklin pointed out the bad effects of slavery upon social conditions in his "Observations concerning the Increase of Mankind". Soon there were petitions against the importation of slaves in Massachusetts, but not until long after the Quakers had taken a determined stand on the subject. In 1729, members of the sect in Pennsylvania and in New England acting together, opposed the purchase of slaves already imported.[1] The period of the French and Indian War saw many meetings of the Friends taking action against the trade and holding of slaves. The "Yearly Meeting" communicated with its constituents; traveling Quakers like John Woolman and Peter Andrews influenced those in other colonies. Woolman made a trip through New York to New England stopping at Boston, on which he expressed himself as opposed to slavery. He argued against the unchristianlike conduct of slave-keeping on Long Island, and pleaded his cause in Virginia and Carolina as well. Into one of the busiest slave marts on the continent, at Newport, Rhode Island, plunged the gentle crusader; New York was touched by the sincerity of his convictions. Woolman's "Considerations on keeping Negroes" was sent to Virginia, New York and Newport.[2] Anthony Benezet proposed a cessation of slave imports, then to declare free by law those already purchased after a period of service, and suggested the territory west of the Alleghanies as a suitable place for colonization. His own philanthropy proved the capacity of the negro for usefulness. Among the congregationalists, the Rev. Samuel Hopkins and Ezra Stiles opposed slavery.[3]

[1] M. S. Locke, *Anti-Slavery in America, 1619-1808* (Boston, 1901, *Radcliffe College Monographs,* no. 11), 33-34, 50, 17-18.

[2] *The Works of John Woolman* (Phila., 1800), pp. 44, 110-111, 132-153; W. T. Shore, *John Woolman, His Life and Our Times* (London, 1913), pp. 117, 137, 163-168.

[3] Locke, *op. cit.,* pp. 31-32, 40, 56.

The Revolutionary philosophy so much in vogue after 1761 had implications undermining the supports of slavery. In the early Quaker discussions, religion was the source of argument, but in the 1760's the doctrine of natural rights was invoked. The argument of James Otis against the "Writs of Assistance" included generally the rights of negroes too, as being born free in a state of nature. A thesis submitted for the Harvard M. A. the same year, denied that it was "lawful to subject Africans to perpetual bondage".[1] It was the Stamp Act controversy which gave a greater impetus to the opposition literature. Nathaniel Appleton in Boston urged the abandonment of slavery at any cost. In his "Considerations on Slavery," having in mind the " Negro plot " in New York in 1741, and the South Carolina insurrection two years before, he pointed out that the "slaves, as the experience of New York and other colonies has recently proved, 'instead of being a defence . . . . of the Commonwealth are often its terror and sometimes its destruction.' "[2] Dr. Benjamin Rush wrote " An Address . . . . upon Slave-keeping" which went into two editions in Philadelphia and was reprinted in New York, Boston and Norwich. He took account of the volume of literature already presented on the subject, and substantiated the claim of the negro to freedom by a reference to the literary achievements of Phyllis Wheatley, the colored Boston poetess. A disputation at the Harvard commencement opposed slavery on a natural rights basis, but Boston had already agitated a bill for its abolition; signs of disapproval were seen in New Jersey and Delaware. Pennsylvania placed a prohibitive duty on the importation of slaves, while the Quakers in New England, New York and Philadelphia began to disown those members who continued to hold slaves. Prohibitory

[1] Locke, *op. cit.*, pp. 27, 46-49; *Mass. Hist. Soc. Proc.*, i, vol. xviii, p. 139.
[2] Locke, p. 50, pp. 19-20.

duties were also levied in Rhode Island and Connecticut.[1] Benezet, who influenced many in the opposition group, wrote Franklin, urging his cause and pointed to supporters in New England and Virginia.   He and Woolman had English well-wishers too, notably Dr. John Fothergill.[2] Economic forces eventually were to succeed where humanitarian ideals faltered, but for a brief moment the vision of a finer existence floated before the negroes because of the dreams of some practising Christians.

It is evident that there are far more strands than have hitherto been counted when tracing intercolonial relationships.   Ties of blood and of spirit knotted widely separated groups, and narrow provincialisms in contact with the larger colonial world tended to be sloughed off.   The general participation in diversions with a universal appeal resulted in the formation of common attitudes.   Clubs and other organizations, outgrowths of a rapidly developing social consciousness, were the means whereby isolated individuals might be awakened to the contemplation of a larger social unit.   In the process of this awakening the less fortunate members of the community were not lost to sight.   Sharing pleasures in common suggested sharing burdens too, and humanitarian appeals touched responsive chords.   All these agencies for promoting group feeling appear weak enough, when compared with their modern counterparts, yet their importance in jostling the lonely colonial out of provincial isolation cannot be denied.

[1] Evans, 12990 (1773) ; Locke, *op. cit.,* pp. 53, 56, note 3, pp. 35-36, 71.

[2] Franklin, *Calendar of Papers,* vol. ii, p. 132; R. H. Fox, *Dr. John Fothergill and His Friends* (London, 1919), pp. 222-223.

CHAPTER III

RELIGIOUS CONTACTS

The social contacts, which in increasing measure were cutting across colonial boundaries, were only a phase of the general American process of learning about the neighbors. The eighteenth-century Americans of almost any locality were also very much interested in the religious life of fellow colonists, which led sometimes to mutually helpful endeavors and just as often to mutually bitter reproaches. But then, of course, the knowledge that comes in any learning process may be welcome or unwelcome, depending on the strength of original prejudices. It is frequently stated that among the prejudices which fostered antagonism between the colonies, religion loomed large. It is explained that New England was cut off from the rest of America especially because of a different religious affiliation. To a large degree the statement is probably true, but qualifications considerably weaken its strength. Here and there are indications of a community in spiritual interests with southern areas. Among the middle colonies, particularly, there was a close interweaving of these associations. Many ministers had attachments in more than one locality, and religious books having an extensive circulation assisted in welding common bonds.

The relations within some of the sects were fairly close, religious ties being augmented by those of kinship. The period 1750-1776, witnessed the migration of a number of New York Jews to Philadelphia, Newport and Charlestown. Several families of note located in Philadelphia were connected with the New York Jews, some through intimate commercial and family relations, as in the case of the Franks.[1] The social amenities were observed within this racial group. Isaac Solomon from Boston sent New Year greetings to the family of Mordecai Gomez in New York. Nathan Levy from Boston, corresponded with a member of the same religious persuasion in his former home, Philadelphia. Judah Monis, formerly a rabbi in New York and elsewhere, taught Hebrew at Harvard and published the first Hebrew grammar in America. There was much friendly intercourse between the New York and Pennsylvania Jews. Isaac M. Seixas wrote to Joseph Symons of Lancaster, introducing his son Gershom; best wishes were added on the marriage of Miss Symons to Michael Gratz. A community in Reading, Pa. borrowed the scroll of the Law from the New York congregation through the influence of leading Philadelphia Jews. At the same time New York furnished financial assistance to build a synagogue at Newport, and revealed an interest in the proposed erection of a house of worship in Philadelphia.[2] When the Revolution broke out the Rev. Gershom M. Seixas left New York with others, and went to Philadelphia to take charge of the congregation. Rabbis from other lands traveling through the colonies established some ties among the scattered groups. So too, some of the domestic religious leaders like Rabbi Touro of Newport, well known in New York, and Gershom Seixas, who, some years before his final removal, had visited Philadelphia to open up a new synagogue, performed similar services.[3]

[1] C. P. Daly, *The Settlement of the Jews in North America* (N. Y., 1893), pp. 52, 58; H. P. Rosenbach, *Jews in Phila. Prior to 1800* (Phila., 1883), pp. 11-13; *Amer. Jew. Hist. Soc. Pub.*, vol. iv, p. 197.

[2] L. M. Friedman, "Early Jewish Residents in Mass.," *Amer. Jew. Hist. Soc. Pub.*, vol. xxiii, p. 82, note 22, p. 85, note 37; *ibid.*, vol. xxii, pp. 2-11 and note 9, pp. 3-4; vol. xxvii, pp. 170-171, 20-21, 177-182; Rosenbach, *op. cit.*, p. 6.

[3] Morris Jastrow, "Jews in Phila.," *Amer. Jew. Hist. Soc. Pub.*, vol. i, p. 51; Stiles, *Diary*, July 18, 1771.

The difficulties confronting the Catholics are too well known to rehearse again. These seemed to increase in direct proportion to the distance one traveled north or south from Philadelphia. Because of the tolerant spirit that prevailed here, with other advantages, a letter to Rome suggested that Philadelphia be made the central seat of Catholicism in the English American colonies. Bishop Challoner wrote

... it is a very populous city and is moreover, a seaport, and consequently is convenient for the easy exchange of letters with the other provinces of the mainland as also with the islands. To these various reasons may be added the fact that there is no place within the English dominions where the Catholic Religion is exercised with greater freedom.[1]

It should be remembered however, that despite the open hostility toward this church, Catholics and Protestants before the Revolution had joined together in a Boston charitable society. New York copied a Catholic item from a Boston newspaper, and the death of a Philadelphia priest was chronicled in New York. John Leary, a turfman and popular with the gentry in the latter town, went every Easter to Philadelphia for confession. Gradually the Jesuit fathers extended pastoral visits to members of the faith in New Jersey, and reached New York just before the outbreak of military hostilities in 1775.[2]

The Quakers had very intimate religious and family ties for they moved around more freely than people of other sects, always assured of an hospitable reception among the brethren. The intermarriage among them was comparatively large; several Franklins in New York took Philadelphia inhabitants for spouses. The daughters of John Rodman of

[1] Peter Guilday, *The Life and Times of John Carroll* (N. Y., 1922), vol. i, p. 62 (1763?).

[2] *U. S. Catholic Hist. Mag.*, vol. ii, pp. 93-98; J. G. Shea, *Catholic Churches of New York City* (N. Y., 1878), pp. 28-30.

Long Island found new homes in Philadelphia and Boston.[1] The Friends' meetings kept the members in close touch with one another.   In 1772, for example, there were 180 "Particular meetings" of districts with centers in Newport (which included Boston), Flushing, New York, Philadelphia and elsewhere; these offered many points of contact.   Robert Barclay's Quaker "Catechism and Confession of Faith" was reprinted in Newport and in the two principal cities of the middle colonies.   The Society of Friends published "An Epistle" in Philadelphia and Boston.[2]   Quaker preachers traveled throughout the colonies often doing very effective work, none more than John Woolman.   European Friends at times visited America, less frequently colonials returned the compliment.   Samuel Fothergill, a brother of the helpful Dr. John, whose generosity assisted many American enterprises, was in the colonies in 1754 where he did much to raise the tone of religious life among the Quakers, who were becoming negligent.   He visited many of the provinces and the next year addressed a gathering of 2000 persons in Boston.[3]

Pennsylvania was the pivotal point in the intercolonial plans of several sects.   The Philadelphia congregation of the German Reformed Church was organized in 1727 by the Rev. George M. Weiss, who was likewise responsible for its establishment in New York.   About a decade later the Dutch Reformed ministers of New York and the German Reformed of Pennsylvania tried to organize a coetus, an attempt which resulted only in separate associations.   An-

---

[1] " N. Y. Marriages from Friends' Records of Phila.," *N. Y. Genea. and Biog. Rec.,* vol. iii, pp. 51-52, vol. v, p. 38, vol. iv, p. 194, vol. vi, pp. 101-103, 106; vol. vii, p. 41.

[2] *Bulletin of Friends' Hist. Soc. of Phila.,* vol. iv, no. 1, March, 1911; Evans, 6812-14, 8859-60.

[3] James Bowden, *History of the Society of Friends in America* (London, 1850-54), vol. ii, pp. 237-38, 291, 292; Fox, *op. cit.,* pp. 243-44.

other effort at union with the Presbyterian and Dutch Reformed churches also failed. Like other churches this had its energetic personalities known almost everywhere. John Philip Boehm was a connecting link binding all members of the church; the Rev. Michael Schlatter was another who made close contacts in the three largest cities. Schlatter went to New York to confer about the founding of a synod for the Germans, and when his new church was building at Philadelphia, the Dutch Reformed congregation in the former province sent him a generous sum. The Rev. Frederick Rothenbuhler was preaching to a Reformed congregation in New York when Philadelphia called him.[1] By recognizing each other's licenses to preach, the Dutch Reformed Churches in the middle colonies kept in rather close touch. In the middle of the century a suggested union between the Dutch and Germans with the Presbyterians of New York and Philadelphia awakened much discussion. The New York coetus, troubled by problems like those of the Anglicans, especially the question of local ordination of ministers, sent a circular letter to the churches proposing a classis for more self-government in America, but nothing of great moment was accomplished.[2]

The first Lutheran synod in America was founded by Heinrich M. Muhlenberg and included Pennsylvania and New York. A later organization enlarged the area of activity, especially through the efforts of Pastor Johann Christian Kunze who had removed from Philadelphia to New York; John C. Hartwig was another Lutheran minister known to both cities.[3]

[1] J. I. Good, *History of the Reformed Church in the United States,* 1725-1792 (Reading, Pa., 1899), pp. 332, 473, 310-328, 535.

[2] *Ecclesiastical Records of the State of New York* (Albany, 1901-16), vol. v, pp. 3164, 3278, 3165, 3301, 3336-37, 3493, Sept. 19, 1754.

[3] Faust, *German Element in the U. S.,* vol. ii, p. 410; W. B. Sprague, *Annals of the American Pulpit* (N. Y., 1857-69), vol. ix, pp. 29-31.

Like other groups, the Dutch founded a college, Queen's, in New Jersey, backed also by New York.. The problem that faced the Dutch was similar to that fronting the Anglicans, who were seeking the establishment of a native episcopate. It was the question of independence from the church in Amsterdam with the right to ordain colonial ministers; they were also interested in the erection of a school to prepare men for the pastorate. John Frelinghuysen, a member of the famous New Jersey family, was already teaching young students the fundamentals necessary to ordination, in his home at Raritan. One of these students, Jacob Rutsen Hardenburgh, wrote the classis of Amsterdam asking its aid in procuring a charter (1764), "Our ability to raise an endowment is much greater than was that of either the Episcopalians or the Presbyterians when they established their Seminaries. Why, then, may we not establish a school as well as they?" The letter indicated a movement already under way to prepare a college foundation independent of ecclesiastical authority.[1]

At the same time there were forces at work stimulating the growth of a more intense consciousness among the separated communicants of the Anglican Church. In the middle colonies where it was comparatively strong, there was much mutual intercourse, but contacts were maintained with branches of the church in other areas as well. A sermon delivered by John Beach before the Anglican clergy in New Haven was printed in New York. Gov. William Shirley of Massachusetts suggested that Gov. Morris of Pennsylvania contribute his share of a lottery fine to help build an Anglican church in Connecticut.[2] The S. P. G. attempted to keep the churches in touch with one another and to correct backsliding

[1] W. H. S. Demarest, *A History of Rutgers College* (New Brunswick, N. J., 1924), pp. 26, 44-46, 53-54.

[2] Evans, 8538; Martin, " Lotteries in Pa.," *loc. cit.*, p. 312.

members of the Establishment. The Rev. Robert Jenney, a missionary of the Society in New York, was invited to head Christ Church, Philadelphia. Letters passed to and from Boston and Philadelphia, relative to church affairs in which the Rev. William Smith of the Pennsylvania college took a leading part.[1] A watchful eye was kept on New York arrangements. When the new St. Peter's was erected in Philadelphia, it was governed by the wardens and vestry of Christ Church, and the ministers were to officiate alternately, as at New York. The "Pennsylvania Magazine" noted the installation of the Rev. Mr. Vardill as the first professor of divinity in King's College. In a report to the Archbishop of Canterbury on the state of the church in Philadelphia, it was asserted that

on the whole the Church is on as good a Footing in this Seminary even as at New York. For tho' the President of New York College is by charter of the communion of the Church ... the Dissenting Ministers of all different Denominations in the City are ex-officio . . . Governors of the College; whereas in Philadelphia there can be none made Trustees or Governors of the College but by the Election of the present Trustees.

Both colleges were mentioned for their possibilities in educating missionaries to serve the S. P. G.[2] Long before, pleading for a college in New York, Trinity had written to the S. P. G. that the dissenters already had three seminaries advocating their own ecclesiastical preferences. Dr. Johnson of King's College noticed the sad state of the Anglican clergy in most of the colonies, although he felt free to write that those in New Jersey, New York and New England,

---

[1] Benjamin Dorr, *An Historical Account of Christ Church, Philadelphia* (Phila., 1859), pp. 76-79; W. S. Perry, *Papers Relating to the History of the Church in Pennsylvania, 1680-1778* (Hartford, 1871), p. 320.

[2] *Ibid.*, pp. 332, 571, 573 *et seq.*; *Penn. Mag. or American Monthly,* Jan. 24, 1775, p. 41.

"generally speaking," were "virtuous and faithful persons."
Dr. Cutler at Boston was characterized as a "learned and
faithful divine" while Mr. Caner was said to be an excellent preacher. Johnson, who was a sort of rallying point
for members of the Church, wrote Franklin that he had pupils
in the leading pulpits of Connecticut, Boston, New York and
other places.[1]

There was less traveling among the Anglicans apparently
than among their contemporaries, but some has been traced.
Samuel Auchmuty, a native of Boston and a Harvard
graduate, became a minister of Trinity and was granted an
honorary degree by King's College. The Rev. Charles
Inglis at Philadelphia, after a first declination, accepted the
post of assistant to Auchmuty.[2] The Rev. William Mc-
Clenahan, who had been converted to Anglicanism at Boston, became rector of St. Paul's in Philadelphia. New
York was frequently visited by the Anglican clergy of
other cities. The Rev. Richard Peters of Philadelphia, who
preached to large and enthusiastic audiences in Trinity
Church and St. George's chapel, and the Rev. William
Smith, were the most conspicuous among those whose
ministrations transcended local boundaries in the interest of
a more inclusive religious brotherhood.[3]

Presbyterian worship was begun in New York City in
1707, where soon after the Wall Street congregation was
formed and joined with the Presbytery of Philadelphia. As
a young preacher, Jonathan Edwards served this church.

---

[1] Dix, *Trinity Church*, pp. 271-73, 288-89; *N. Y. Col. Doc.*, vol. vii,
p. 397; T. H. Montgomery, *A History of the University of Pennsylvania
to 1770* (Phila., 1900), p. 513.

[2] Dix, pp. 246, 309-11.

[3] N. S. Barratt, *Outline of the History of Old St. Paul's Church,
Philadelphia* (Phila., 1917), pp. 66-72; *N. Y. Gaz. or Weekly Post-Boy*,
July 22, 1754, *N. Y. Mercury*, Sept. 3, 1764, in *N. Y. Hist. Soc. Coll.*,
1870, pp. 169-170, 189.

The Boston Presbyterians who organized "The Synod of New York and Philadelphia," wielded considerable influence; for many New Englanders had migrated to the middle and southern colonies, carrying with them a strong religious strain which sought a modified Presbyterianism.[1] Many of the ministers were known to several congregations. The Rev. John Pemberton, a Harvard graduate, was an influential figure in the New York church for many years before he removed, about 1754, to Boston where his father had been connected with the Old South Church. Alexander Cumming, a colleague in New York, was brought to Boston, probably by Pemberton. The Rev. David Cowell was also of Harvard, and in 1736, he was ordained by the Presbytery of Philadelphia. John Murray was an effective preacher in Maine, New York, and Philadelphia where he succeeded Gilbert Tennent. Elihu Spencer was ordained in Boston, but was known in New York and New Jersey. The Rev. Samuel Blair in Boston, married a daughter of Dr. William Shippen of Philadelphia, which, coupled with religious differences at home, induced him to leave for the latter city.[2] When the Rev. Alexander McWhorter, whose wife was sister to Cumming, visited Boston, he was invited to preach, a practise not uncommon for visiting ministers in the local pulpit of the learned Samuel Cooper. Cooper's diary recorded that " Mr.. Pemberton of N. York " preached for him on the morning of Sept. 16, 1753.[3]

[1] Rev. W. H. Benham, " Churches and Clergy of Colonial N. Y.," *N. Y. State Hist. Assn. Proc.,* vol. xvi, p. 100; F. W. Loetscher, " Presbyterianism in Colonial New England", *Presbyterian Hist. Soc. Journ.,* vol. xi, pp. 107-108, 113.

[2] H. A. Hill, *History of the Old South Church Boston* (Boston, 1890), vol. ii, pp. 46-47, 95, 104-11; Loetscher, *loc. cit.,* pp. 108-09, 112-13; John McLean, *History of the College of New Jersey* (Phila., 1877), vol. i, pp. 104, 112.

[3] " Notes from Rev. Sam'l Cooper's Interleaved Almanacs, 1764, 1767," *New Eng. Hist. and Genea. Reg.,* vol. lv, pp. 145-149; " Diary of Sam'l Cooper ", *ibid.,* vol. xli, p. 390.

The Synod of New York and Philadelphia, religious publications and programs of expansion obviously brought ministers and congregations in touch with one another. A sermon preached by Samuel Finley in Philadelphia went into a second edition and was sold in New York. Proposals were made to print the sermons of Samuel Davies, the eloquent late president of the New Jersey college; subscriptions were taken in by ministers and booksellers of Boston, New York and Philadelphia, in which places his writings were evidently well known, having been printed some years before. The suggestions for improving public worship in the Church of Scotland by John Witherspoon, printed in London, had reprints in two of the middle colonies. When the New York Presbyterians wished to build a new house they sought the aid of Boston. Boston was again appealed to when Philadelphia coreligionists sought funds to build a new meeting house, and Colonel Wendell, a public-spirited citizen with intercolonial interests, was asked to enlist his friends in behalf of the subscription.[1]

Among the most effective agents in building up a more vital religious spirit in the Congregational and Presbyterian churches, the publications of Dr. Isaac Watts must be accorded a high place. The influence of his " Hymns and Spiritual Songs," and " The Psalms of David Imitated " on "Protestant worship in England, and later in America, for one hundred and fifty years, can scarcely be overstated," is the recent verdict of a careful student.[2] The " Psalms " was reprinted in Philadelphia by Franklin in 1729, and from thence to 1760, five reprints appeared in that city alone. The edition of 1753 was also sold in New York by Noel, the

[1] Evans, 8122, 8831-36, 9881; *Pa. Journal*, March 16, 1769, in *N. J. Archives*, ser. 1, vol. xxvi, pp. 399-400; Stokes, p. 595; *New Eng. Hist. and Genea. Reg.*, vol. xxi, p. 23.

[2] E. S. Ninde, *The Story of the American Hymn* (N. Y., 1921), pp. 29, 30.

local bookseller. New England, which naturally printed more of Watts than the southern colonies, issued his "First Sett of Catechisms and Prayers," followed several years later by a new edition of the "Psalms," published also in Philadelphia.[1]

Meantime there was under way a tremendous religious movement, begun in continental Europe which was to affect all churches intensely. Known as " Pietism " in Germany and the " Methodist revival " in England, it was expressed in the colonies as the " Great Awakening "; it proved to be a force remolding almost every aspect of American life —an emotional earthquake that left scarcely a home unaffected.

Nourished " by the spirit of German Pietism," " a more individualistic and emotional type of religion " emerged, expressing itself on " its subjective side in a new hymnody and on its objective " in the " beginning of philanthropic enterprises." To rekindle a vital religious feeling in the heart of the individual, now dulled by an exacting formalism, was the motive behind this revival in the eighteenth century. It

... witnessed in the Lutheran Church of Germany; in the Established Church of England and among the Protestant sects of America a religious movement which led not only to a decided modification in the character of Protestant Christianity, but also to far reaching consequences in the domain of national culture. Although German Pietism, English Wesleyanism and the Great Awakening in America, strictly speaking, started independently of each other, yet in their inmost essence, as well as in some of their outward characteristics, they were really one and the same.

The Lutheran court chaplain in London, A. W. Boehm, was a connecting link between the English and German religious

[1] L. F. Benson, "Early Editions of Watts' Hymns," "American Revisions of Watts' Hymns ", *Presbyt. Hist. Soc. Journ.*, vol. i, ii; Evans, 6965, 7135, 7846-47.

forces.   Boehm also brought Cotton Mather into correspondence with A. H. Francke at Halle, the first direct tie between
American Christianity and German Pietism.   Johann Arndt's
"True Christianity' which had a great vogue in Germany,
influenced Whitefield and others in England, while in the
colonies a German edition came from Franklin's press.   The
German mystics imparted to Wesley and Whitefield the
notion of a more personal religion, and these in turn transmitted it to the American provinces.[1]

Among the Dutch the preaching of the first Frelinghuysen
was the spark that lit the evangelical revival.   Although
immediately opposed by many groups, in time he won them
over so that not only the laity but also church officials
became converted.   Even the support of the conservative
Dominie Du Bois, senior pastor of the collegiate church in
New York City, was finally won for Frelinghuysen.[2]   The
Moravians received a direct impetus from the continent.   In
New York they built the ship "Irene," which for nine years
plied between that port and England and Holland, carrying
goods and passengers.   The latter were for Pennsylvania,
but always disembarked at New York because the captain
could get freight there for his vessel.   Bishop Spangenberg
and David Nitschmann introduced the Moravian Brethren
to New York, receiving help from Thomas Noble, a local
merchant.   The Moravians had worked their way north
from Georgia, and James Burnside, a lay evangelist, married
one of the first of the new converts in New York.   John
Jacob Boemper, the agent of the Georgia Moravians in
New York, played host to Spangenberg and Nitschmann,

[1] J. P. Hoskins, "German Influence on Religious Life and Thought in
America, during the Colonial Period", *Princeton Theological Rev.,* vol.
v, pp. 60-61, 211-213, 223; Kuno Francke, "Cotton Mather and A. H.
Francke" (*Harv. Studies and Notes,* vol. v), pp. 57-67.

[2] C. H. Maxson, *The Great Awakening in the Middle Colonies* (Chicago,
1920), pp. 11-19.

who also made the acquaintance of others in the city. An undenominational society ministered to by evangelists from Bethlehem, Pa., was organized by Peter Boehler in New York.[1]

Count Zinzendorf, who played a part among the Germans similar to that of George Whitefield among the English, bound his people together especially through his efforts in extending the influence of the Moravian Association of New York between 1741 and 1743. He organized the church in Philadelphia where he was the guest of J. S. Benezet. This included members originally from New York, to which some communicants returned, while others left for Boston.[2] A synod held at Bethlehem voted to extend the visits of Moravian evangelists to New England, as a result of which Jasper Payne and Christian Fröhlich went through Connecticut to Boston and beyond, as missionaries. Unbroken intercourse was maintained among the Associations, especially through the efforts of Bishop Spangenberg who assumed full charge of the work of the church in 1744. The year before, Zinzendorf had conferred in New York with the local Moravians concerning the extended prosecution of the work of the church in the province and in Pennsylvania, where Franklin's press was engaged to serve the cause. Thomas Noble was the center of New York activities; for four years the local Society met at his house until the first Moravian congregation was organized there in 1748, to which a school was soon attached. Brethren passing through New York were entertained by the Noble and Horsfield families; a boarding school for girls at Germantown was attended by

---

[1] J. W. Jordan, "Moravian Immigration to Pennsylvania, 1734-1767," *Moravian Hist. Soc. Trans.*, vol. v, pp. 51-90; *Trans.*, vol. i, pp. 419-420; H. E. Stocker, *A History of the Moravian Church in New York City* (N. Y., 1922), pp. 35-36, 42-44, 28.

[2] Abraham Ritter, *History of the Moravian Church in Philadelphia* (Phila., 1857), 19; *Moravian Hist. Soc. Trans.*, vol. i, pp. 373-74, 376-80.

pupils from New York.[1] Noble, who sent his five children
to the school in Bethlehem, had personally visited the congregation. These educational and religious connections, as
in other sects, were strengthened by those of marriage. A
number of the Society in New York visited Bethlehem, some
to stay, others to leave in order to take a more active part
in spreading the doctrines of the faith. In the work of
preaching and teaching, the Bethlehem community employed
many individuals scattered through New England, the middle
colonies and the Carolinas.[2]

The Baptist church in Pennepek, Pa., mothered many of
that denomination in the middle colonies. The Philadelphia
Baptist Association, formed in 1707, shortly included
churches as far north as Dutchess county, New York, east
to Greenwich, Connecticut, and south to Virginia. The
church in New York City owed its foundation to a certain
Mr. Ayres and two New Englanders. For two years the
group met in the house of the former, until by 1724 a
church had been constituted over which Ayres presided. He
was ordained pastor by Elders from Groton and Newport,
and when his congregation began to build a house it solicited
aid from Providence. Ayres moved to Newport and soon
after his church dissolved, but a new one was shortly organized which was received into the Philadelphia Association.[3]

[1] Stocker, op. cit., pp. 30, 52-53, 57, 76, 95; Moravian Hist. Soc. Trans.,
vol. i, pp. 419-420, 380; vol. iii, pp. 207, 195-196; vol. v, p. 323; Oswald
Seidensticker, The First Century of German Printing in America (Phila.,
1893) p. 14.

[2] Stocker, pp. 59-76; Trans., vol. i, p. 422; "Report of Members and
Activities of Bethlehem Moravians, 1756", in Penn. Archives, 1756-1760.

[3] The Bi-centennial Celebration of the Founding of the First Baptist
Church of Philadelphia (Phila., 1899), pp. 17, 33-35; William Parkinson,
Jubilee, a Sermon Containing a History of the Origin of the First
Baptist Church in the City of New York (N. Y., 1813), pp. 9-11;
David Benedict, General History of the Baptist Denomination (Boston,
1813), vol. i, p. 537 note.

The revival movement gave a decided impetus to the growth of the Baptists, receiving accretions from New Englanders and Southerners who had separated from original affiliations. The Warren Association, formed in Rhode Island in 1767, as a center for Baptist activities, was greatly encouraged by the Philadelphia Association which sent three ministers to the younger group; in general the older organization acted the part of guide for sectarian functions which it coordinated through a large correspondence. Three years earlier, the Rev. Samuel Stillman, a native of Philadelphia with a degree from the college there and an M. A. from Harvard, was called to the First Baptist Church in Boston where a fellow alumnus, John Davis, headed the pastorate of the Second Baptist Church. Isaac Skillman, a Princeton graduate, ordained in New York, was another pastor of the last named church. In other ways a mutual interest was stimulated. John Gano preached alternately at Baptist churches in New York and Philadelphia; John Comer, educated at Harvard and a preacher in Rhode Island, traveled widely in search of materials for a history of the Baptist churches and entered into correspondence with men of that denomination in all of the colonies. Probably the person most influential in uniting the members of this sect throughout colonial America was Morgan Edwards, its historian.[1]

The Methodist group, whose rapid growth was accelerated by the revivalist movement, had centers in New York and Philadelphia whose religious work was closely interrelated. Methodism derived an early importance from the number of reputable and, in many instances, wealthy people who lent it support, although in the main it had a popular appeal. The mutual helpfulness was very marked. Methodists in Phila-

---

[1] Benedict, *op. cit.*, vol. i, pp. 508-509, 595, 408-409; N. E. Wood, *The History of the First Baptist Church of Boston* (Phila., 1899), p. 244; Sprague, *Annals*, vol. vi, pp. 117, 64, 39-43; Stiles, *Diary*, vol. i, p. 330.

delphia sent thirty-two pounds to their New York core-
religionists although they lacked a church themselves. Capt.
Thomas Webb, a Methodist leader, was in Philadelphia in
1769 to receive Joseph Pilmoor, minister to the local district,
and Richard Boardman, destined for New York, when
these preachers arrived from England. These newcomers
spent two or three months alternately preaching in Philadelphia and New York. That same year, Robert Williams
preached in the latter city and then went to the Pennsylvania
metropolis, returning to New York two years later. Francis
Asbury, soon to be the dominating personality among the
Methodists, visited both centers which often exchanged
preachers. Boardman went to Boston and Providence in
the spring of 1772, the first time organized Methodism was
introduced to New England.[1]

The " ,Great Awakening " hardly got into full swing before
the advent of George Whitefield, for the activities of Jonathan Edwards in New England had no direct or immediate
effect to the southward. Even before the coming of Whitefield, the Presbyterian church had given evidence of a split
into two groups, an evangelical and a conservative, to be
known later as the "New Lights" and "Old Lights," respectively. Many of the former party of New England
origin were located in Long Island and East New Jersey
where their pastors, converted during the Edwards' revival,
responded to the newly quickened interest in a throbbing
religious life. Aaron Burr of Newark was a stimulating
figure who took the lead in these local revivals.

The colonies were prepared for Whitefield by descriptions

---

[1] S. E. Seaman, *Annals of New York Methodism* (N. Y., 1892), pp.
23-24, 65-66, 30-33, 35, 44-47, 53, 65-66; J. M. Buckley, *History of
Methodism in the United States* (N. Y., 1897), vol. i, p. 136; J. B.
Wakeley, *Lost Chapters Recovered from the Early History of American
Methodism* (N. Y., 1858), p. 204; Rev. S. W. Coggleshall, "Introduction of Methodism into Boston", *New Eng. Methodist Hist. Soc. Trans.*,
1859, pp. 5-16.

of his activities in England which had been transcribed by the colonial newspapers. But they were temperamentally prepared also. Some years before, William Tennent had preached in New York and Pennsylvania with great effect. In 1726 he settled at Neshaminy with his "Log College" whose graduates wielded a tremendous influence. He transmitted his own fervor to his students, among whom were three Tennents, his sons, all capable preachers. Revivals restricted in territorial extent were carried on, but the leaders were in close touch with one another, and the wide publicity given these operations through the medium of the press, promoted a mutual interest. It was Whitefield however, who gave universality to this movement. His hold on his hearers was magnetic, and there were few who did not feel the powerful attraction of his personality. It was estimated that between thirty and forty thousand converts were made in New England alone, showing how well prepared the colonists were for the itinerant Methodist preachers who came some years afterward.[1]

In November 1739, Whitefield preached to vast numbers in Philadelphia where he had friendly conversations with the elder William Tennent. On the way to New York where he was to be the guest of William Smith, a well known Presbyterian, Whitefield stopped to preach in Burlington and New Brunswick. In the city of his host he was attacked by Jonathan Allen and defended by Smith and Mangus Falconer of Philadelphia; both defenses appeared in the "American Weekly Mercury." Letters, sympathetic and antagonistic, were copied from one paper by another, until the question assumed the aspect of an intercolonial debate. It attained international proportions when colonial printers republished English and Scottish tracts, and American publications appeared in Glasgow and London. During

---

[1] Maxson, *op. cit.*, pp. 25-42; Abel Stevens, *History of Eighteenth Century Methodism* (N. Y., 1858-61), vol. i, pp. 477-79.

a few days in New York, Whitefield claimed a great popular following and then left for Philadelphia. On his return trip he stopped again at New Brunswick to meet several leaders in the movement, Dominie Frelinghuysen, John Cross and James Campbell.[1]

The decade beginning 1740 saw the Great Awakening at flood tide. The newspapers of that period reveal the widespread influence of Whitefield and of Gilbert Tennent, who was accounted second to the great preacher in power. The former's sermons were printed in German by Franklin, and other printers, watching the drift of the public literary taste, applied to Whitefield for sermons to publish.[2] "The Christian History, containing accounts of the Revival and Propagation of Religion in Great Britain and America," published in Boston, ran for two years, printing letters about the movement in all of the colonies. The first three months of 1740 marked the height of the revival in Newark under Burr and Dickinson; that spring saw a revival in the highlands of New York under William Tennent Jr. and others. Samuel Blair's congregation at Fagg's Manor, Pennsylvania, went through a similar experience. Whitefield repeated his journey through the middle colonies to collect funds for his orphan house in Georgia, and at the same time pleaded for kindlier treatment of the negro. The Moravians and the Dutch were stirred once again. Daniel Rogers, a tutor at Harvard and a recent convert, in company with Whitefield, brought to Gilbert Tennent at New Brunswick an invitation from some prominent New England ministers to visit Boston. Tennent accepted and preached to large audiences in Boston and elsewhere in New England, making a deep

---

[1] Maxson, pp. 3, 46-51.

[2] N. J. Archives, ser. 1, vol. xii, extracts of newspapers, 1740-1750; E. P. Oberholtzer, The Literary History of Philadelphia (Phila., 1906), p. 38; Seidensticker, op. cit., p. 12; Joseph Tracy, The Great Awakening (Boston, 1842), p. 53, note.

impression. In New Haven, some students who were converted entered the ministry of the Presbyterian church to work in the middle colonies, and one of them, James Sprout, later became a pastor in the church established by Tennent in Philadelphia. Whitefield was in New England again in the fall of 1740, strengthening the attachments Tennent had already made.[1]

The years between 1741 and 1746 were concerned with the expansion and organization of these activities. The Second Presbyterian Church of Philadelphia, founded under the inspiration of Whitefield, became a leading protagonist of the "New Lights" and chose Gilbert Tennent for its first pastor. Tennent wrote Prince of Boston, about the remarkable achievements of Theodore Frelinghuysen, freely acknowledging his own debt to the latter.[2] In 1742 the Synod of Philadelphia met and a greater number of representatives of the New York Presbytery attended than hitherto. Three years later, a New York Synod with representatives from New Jersey and Pennsylvania, was organized in the former province at Elizabethtown. As has been noted, a division existed between the more conservative church members and those inclined to the evangelical movement, a breach which thoughtful leaders early sought to heal but failed. Gilbert Tennent published his "Irenicum" in 1749 exhorting peace, and the Synod of New York made proposals of union to Philadelphia. Negotiations extending over a period of nine years achieved this result, and Tennent was made moderator of the newly organized Synod of New York and Philadelphia, a consummation which was in reality a victory for the evangelists, since the "Old Sides" were now committed to the aims of their rivals.[3]

---

[1] 1743-1745; Maxson, pp. 54-59, 64-65; Tracy, pp. 114-120.

[2] E. R. Beadle, *The Old and the New: the Second Presbyterian Church of Philadelphia* (Phila., 1876), pp. 21-23; Demarest, *Rutgers College*, 25; Hoskins, *loc. cit.*, pp. 227-29.

[3] Maxson, pp. 88-89, 114-116.

Whitefield reappeared in New York and Philadelphia during 1763, a source of great worry to the Anglicans. The Rev. Samuel Seabury wrote to the S. P. G. that the revivalist's influence was greater than formerly; there had been a continual "succession of Strolling Preachers & Exhorters" harmful to the Anglican Church. Twenty years before, the Rev. Robert Jenney noted that New York had made a fine stand against Methodism and Moravianism because of the work of "Mr. Charleton in the way of Catachising" and, with the same end in view, asked that a catechist be sent also to Philadelphia. After a delay of a few years, William Sturgeon, educated in New England and recommended by the Rev. Henry Barclay of New York, was sent to assist Jenney.[1]

Whitefield attained a public recognition which in more modern times seems reserved for political or athletic luminaries. A wax figure of him, modeled by Mrs. Patience Wright, was placed on exhibition; a mezzotint of the preacher was sold in Boston. His death in 1770 occasioned widespread expressions of genuine sorrow, even among those originally hostile; for by this time, the acerbity had been considerably dulled. The evangelist, whose voice was stilled, had done much to stimulate a spirit of cooperation among the churches, transcending provincial limits. And while it is true that denominationalist tendencies were strengthened, it is likewise true, writes Hoskins, that

in the fervor of the revival, the continent awoke to the consciousness of a common spiritual life. Whitefield's extensive travels and his ministrations to all sects alike formed a link which bound all denominations to each other in a common religious purpose. The preaching of Gilbert Tennent in New England, the calling of Dickinson, Burr and Edwards from

[1] *Ecclesiastical Records of N. Y.*, vol. vi, 3952; Perry, *op. cit.*, Jan. 26, 1744, Nov. 14, 1745, May 28, 1747; Dorr, *op. cit.*, pp. 90-91.

New England to labours in New Jersey served further to strengthen the good understanding and mutual fellowship.[1]

Publications with an intercolonial sale emphasized the universality of the movement. A sermon delivered by Aaron Burr in Newark was printed in Boston and New York and went into three editions. On Burr's death, when William Livingston published a eulogy, a reprint appeared in Boston. An account of the revival as it affected students in the College of New Jersey (Princeton) had five editions, being reprinted in Boston and Hartford. There were various printings of "Thoughts (on) the Present Revival of Religion in New England" by Jonathan Edwards; his other writings including a Dutch publication of a Newark sermon, secured a cosmopolitan audience.[2]

In other spheres of activity, the influence of this movement is easily traceable. The Moravians taught John Wesley the worth of hymns in socializing the Gospel, a lesson which resulted in the compilation of a hymn book which was used in the Anglican Church. This work which charts a new departure in English hymnody was, interestingly enough, printed in Charlestown, S. C., when Wesley was in America. "The Psalms of David" by Isaac Watts, supplanted the older psalmody, and furnished a transition to the more attractive hymnody nurtured by the Germans. The work of Watts, we have noted, had been issued before the religious revivals were begun; but it needed the impulse of the Great Awakening, writes E. S. Ninde, to make "the

[1] *N. Y. Gaz. and Weekly Post-Boy*, June 10, 1771; *Boston Gaz. and Country Journal*, June 3, 1771; *ibid.*, poems, Oct. 8, 1770, and in *Boston Eve. Post*, Oct. 15, 1770; Hoskins, *loc. cit.*, p. 78; A letter from Dr. Spencer to Ezra Stiles, "An Account of the Dissenting Interest in the Middle States 1759", is an example of this intercolonial interest, *Mass. Hist. Soc. Coll.*, 2, vol. i, pp. 156-157.

[2] Sedgwick, *Memoir of Livingston*, pp. 113-114; Evans, 7863-64, 9629, 10276-77, 10888, 7187.

people thoroughly dissatisfied with the dull lifeless mode of singing which had been so long in vogue." A Presbyterian, Samuel Davies in Virginia, and a Congregationalist, Mather Byles in Boston, were stimulated to write hymns, and church singing in New England underwent a drastic reform. Singing schools and the efforts of men like William Billings, whose "New England Psalm Singer" had a sensational appeal, set congregations to singing as they had never sung before.[1] A stimulus was given to literature concerned with Biblical subjects, and publications with a preceptive moral ideal. Solomon Gessner's "Death of Abel" was exceedingly popular; Philadelphia and Boston reprinted it in 1762, a seventh edition was printed in New York four years later, and a like period had elapsed when two reprints appeared in the Quaker capital. The central seat of German Pietism at Halle, furnished the model for Wesley's school and orphanage in England and for Whitefield's orphan house at Savannah, Georgia. It was the reaction against the doctrine of salvation by faith alone, that prompted participation in good works and encouraged the development of an humanitarian spirit.[2]

Colonial newspapers noted the efforts that were made in behalf of the negro, to a large degree inspired by Whitefield. Education was largely indebted to the spirit evoked by the Great Awakening, as seen not only by the actual establishment of new colleges in the middle colonies and in New England, but also in the more liberal tone that permeated some of them. It was probably the temper of the times, coupled with the persistent attacks of William Living-

[1] Hoskins, *loc. cit.*, pp. 230-34, 77; Ninde, *Story of American Hymn*, pp. 30-31, chaps., iii, iv.

[2] Hoskins, *loc. cit.*, pp. 236, 62, 65; Evans, 9125; F. H. Wilkens, " Early Influence of German Literature in America ", *German American Annals*, Benedict, *op. cit.*, vol. i, pp. 408, 508-509.

ston, that caused the charter of King's College to be among the very first to establish religious freedom for its students and instructors. Friendly cooperation with the Dutch Reformed Church, which was to be represented by a professorship in its theology, was part of this new collegiate policy. Students entering Queen's College were assured that they "may expect to be treated . . . . without any Discrimination with Respect to their Religious Sentiments."[1] The charter of Rhode Island College, characterized as a " Catholic Comprehensive and Liberal Institution," was more generous than its contemporaries in "rejecting religious tests for members of the Faculty and providing definitely for broad representation on the governing board," writes its historian. William Ellery, a signer of the Declaration of Independence from the same province, discussed with Ezra Stiles the possibility of erecting another college with "Equal Liberty to Congregationalists, Baptists, Episcopalians, Quakers."[2] Massachusetts churches began to seek their pastors beyond Harvard walls; Princeton and Yale were especially favored. The Old South in Boston had three ministers before the Revolution who were graduates of the college in New Jersey.[3]

Agitation for religious liberty was hastened by the evangelical movement. "It is with great pleasure I can say that religious liberty daily gains ground," wrote Andrew Eliot, a learned Boston Congregationalist. The Warren Association of Baptists which was very active in promoting religious toleration throughout the colonies, chose John Davis as an

---

[1] Maxson, p. 91, note 2; *The Charter of the College of New York in America* (N. Y., 1754), p. 10; Demarest, *op. cit.*, pp. 33, 82.

[2] W. C. Bronson, *The History of Brown University* (Providence, 1914), pp. 30-31, charter reprinted, p. 505; Stiles, *Diary*, Feb. 23, 1770.

[3] H. A. Hill and G. F. Bigelow, *An Historical Catalogue of the Old South Church, (Third Church) Boston* (Boston, 1883), pp. 1-2; Hill, *Old South Church*, vol. ii, p. 86.

agent to further the cause in Massachusetts and London.[1]
Leaders of the Presbyterians and Baptists in New York
City formed a " Society of Dissenters " to organize all
so disposed in the colonies against the Anglican Church.
Should the neighboring provinces establish societies, they
were to send delegates to the New York group. A
committee of correspondence made up of men known in
New Jersey and Philadelphia was elected, and a circular
letter was drawn up urging religious liberty and expressing
alarm at the possible introduction of episcopacy.[2]   Colden
wrote that dissenters were more numerous than Anglicans
in the middle colonies and were clamoring for equal rights.
"A brief review of the State of religious Liberty in the
colony of New York, read before . . . . Delegates (of)
. . . . the Churches of Connecticut and the Synod of New
York and Philadelphia" at Stanford in 1773, revealed a
common colonial interest in an engrossing topic.[3]   The question of the relations between church and state was brought
nearer a solution; the New England theocracy grimly holding fast now began to disintegrate much more rapidly.
Much as he served the church, Wesley served democracy far
more, for to society's lower depths long neglected, he carried
the gospel of eternal salvation.   The revival, J. T. Adams
writes,

cut across the boundaries of colonies and sects, and for the
first time united great numbers in all of them in a common and

[1] *Bancroft Transcripts*, Andrew Eliot, Jonathan Mayhew, Thomas Hollis
Correspondence 1761-1776; to Archdeacon Blackburne, May 13, 1767;
Benedict, *op cit.*, vol. i, pp. 408, 508-509.

[2] H. L. Osgood reprinted the minutes (1769) in *Amer. Hist. Rev.*, vol.
vi, pp. 499-507.

[3] Colden to Lords of Trade, *N. Y. Col. Doc.*, vol. vii, pp. 585-86; *Mass.
Hist. Soc. Coll.*, 2, vol. i, pp. 140-156.

emotional experience . . . of fundamental and far-reaching import. Those throughout the colonies who separated from the old churches were bound together by a common opposition to the privileges conferred by a union of church and state.

It was a unifying influence among a large group with "democratic tendencies," a "movement . . . . of discontent . . . . against an established order." [1]   It broke down the barriers that separated the seemingly discordant polyglot population in the middle colonies, which linked the provinces by religious, social and political bonds.   Nor must the movement of population be overlooked in tracing the growth of a common spirit; New England Separates and Baptists who migrated to Vermont and New York were not the least of such influences.

Finally, the political implications deserve a word.   It is not a mere coincidence that those religious groups which had the most intimate intercolonial contacts were the most firmly united in their political convictions.   Writing at the time of the first Continental Congress, Ezra Stiles observed that "The Defence & Conservation of the public Liberty stands on the Union of the Southern Episcopalians (who differ on this point from their Northern Brethren) and the grand universal Body of Congregationals & Presbyterians throughout the continent . . . . Perhaps the Baptists may [also] open their Eyes." [2]   The Presbyterian Synod and the Connecticut Consociation of Congregational Churches met together in annual assembly for ten years before the Revolution, an experience of no little value in producing a sentiment of solidarity.   These "joint assemblies," a recent student has suggested, "did much to forward the union of the colonies,"

[1] J. T. Adams, *Revolutionary New England, 1691-1776* (Boston, 1923), pp. 177-178.

[2] *Diary*, Nov. 30, 1774.

for "they afforded a training in the utilization of national institutions." [1]

The stressing of religious divergences among the colonists in order to account for their mutual antagonisms has been traditional in American history, and there is much to be said in justification of such an interpretation, but the facts stated in the foregoing pages should modify it considerably. The reading of a common literature and the singing of the same hymns must have assisted in breaking down the barriers separating some of the sects.   Correspondence between corcligionists in remote places promoted a feeling of oneness which expressed itself in mutually helpful enterprises.   A few individuals like Dr. Samuel Johnson among the Anglicans, John Philip Boehm among the German Reformed, and Morgan Edwards among the Baptists, were wells of religion from which their respective communions drew spiritual sustenance.   Most important of all in the process of interweaving bonds among all colonials was, of course, the Great Awakening.   In many ways it stimulated communal thinking, resulting in sharpening ecclesiastical differences while it mitigated the harshness of theological principles.   It hastened the growing realization of a larger humanity, which found an outlet in beneficent undertakings. In the gradual wearing away of religious exclusiveness, a prophetic eye might have discerned intimations of a sequel in the political sphere.

[1] E. F. Humphrey, *Nationalism and Religion in America 1774-1789* (Boston, 1924), pp. 22-23; see A. M. Baldwin, *The New England Clergy and the American Revolution* (Durham, 1928), chaps. v-viii.

CHAPTER IV

PRINTERS AND PRINTING

Next to personal exhortations the press was the greatest single force that stirred the American colonists in the eighteenth century to reexamine many of their religious habits. A multitude of pamphlets, a magazine and controversial letters in newspapers suggest that the colonies had become one gigantic forum wherein debates extending over many years left some more confirmed than ever in their original beliefs, while others struggled to what seemed a clearer light. Other ideas, especially political, were to be subjected to minute analyses, and through the medium of an intercolonial press were to dig new channels for provincial thought. The development of this press, which from an early period played a very significant part in American life, reveals a mutual colonial indebtedness, and a more rapid transfer of influences than historians have usually admitted

There is much interweaving of relationships, nevertheless certain unmistakable sources from which abundant ink flowed may easily be traced. William Bradford, if only by reason of his priority, claims immediate attention. There were few printers in the middle colonies who had not learned their lessons at his press, or been associated with him in some capacity in Philadelphia or in New York. The Bradfords—there were several—monopolized the printing activities of New Jersey for fifty years, doing their work in Philadelphia or New York. To William Bradford must be laid the paternity of the press in the middle provinces; there he also fathered the art of bibliopegy, (bookbinding).[1]

[1] Frederic Hudson, *Journalism in the United States, from 1690 to 1872*

The first issue of the "New York Gazette" in October, 1725, followed some years after Bradford's removal from Philadelphia, and in his new office his publications took notice of events in Boston as well as in his old home. Reinier Jansen had been left in charge of a press when Bradford moved to New York where his son Andrew lent assistance. Father and son later journeyed to Philadelphia to secure the privilege of printing the assembly laws, and the successful issue of this application probably marks the establishment of Andrew there about 1712. Both William Bradford in publishing the "Gazette" and Andrew in publishing the "American Weekly Mercury" used Ritten-house paper, made in Pennsylvania by the forbear of the early American scientist, David Rittenhouse. By 1728 Bradford, the elder, had secured control of a mill at Eliza-bethtown, New Jersey, which supplied the family needs, and in other respects there was naturally a close understanding between the two printers which for a time took the form of a partnership. The younger Bradford had not only profes-sional but also domestic relations with New York, his second wife being Cornelia Smith of that city. To judge from the printing trade the place of eighteenth-century woman was not exclusively in the home, for like many another Cornelia succeeded her husband in a business which also included selling books.[1]

(N. Y.,1873), p. 94; Wm. Nelson, " New Jersey Printers of the Eigh-teenth Century ", *Am. Antiq. Soc. Proc.*, vol. xxi, p. 16; J. W. Wallace, *Address (on) 200th birthday of Mr. William Bradford* (Albany, 1863), p. 47.

[1] C. R. Hildeburn, *Sketches of Printers and Printing in Colonial New York* (N. Y., 1895), pp. 1-18; Isaiah Thomas, *The History of Printing in America* . . . (Worcester, 1810), vol. ii, pp. 25, 27-29, 32; negotia-tions previously entered into sought to place Andrew as printer to the province of Rhode Island, Wallace, *op. cit.*, pp. 84-85; Weeks, *Paper Manufacturing in the U. S.*, pp. 9-10, 17.

The family tree has still another important branch. William Bradford 3rd, grandson of William the first, was born in New York and adopted by his uncle Andrew, who taught him the art in Philadelphia. In time this William Bradford became official printer to New Jersey. Another debtor to William Bradford the elder, was John Peter Zenger, the center of the famous trial for libel. Zenger was apprentice, then a partner and finally the independent publisher of the second newspaper in New York. Henry De Foreest, the first native printer, also learned his art from the same Bradford whose partner he shortly became. The late apprentice then took over the management of his master's paper, which he now called the "New York Evening Post," winning for it the distinction of being America's first afternoon paper.[1]

Another source from which much ink flowed directly or indirectly was Benjamin Franklin, whose center of activities was in Philadelphia, where his first professional employment was in the shop of Samuel Keimer, a printer of almanacs. For a short time Franklin printed money for New Jersey at Burlington, one of many positions he secured through the intercession of influential men like Andrew Hamilton, the most distinguished lawyer in the colonies.[2] Franklin's connections with other printers extended almost the entire length of colonial America. A nephew James who had been taken into the Philadelphia office, inherited the family business, and with his mother, conducted the "Newport Mercury."[3] James Parker, of many addresses, was greatly in-

[1] Thomas, vol. ii, pp. 52, 48; J. W. Wallace, *An Old Philadelphian, Col. William Bradford* . . . (Phila., 1884), p. 21; Livingston Rutherford, *J. P. Zenger* (N. Y., 1904), Hildeburn, pp. 55-57.

[2] J. C. Oswald, *Benjamin Franklin, Printer* (N. Y., 1917), pp. 37, 61, 65.

[3] H. M. Chapin, "Ann Franklin of Newport, Printer" (1736-1763) in *Bibliographical Essays; A Tribute to Wilberforce Eames* (Cambridge, 1924).

debted to Franklin.   In 1733 he was a runaway apprentice of the elder William Bradford, and eventually found himself in Philadelphia employed with Franklin.   A few years later, Franklin and Parker were partners in New York, the latter to do the actual work on the press, types and materials furnished by the former from Philadelphia.[1] Parker was to get two-thirds and Franklin one-third of the proceeds.   In 1745 Parker was the publisher of the "New York Gazette revived in the Weekly Post-Boy," and Hugh Gaine, a recent Irish immigrant assisted its publication for a time, till he began his own "New York Weekly Mercury," which later became "The New York Gazette and Weekly Mercury."   An associate of James Parker, some years after, was a nephew Samuel, who took over the New York business in 1759.   In the interim, William Weyman of Philadelphia, whose first printing lessons were secured in the shop of William Bradford the younger, had become a partner of Parker.   Still another associate of later date, recommended by Franklin, was John Holt whose publishings subsequently did much to hearten the radicals of the revolutionary period.[2]

James Parker's field of operations included Connecticut and Woodbridge, New Jersey, where he established the first printing office of some permanency.   In 1765 this was turned over to Samuel F. Parker, and James started another at Burlington.   At New Haven, Parker's printing establishment was under the care of John Holt, who in addition was postmaster and bookseller.   In 1755 the former began the "Connecticut Gazette" which lasted for some five years, when Holt was

[1] Nelson, loc. cit., p. 18; N. Y. Genea. and Biog. Rec., 1898, p. 192; " Parker to Franklin Letters ", Mass. Hist. Soc. Proc., ser. 2, vol. xvi, pp. 186-189; this division of proceeds was an old practice.

[2] P. L. Ford, The Journals of Hugh Gaine, Printer (N. Y., 1902), vol. i, p. 3, et seq.; Hildeburn, pp. 34-40, 61; V. H. Paltsits, " John Holt, Printer and Postmaster ", N. Y. P. L., Bulletin, Sept. 1920.

recalled from New Haven to take charge of the New York office. Thomas Green, a former employee of Parker, who then took over the paper, was related to the well known Greens, printers in Boston. For some four years, Holt, a silent partner, practically ran Parker's "Gazette," until the latter resumed a control which lasted to 1770. Holt had already begun "The New York Journal," strongly tinctured with a Whig flavor.[1] The successors to the "Gazette," were Samuel Inslee and Anthony Car, the latter of whom had learned his printing under Parker. When his partnership with Inslee was severed, Car found employment with Isaac Collins of Trenton, New Jersey. Collins himself had worked with Goddard and others in Philadelphia, and when Parker died he succeeded to the latter's place in Burlington.[2]

Franklin's aid to colonial printing is further traceable. Benjamin Mecom, another nephew, had learned his trade in the Philadelphia office, whence he wandered to the West Indies where he published "The Antigua Gazette." By 1756 he was home again in Boston, where his issues included 30,000 copies of "The Psalter" for the booksellers, and a short-lived "New England Magazine." In 1763 he was on his way again, stopping long enough in New York to issue the "New York Pacquet." The next year New Haven claimed him for a time, during which he bought out James Parker & Co., to revive the "Connecticut Gazette." Shortly after, Samuel Green bought Mecom out, and the latter was off again for Philadelphia. Here his "Penny Post" soon failed, and then he entered a connection with Will-

[1] William Nelson, *Check-list of the Issues of the Press of New Jersey, 1723 . . . 1800* (Paterson, 1899) ; Hildeburn, pp. 46, 89 *et seq.;* A. C. Bates, " Thomas Green ", *New Haven Col. Hist. Soc. Papers,* vol. viii, p. 290.

[2] Philip Freneau, *The American Village, a Poem ... with introduction by H. L. Koopman, bibliographical data by V. H. Paltsits* (Providence, 1906), p. 57; Thomas, vol. ii, pp. 123-124.

iam Goddard, publisher of "The Pennsylvania Chronicle."
The much-traveled Mecom next found employment with
Isaac Collins at Burlington, New Jersey, where he rested
for a while.   An eccentric and interesting character, worry-
ing poor Parker to his grave, "Benny" Mecom was known
to nearly all the printers, and is an excellent example that
suggests the intercolonial nature of his profession.[1]

Franklin touched colonial printing in many other ways.
He placed Thomas Whitemarsh in business to found the
" South Carolina Gazette," and was a useful link between
the Charlestown and Philadelphia newspapers.   Charlestown had previously been indebted to Boston which sent
the southern capital its first printer.   James Davis, whom
Franklin appointed postmaster, published North Carolina's
first newspaper.[2]   The press for the "Connecticut Gazette,"
the colony's first news sheet, was set up by Franklin
at the request of Yale's president; William Weyman in
New York, used large quantities of his paper.   As an
intermediary, Mecom delivered ten reams of paper to Samuel
Kneeland in Boston, while a keg of ink from Philadelphia
helped make Newport literary history.[3]   Franklin and Christopher Saur, the German printer, were interested in casting
type, an art in which Abel Buell of Connecticut proved himself so proficient, that his work, which had been sent to
Boston, was used as a standard to judge similar products.[4]

[1] Hildeburn, pp. 65-72; William Beer, " Check-list of American Periodicals ", *Amer. Antiq. Soc. Proc.,* 1922, p. 340; Thomas, vol. i, pp. 349-
352; " Parker to Franklin Letters," *loc. cit.*

[2] E. C. Cook, *Literary Influences in Colonial Newspapers, 1704-1750*
(N. Y., 1912, *Col. Univ. Studies In English and Comp. Lit.*), pp. 230-37;
McCrady, *op. cit.,* p. 146; S. B. Weeks, *The Press of North Carolina in
the Eighteenth Century* (Brooklyn, 1891), pp. 9-16.

[3] Franklin, *Calendar of Papers,* vol. v, pp. 177, 180, 183.

[4] F. W. Hamilton, *Type and Presses in America* ... (Chicago, 1918);
L. C. Wroth, " The First Work with American Types ", *Bibliog. Essays
to Eames; Itineraries and Corr. of Ezra Stiles,* pp. 448-49.

Franklin's professional contacts were not only intercolonial; they also reached across the Atlantic. He took into his employ David Hall who had been sent to him by William Strahan, the well known English printer. An oceanic correspondence grew up around Cadwallader Colden's proposals for a new method of printing (stereotyping), on which Franklin made some observations. Franklin, who was very friendly with John Baskerville, the famous English type-founder and printer, used his influence to acquaint Americans with the latter's work, both the types and the imprints.[1]

The master of the colonial printing trade was a mentor of Anton Armbruster who, in turn, tutored Frederick Shober. The latter and Robert Hodge, who had worked for two years in the Philadelphia house of John Dunlap, became partners in a Baltimore printing enterprise, a partnership which shortly wandered to New York. Here they printed mainly for the booksellers, particularly Noel and Hazard, but Hodge felt impelled to travel again, sold out to Shober, and found employment in Boston.[2] The latter then entered into another partnership with Samuel Loudon, a good example of eighteenth-century versatility. "From merchant to printer and patriot" is the fictional title of a real career, which included bookselling and publishing an important newspaper, "The New York Packet and the American Advertiser."[3]

The Boston printers were fairly well known to their southern contemporaries, especially the Green family tree

---

[1] *Colden Papers,* vol. iii, pp. 58-59; *ibid.,* Nov. 4, 1743; J. H. Benton, *John Baskerville, Type-Founder and Printer* 1706-1775 (Boston, 1914); Franklin, *Calendar of Papers,* vol. ii, p. 151.

[2] Seidensticker, *First Century of German Printing in America,* p. 63; L. C. Wroth, *A History of Printing in Colonial Maryland 1686-1776* (Baltimore, 1922), p. 115; Hildeburn, pp. 144-147.

[3] A. J. Wall, "Samuel Loudon (1727-1813), Merchant, Printer and Patriot", *N. Y. Hist. Soc. Quarterly Bull.,* Oct. 1922.

which was rooted in Boston and had offshoots in Annapolis, New London, New Haven and Philadelphia. Jonas Green, a descendant of the printer of Eliot's famous Indian Bible, had been with his brother (of Kneeland and Green, Boston), before locating in Philadelphia where he worked for Franklin and Bradford. A more attractive field beckoned in Annapolis where Green's printing, which included the second " Maryland Gazette," is said by the historian of the local press to have achieved "a high degree of excellence." Through another connection Boston further assisted the growth of the colonial press. James Robertson, who published "The New York Chronicle" in 1768, had worked four years earlier in Boston as a journeyman, where he counted among his friends, John Fleming, a partner of the energetic loyalist publisher John Mein. Scenting new opportunities, Robertson moved to Albany to publish "The Albany Gazette," and in conjunction with John Trumbull printed "The Norwich Packet" in Connecticut.[1]

These interprovincial relationships among the printers are nowhere more strikingly illustrated than in the life of William Goddard. This restive person, of various places in his varied career, worked in the New Haven office of Parker and Holt, whence he eventually drifted to New York. By 1762 he had traveled to Rhode Island to publish the "Providence Gazette and Country Journal," which was soon taken over by his mother, "Sarah Goddard and Company." Goddard had already joined Holt in New York, but disagreements between the latter and Parker caused the new assistant to move to Philadelphia. To assist his mother, who was also a student of languages and mathematics and was known in several colonies, Goddard sent John Carter,

---

[1] C. F. Heartman, *Check-list of Printers in the United States ... to the Close of the War of Independence* (N. Y., 1915, *Heartman's Hist. Ser.*, no. 9), pp. 24-27; Wroth, *op. cit.*, p. 75 *et seq.*; Thomas, vol. ii, p. 109; Hildeburn, 98 *et seq.*

formerly with Franklin and Hall. Carter purchased the Providence office soon after, and Mrs. Goddard moved to Philadelphia to invest again in her son's enterprise, which had been joined by Joseph Galloway and Thomas Wharton, local dignitaries. In his latest home Goddard issued "The Pennsylvania Chronicle and Universal Advertiser," assisted by a journeyman Benjamin Towne, who later became a partner. Probably Goddard was also acquainted with J. D. MacDougall, who had come to Philadelphia after working in the house of Sarah Goddard at Providence. The ubiquitous William found himself in 1773 publishing "The Maryland Journal and Baltimore Advertiser," but the struggle for separation from England which was drawing near involved the ever active Goddard, and he relinquished control of the paper, now to be managed by his sister Mary.[1]

These migrations and intercolonial contacts doubtlessly had significant political consequences later, but some other contributions of the printers will first be considered. The first William Bradford is credited, besides his newspapers, with other issues, notably, Colden's " History of the Five Indian Nations," a work that is still useful. Both Franklin and Parker reprinted Richardson's " Pamela; " no copyright laws protected the American rights of eighteenth-century authors. Under the imprint "Parker and Weyman," Jared Eliot's " Essay upon Field-Husbandry . . . . in New England," was sold in New York. They also printed the writings of William Smith, including his " General Idea of the College of Mirania," which was to launch him into American academic life. Francis Hopkinson's musical arrangement of the English translation of Psalms for the Dutch church came from Parker's press. Perhaps it is

---

[1] Wroth, chap. x; Thomas, vol. i, 430, vol. ii, 108; Wilkins Updike, *Memoirs of the Rhode Island Bar* (Boston, 1842), p. 256; Albert Mathews, *Col. Soc. of Mass., Trans.,* vol. xi, p. 442.

no exaggeration to state that Parker in the period of the 1750's had the most extensive publishing business in the colonies. William Weyman, who was associated until 1759 with Parker, issued in that year his own "N. Y. Gazette," and to him are attributed the first volumes of Jewish prayers in the colonies.

The close associations among the American fraternity of the press reveal how ideas filtered through from place to place. In 1760 Mecom published in Boston a separate edition of the " Wisdom of Poor Richard," collected by Franklin two years earlier under the heading of "Father Abraham's Speech." Hugh Gaine had a prolific press, numbering some medical discourses and many almanacs among his issues. He catered to military tastes and his importation of more progressive children's books, which rendered obsolete the old primers, was materially well rewarded. Shober and Hodge in New York, brought out Garrick's "Irish Widow" and Goldsmith's "She Stoops to Conquer," while Inslee and Car sponsored Freneau's "The American Village," a youthful publication. The first American edition of "Josephus" was a cooperative enterprise as a result of the removal to New York of J. McGibbons, a bookseller, who had originally ordered it in Philadelphia. The Bradfords issued the first volume there; Shober and Hodge brought out the second in New York, followed by the third and fourth which bore the stamp of "Shober and Loudon." [1]

The younger William Bradford was an able and active person. "As an editor and printer of a newspaper, Bradford was not behind Franklin," writes his biographer, and "in the department of news" it is claimed that he was Franklin's superior. From a trip to London he returned

[1] Hildeburn, pp. 16, 40, 61-65, 143, 146-147; Evans, 6999, 8131, 13357; Ford, *Journals of Hugh Gaine;* R. V. Halsey, *Forgotten Books of the American Nursery* (Boston, 1911), p. 64.

with probably the largest assortment of books in the middle colonies, and his reputation as printer and bookseller was further enhanced by the publication of James Hervey's "Meditations," which had a large sale. Bradford had met in London, James Rivington a printer of some prominence who came to the colonies in 1760, and opened a bookstore in Hanover Square, New York, announcing himself as the "Only London Bookseller in America." The next year he left this establishment in charge of Samuel Brown, a bookseller of some standing, and went to Philadelphia where his friendship with William Bradford was doubtless of considerable advantage. Almost immediately Rivington extended his business to Boston under care of an agent, but this office was discontinued in 1765, and that in Philadelphia a year or so earlier; thenceforth he confined most of his activities to New York. Two volumes of Cook's "Voyages" came from his press here, where his newspaper "Rivington's New York Gazeteer," took an important place on the loyalist side of the impending storm.[1]

Eighteenth-century printers engaged in a multifarious round of operations which kept them in touch with nearly all phases of colonial life. Besides forming a bookselling partnership with Weyman of Philadelphia, Hugh Gaine sold arms, advertised "Philadelphia white-brown paper, fit for Shop-Keepers" and a long list of other articles. Auctioneering, an avocation which often took them far afield, was another of the services performed by Thomas Fleet, printer of the "Boston Evening Post." Samuel Dellap of Philadelphia made frequent visits to New York to advertise and sell his publications, returning with large collections of old books to be sold at auction.[2] Robert Bell with his Quaker

[1] Wallace, *Col. William Bradford*, pp. 356, 13; Hildeburn, chap. vii and p. 58; Thomas, vol. ii, p. 112.

[2] Ford, *op. cit.*, vol. i, p. 4; J. T. Buckingham, *Specimens of Newspaper*

hat, was a well known figure in the colonial book market, especially in New York where he was wont to auction large numbers of books which he had brought from Philadelphia. He performed the same function in Boston and Salem, specializing in the literature of "physick and surgery." Appealing to the prevailing passion for "made in America" articles, Bell stated that his books were either of native manufacture or had been imported before the adoption of commercial non-importation agreements.[1] The printer might also be a tavern owner. The versatile Bradford's "London coffee house for Merchants and Traders" in Philadelphia, was a center at which much news and gossip were retailed, culled perhaps from the newspapers of other colonial cities around which an eager audience gathered.[2]

The advantage of being a newspaper owner and a postmaster at once was too obvious to escape notice. "For fifty years (1704-1754) every Postmaster of Boston was also a publisher of a newspaper; of the seven Postmasters during that period five were connected with the 'Boston Gazette,' " writes a New England student. James Parker, Holt and Franklin were others closely connected with the post office. The advantages were decidedly positive, for on more than one occasion a rival was injured because he found his papers unmailed; it is said on good authority, that Franklin's appointment as postmaster undoubtedly assisted his "Gazette" to surpass the circulation of Bradford's "Mercury." Up to 1758, newspapers were distributed free of charge, but the instructions of the new Deputy-Postmasters General,

Literature (Boston, 1850), vol. i, p. 144; Thomas, vol. ii, pp. 79-80; Dellap advertised an auction in *N. Y. Gaz. and Weekly Mercury*, Jan. 25, 1773.

[1] " Parker to Franklin Letters," *loc cit.,* p. 221; *Boston Gaz. and Co. Journal,* July 2, July 16, 1770; J. P. Felt, *Annals of Salem* (1849, 2nd ed.), vol. ii, p. 29.

[2] Wallace, *Col. William Bradford,* pp. 48, 54.

Franklin and Hunter, indicate that these publications had become burdensome to post-riders and a small charge would have to be made. The enterprising Goddard, charged one pound a week for the delivery of three hundred and fifty papers to places outside of Philadelphia, established his independence of the post office by having his own system of post-riders.[1] An alert New York printer, Samuel Farley, wished to speed up the news-gathering service by having advance sheets released by the owners of newspapers in other cities, but his suggestion went unheeded.[2]

Circulation figures of newspaper owners have been proverbially unreliable. In 1773, Rivington announced that 3600 copies of his paper were distributed through every colony of North America and elsewhere. Gaine's "Mercury" claimed to be sold throughout New Jersey, Connecticut, Rhode Island and in the leading towns of other colonies. It is certain that Franklin's "Gazette" became very profitable, having an extensive circulation in Pennsylvania and neighboring colonies. Andrew Bradford's "Mercury," published in Philadelphia was also obtainable in New York. His nephew's "Pennsylvania Journal" numbered among its subscribers "leading planters, merchants, statesmen, . . . and literati, in all parts of America." [3] J. H. Miller, publisher of the "Staatsbote" in Philadelphia, depended for widespread circulation on agents scattered through the colonies; it was estimated that 6000 subscribed for the paper printed by the famous German, Saur. That many did not circulate is proven by the fact that, of seventy-eight printed between

---

[1] Albert Mathews, " Check list of Boston Newspapers 1704-1780," *Col. Soc. of Mass., Trans.,* vol. ix, bibliographical notes, p. 440; Oswald, *op. cit.,* p. 109; Thomas, vol. ii, p. 328; Ford, *op. cit.,* vol. i, pp. 38-39.

[2] J. M. Lee, *History of American Journalism* (Boston, 1923), p. 66.

[3] Thomas, vol. ii, pp. 316, 328, 39; C. S. Brigham, " Bibliography of American Newspapers ", *Amer. Antiq. Soc. Proc.,* vol. xxxii, p. 85; Oberholtzer, *Literary History of Phila.,* p. 14.

1705-1775, only one half survived to the Revolution.[1]   One may be skeptical of the figures enumerated, but the growth of an American mind was certainly stimulated by the interchange of newspapers and the mutual transfer of items, which frequently betrayed an interest in local affairs by distant readers.

Another activity indicating many colonial contacts was the printing and selling of almanacs.   Daniel Leeds, who published an almanac at Philadelphia in 1687, was also New York's first almanac maker, using Bradford's press.   Titian Leeds evidently inherited the Philadelphia almanac, which was printed by Andrew Bradford and then by Keimer.   In 1727 a parcel of these almanacs was sent to Boston, Newport and other towns where they sold well; the New York publication was taken over by a brother, Felix Leeds.[2]   Nathaniel Whittemore's almanac for 1724, Boston, stated that it was acceptable as far as New York where the compilations by Daniel Travis, a fellow townsman, had previously been printed over a stretch of ten years.[3]   William Birkett's almanac was sold in New York and Philadelphia by the Bradfords.   Long before his more illustrious brother, James Franklin had issued an almanac containing much of the sprightliness characteristic of "Poor Richard."   Three years earlier in 1725, Nathaniel Ames brought out his "Astronomical Diary and Almanac," which was to live through three generations.   It possessed nearly every excellent feature that was to make its contemporary "Poor Richard" so famous; in fact it has been adjudged even

[1] C. F. Dapp, *The Evolution of an American Patriot ... John Henry Miller* ... (Phila., 1924), pp. 11-14; Thomas, vol. ii, p. 397; on circulation, see S. N. D. North, *History and Present Condition of the Newspapers and Periodical Press of the United States* (Wash., 1884), p. 19.

[2] A. J. Wall, "New York Almanacs 1694-1800," *N. Y. P. L., Bulletin*, vol. xxiv, p. 288.

[3] C. L. Nichols, "Massachusetts Almanacs 1639-1850," *Am. Antiq. Soc. Proc.*, vol. xxii, p. 29.

better than Franklin's.[1] Roger Sherman's almanacs for
New York and Boston, which contained items mutually advantageous, were printed on occasion by De Foreest and
Parker in the former city, and in the latter by D. Fowle.
In organizing his almanac, Sherman acknowledged his indebtedness to Ames, with whom he assumed his readers were
"well acquainted."[2] Parker also printed for a time, succeeded by Thomas Green, some of the issues of Nathaniel
Ames, which likewise appeared in Boston. "Father Abraham's Almanac," 1759, the first "Weatherwise" almanac,
was printed by William Dunlap in Philadelphia for booksellers in New York and Boston. A decade later, Sarah
Goddard and John Carter published an almanac whose name
was taken from that of Dunlap, with which Carter had been
familiar in Philadelphia.

Both Andrew Bradford and Franklin appealed to the
large German element in Pennsylvania with almanacs in
their native language. The latter was very successful in
selling his publications; " Poor Richard's Almanack " ap-
proximated ten thousand each year, and " Poor Richard
Improved " gained an equally large audience; over 141,000
copies were printed between 1752 and 1765. The circulation figures for Ames's almanac seem unbelievable, reaching an average annually of 60,000 copies between the years
1726 and 1764.[3] Almanacs seem to have been more widely
read than newspapers but both agencies played important
parts in the cultivation of a common sentiment.

[1] Samuel Briggs, *The Essays Humor and Poems of Nathaniel Ames,
Father and Son, of Dedham, Massachusetts, from their Almanacks 1726-
1775* (Cleveland, 1891) ; M. C. Tyler, *A History of American Literature* (N. Y., 1895, Agawam ed.), vol. ii, p. 122.

[2] V. H. Paltsits, "Roger Sherman's Almanacs 1750-1761," *Am. Antiq.
Soc. Proc.,* vol. xviii, pp. 217, 234; Briggs, *op. cit.,* pp. 222-223.

[3] H. A. Morrison, *Preliminary Check-list of American Almanacs 1639-
1800* (Wash., 1907), pp. 10-11, 94-118; Nichols, *loc cit.,* p. 36; A. M.
Chapin, "Rhode Island Almanacs ", *Am. Antiq. Soc. Proc.,* vol. xxv;
Seidensticker, *op. cit.;* Oswald, *op. cit.,* p. 115; Evans, 9827; Briggs,
p. 20, note 1.

CHAPTER V

Schools and School Books

The importance of common reading material dispensed by newspapers and almanacs in creating a group mind has long been conceded. But a standardized culture is just as much the result of a common educational system which weaves similar patterns of thought in the minds of its students. Of course, better organized attempts have been made since the eighteenth century to give a definite stamp to the products of our schools; but this earlier period, in a less obvious way, was shaping its own "consciousness of kind." Books containing the same substance, schools run on similar lines and colleges with many far-flung associations, have ever been potent factors in constructing a cultural unity.

The universal acquaintance with the New England primer must have been a powerful force in molding youthful mental habits. It was known throughout the colonies; Franklin and Hall printed over 37,000 copies between 1749 and 1766; Z. Fowle of Boston sent forth an edition of 10,000 copies. Practically every printer in the colonies issued a number of these primers, calling them the "Franklin Primer," "Boston Primer," "New York Primer," etc. Christopher Saur in Germantown, reprinted a Boston "New England Primer." The primer at best was not an attractive book but improvements were soon forthcoming. Thomas Fleet recognized the value of entertainment in children's reading, for he included pictures in "The Parents' Gift," a religious work. Franklin encouraged the pictorial feature when he introduced into Dilworth's "New Guide to the English Tongue," known throughout the colonies, a feature called "Select Fables" with cuts. Before 1750 pictures had become an accepted ingredient in children's books. By this time, John Newbery, who began modern books for children in England was known in Philadelphia; in New York, J. Waddell and James Parker were marketing similar publications. Some ten years later Gaine was importing most of Newbery's juvenile literature, and Rivington was selling books of a like pattern. Garrat Noel stocked them in New York where he also sold John Gignoux's "The Child's Best Instructor in Spelling and Reading," printed in Philadelphia; Fowle and Draper in Boston, published children's books and John Mein sold them.[1]

Most of the more elementary schools were closely affiliated with religious denominations, but the primer was a common article of nourishment.[2] The Society for the Propagation of the Gospel, an Anglican body it will be recalled, did a great deal to further education in the colonies, and its teachers like their contemporaries, the printers, traveled from place to place. The Rev. Robert Jenney, who had worked as a schoolmaster in Philadelphia, conducted a grammar school in New York for a few years. Charles Inglis, later rector of Trinity Church in New York, taught a "Free School" in Lancaster before 1759; a Harvard graduate, John Rand taught the S. P. G. school at Rye, N. Y. District catechising schools which offered also a training in reading, were opened in New York, Philadelphia and Charlestown. Franklin and the Rev. William Smith were trustees of funds to open institutions under the auspices of the S. P. G. in

[1] C. F. Heartman, *The New England Primer issued prior to 1830* (N. J., 1922, *Heartman's Hist. Ser.*, No. 15) ; P. L. Ford, *The New England Primer; a History of its Origin and Development* (N. Y., 1897), pp. 19, 27; Evans, 7264, 10314; Halsey, *Forgotten Books of the American Nursery*, pp. 38-39, 59-65, 68, 73, 70.

[2] Found its way into Phila. Quaker schools; Thomas Woody, *Early Quaker Education in Pennsylvania* (N. Y., 1920, *Teachers Coll. Contrib. to Educ.*, no. 105), p. 194.

Pennsylvania, where a charity school was closely connected
with the College of Philadelphia.[1] · In 1732 a public school
was established in New York to give instruction in Latin,
Greek and mathematics, a fairly common curriculum.   The
latter city was evidently thought to be in dire need of such
facilities.   Samuel Johnson, later president of King's College, advised Colden to assist the studious Prince of Boston,
who was anxious to set up a school on Long Island to cater
to the New York aristocracy, and added, with a keen eye
to the local deficiency, that it would promote learning in
"your Government" could he teach in it.[2]

The colonial schools offered a fair range of subjects, many
of which were studied for immediate use.   French was
widely taught, texts teaching it by short cuts appeared in
Boston in 1720 and in Philadelphia ten years later.   Noel
and Hazard sold a number of books in French, by far the
most popular foreign tongue, although the teaching of
Italian, Portuguese and Spanish was not neglected.[3]   There
was some demand for German too, for Henry Miller of
Philadelphia announced "A Complete German Grammar" in
the local and New York newspapers.[4]   In an age given to
land speculation and much sea travel, one would expect
plentiful instruction in surveying and navigation.   A
treatise on "Subtential Plain Trigonometry" for use in these
professions, was issued in Philadelphia and delivered to

[1] Kemp, *Support of Schools by the S. P. G.*, pp. 74, 139, 235; J. P.
Wickersham, *History of Education in Pennsylvania* (Lancaster, 1886),
p. 98; S. E. Weber, *The Charity School Movement in Colonial Pennsylvania* (Phila., 190?), pp. 32, 55.

[2] D. J. Pratt, *Annals of Public Education in the State of New York
from 1626 to 1746* (Albany, 1872), pp. 124-125; *Colden Papers,* vol. iii,
pp. 76-77, 104-105.

[3] R. F. Seybolt, *Source Studies in American Colonial Education: The
Private School* (Univ. of Illinois, Bur. of ed. research, bull., 28), pp. 9-
34; *N. Y. Gaz. and Weekly Mercury,* Nov. 18, 1771, supplement.

[4] *Ibid.; Pa. Packet,* Oct. 18, 1773.

subscribers in New York also. Algebra was taught in all the important towns, as were other branches of mathematics, and manuals in these subjects guided a widely scattered student body; John Gordon's " Mathematical . . . . Table," for example, was sold in Philadelphia, New York and Boston. In the private schools these studies were pursued with a view to practical application. Geography and history were taught in many schools of this type, which were also opened for girls whose program included music. These institutions, it is worth noting, did excellent service in liberalizing the academic curricula.[1]

The teachers of these schools were frequently college graduates and were often known in more than one city. Francis Vandale was in Boston, in 1774, and taught in Newport and New York the next year.[2] A man of many travels was William Elphinstone. Teaching in New York in 1753, the following year found him in Philadelphia, whence he returned in 1755. A short stay and he left for Boston, but was soon shuttling between Philadelphia and New York in which latter city he located for a more extended period. He advertised that he had taught a considerable number of "Gentlemen and Ladies" in several parts of America "to write a good legible distinct Hand in five or six Weeks," and now proposed "to teach . . . . Writing and Arithmetick in a Body, at twenty Shillings per Quarter . . . . Nine to Twelve o'Clock in the Forenoon, and from two to five in the Afternoon." For those who could not or cared not to attend the public school, Elphinstone gave lessons privately. He was well known to the gentry and bore a splendid reputation as a teacher.[3]

---

[1] *Penn. Journal*, June 18, 1761, in *N. J. Arch.*, vol. xx, pp. 582-583; Evans, 8140; Seybolt, *op. cit.*, pp. 54-68, 74-75, 102.

[2] *Ibid.*, p. 85, note 16.

[3] *Ibid.*, pp. 84-85; *N. Y. Mercury*, May 29, 1758; *Pa. Archives, 1748-56*, p. 170.

There were also evening schools in the colonies, a fact which has received little or no attention in treatments of colonial history until recently. New York had them before 1700, the "Boston Gazette" advertised one a quarter century later; another ten years passed when the "Mercury" recorded one in Philadelphia, which was followed by others.[1] These institutions were in a real sense the "business colleges" of the colonial period, and were patronized by practically all classes. The subjects embraced nearly all branches of mathematics in their practical aspects, and bookkeeping taught "after the Italian method of double Entry." There were offers made in New York and Philadelphia to supplant the Italian by the London and Dublin styles. "There seems," to quote Seybolt, a painstaking student, "to have been a steady demand for evening instruction in French, Italian, Portuguese and Spanish," the latter language enlisting the pedagogical activities of Noel, the bookseller. Some of the schools offered writing and arithmetic only; a knowledge of reading was assumed.[2] Colonial Americans learnt their arithmetic from reprints of English originals. The manuals of George Fisher and Thomas Dilworth were generally used until 1800, although a few native texts had already secured a more limited acceptance.[3] "The American Instructor," one of a number of texts on letter writing and a general business aid, went through fifteen editions by 1770, being printed one year at Philadelphia, at other times

[1] R. F. Seybolt, *The Evening School in Colonial America* (Univ. of Illinois, Bur. of ed. research, bull., 24), p. 12.

[2] Seybolt, "Evening Schools of Colonial New York City," *N. Y. State Local History Leaflets,* pp. 641-652; *Evening School in Colonial America,* pp. 28-29, 31, 39, 55.

[3] L. C. Karpinski, "Colonial American Arithmetics," *Essays to W. Eames,* pp. 243-48; Herbert Kimmel, *School and Society,* vol. ix, mentions more arithmetics.

in New York, Burlington and elsewhere—an indication of its wide appeal.[1]

Women were admitted to night schools, separately and coeducationally; notices of these institutions appeared in the newspapers. J. and M. Tanner had a boarding school in New York which had classes in writing, arithmetic, needle work, music, dancing and drawing. The mode of education was similar to that obtainable in English boarding schools and was evidently well received. In the same paper Fanny Brian advertised a school that taught reading, writing and needle work.[2] In these schools, it is again noted that French was the most popular language; it was considered fashionable and necessary, and to meet the demand a "French Night School," attended by men and women was opened in one city. Some years later, John Girault had a French school in New York; he taught in homes as well. Lewis Delile, educated at the University of Bordeaux, taught in Boston and Newport, and in at least one instance an ambitious individual left Philadelphia to live with a family in New Rochelle to perfect himself in this foreign tongue.[3]

Most of those who taught in the evening were also masters of day schools. One of the earliest in New York was John Walton, of Yale, who opened up an academy with evening and day classes. An interesting cooperative effort of schoolmasters in Philadelphia was a discussion of evening school problems, with an arrangement of the fees and the academic season (winter term). Most of the terms for apprentices were quarter terms, but John Vinal in Boston had a six

---

[1] Evans, 11859.

[2] *N. Y. Gaz. and Weekly Mercury*, April 18, 1774, supplement; for earlier notices, *Evening School in Colonial America*, p. 17.

[3] *Ibid.*, p. 31; *N. Y. Gaz. and Weekly Mercury*, Sept. 16, 1771; *Boston Gaz. and Co. Journal*, June 22, 1772; Stiles, *Diary*, Aug. 23, 1773; student was Joseph Shippen; McLean, *College of New Jersey*, vol. i, p. 142.

months' schedule. It is certainly worth remembering that the curricula and methods of conducting these schools seem to have reacted upon one another in different cities; the schoolmasters in Boston, for example, were well acquainted with similar institutions in other provinces.[1]

The intercolonial relationships among the business schools and the elementary schools were no more important than those among higher institutions of learning. The many collegiate relationships, found especially in the middle colonies, reveal a lively mutual interest in the problems of education. For many years Harvard and Yale in the north and William and Mary in the south, were the only institutions of collegiate rank. The growth of population, sometimes the advance of the dissenting spirit, and the emergence of a group with strong educational interests urged with varying force the establishment of new schools in New York, New Jersey, Pennsylvania and Rhode Island.

Affecting American life as probably no one before or since, Franklin also lent valuable assistance on its educational side. He played a leading role in founding the College of Philadelphia, later the University of Pennsylvania, with the able assistance of others, including Thomas Lawrence, originally of New York. Samuel Johnson of Stratford, Connecticut, was invited to preside over the College or the Academy, as it was first called. Further correspondence indicated Johnson's interest in the school, but the best he could or would do, was to recommend William Smith for the post. The latter who had also been recommended to Thomas Penn from abroad, was tutoring in New York, where he had written "Some Thoughts on Education and Reasons for erecting a College in New York City." Another of his pamphlets "A General Plan of the College of Mirania,"

[1] Seybolt, *Evening School in Colonial America*, pp. 11, 18-19, 49 and *passim*.

embraced a course of study, somewhat modeled on the scheme of the Philadelphia Academy. Early in 1753 Smith wrote to Franklin about placing his pupils in the school and inclosed a copy of "Mirania." A number of copies of the pamphlet were then ordered from Philadelphia, and the "Pennsylvania Gazette" advertised it for sale. Franklin replied that he and Richard Peters, an active local citizen, had compared notes and had concluded that Smith's plans were practicable. Smith's arrival in June was celebrated with "A Poem on visiting the Academy of Philadelphia," in which allusions were made to the efforts of New Yorkers to establish a college. Within a short time he was ordained in the Anglican communion, and two years later was made Provost of the school.[1]

The story of Princeton reveals most clearly the new influences leavening colonial life. The College of New Jersey, which was its earlier name, founded partly as a reaction against the conservatism of Yale, but more particularly as a guardian of American Presbyterianism, was nursed by many attendants. The New York Presbyterians were interested in its establishment in 1746; there were many in Philadelphia sympathetically concerned. Governor Belcher of New Jersey, an old Harvard alumnus, was an effective medium between the college and New England where it had many friends, whose wealth assisted in the construction of the buildings at Princeton. In fact among the original impulses directing the college founders was that of strengthening the bonds between the Presbyterians in the middle colonies and those in New England, as well as to stem the advance of the Anglicans who were very powerful in New

---

[1] Montgomery, *History of the Univ. of Penn.*, pp. 127, 184, 185-202; Prof. John Winthrop of Harvard, was also suggested as a possible candidate for Provost, pp. 513-514; H. W. Smith, *Life and Corr. of Rev. Wm. Smith*, vol. i, pp. 23-26.

York and Philadelphia.[1] Connecticut raised £13,342 to aid in the building, and the papers in the northern capitals published items relating to the college.   Announcements were made of the brisk sales of lottery tickets in behalf of the college; the lottery which was managed by residents of Philadelphia and New Jersey reported tickets sold in all the principal cities.[2]

Samuel Blair, a tutor at the college for three years and then pastor of the Old South Church in Boston, was offered the presidency of Princeton in case John Witherspoon, a Presbyterian clergyman in the state church of Scotland, should refuse it.   Scotland showed its interest in the college by contributing £1000, and America showed its interest in Scotland by reading Witherspoon's works.   The latter at first refused the call; but after receiving urgent messages from the colonies he accepted it, stopped off in London where he secured a number of books for the college library, and arrived in Philadelphia, August 1768.   His earliest efforts were to place the college on a firmer financial foundation.   He went to New England and, through introductions furnished by Ebenezer Pemberton, a founder of the college, now a minister in Boston, was enabled to add £1000 to its funds.   Rev. Dr. John Rodgers, a well known personality in provincial cities, traveled to the Carolinas in search of funds, while Governor Belcher had begun the foundation of a library by a gift of books to which friends made additions.[3]

[1] McLean, *op. cit.*, vol. i, p. 24; D. W. Woods, *John Witherspoon* (N. Y., 1906), p. 85; V. L. Collins, *President Witherspoon* (Princeton, 1925), vol. i, pp. 76-77.

[2] Barratt, *History of St. Paul's Episcopal Church. Phila.*, p. 40, note 38; Newspaper extracts, *N. J. Archives,* ser. 1, vol. xii, pp. 625, 468-469, 611-612, 590-92, 592, note 1.

[3] Hill, *Old South Church*, vol. ii, pp. 88-89; Woods, pp. 60-73, 98-99, 106; Collins, vol. i, p. 80, note 9, pp. 85, 114, 124; a Rev. Mr. Caldwell was also collecting in S. C.; McCrady, pp. 499-500.

All of the colleges faced the problem of training unprepared entrants, an obstacle which they attempted to overcome by establishing preparatory schools closely affiliated with the parent institutions. In New York, for example, by meeting certain requirements in Latin, Greek, rhetoric, logic and science, students could qualify for the New Jersey college. The school, which was recommended by New Yorkers, had a summer session with a schedule from six to eight, and nine to twelve in the morning, two to four in the afternoon, on the principle perhaps, that the early bird catches the germ of knowledge. A winter term had a program more like its modern counterpart, nine to twelve in the morning and two to five in the afternoon.[1]

Queen's College, now Rutgers, founded by charter in 1766 but not actually functioning till five years later, was originated by the Dutch of New York and New Jersey. It found favor and encouragement among the Episcopalians and especially among the Presbyterians, with whom the Dutch were religiously akin. When the opening of the college was delayed, there was some discussion of a joint use with Princeton of the latter's class rooms; suggestions were also made for a union with King's College.[2]

In the early history of the latter institution we can likewise trace an intercommunity interest. Dean George Berkeley from Newport, Rhode Island, had suggested the establishment of a college in New York years before the first steps were taken in its behalf. Beginning in 1746, plans were made to raise funds for its foundation, but a great controversy immediately flared up as to the nature of the school. William Livingston, an influential lawyer and Presbyterian, feared it might be an appendage of the Anglican Church which actually did happen, and his vigorous

[1] Alexander Miller, *N. Y. Gaz. or Weekly Post-Boy*, Nov. 29, 1764.

[2] Demarest, *History of Rutgers*, pp. 1, 21, 65-67.

attacks delayed the grant of a charter until 1754. The trustees who had already been appointed invited Dr. Samuel Johnson of Connecticut and Mr. Whittlesey, who had tutored at Yale, to come to New York as teachers. Johnson accepted the invitation, and soon after his son, William S., became his assistant. The advertisement in the "New York Gazette" of the opening of King's College indicated that Johnson had been strongly influenced by the proposals for the Philadelphia Academy. Enlarged enrolment necessitated further aid; so Daniel Treadwell, educated at Harvard and highly recommended by Professor Winthrop, became Professor of Mathematics and Natural History. Some years later, Mathew Cushing formerly librarian in Harvard College and teacher in Massachusetts, became master of the grammar school which prepared students for King's.[1]

The desire of the Baptists for an educated ministry caused the organization in 1764 of Rhode Island College (later Brown University), whose Maecenas was Nicholas Brown, the wealthy dealer in spermaceti oil products. Eight years earlier, an academy from which the college later grew had been founded at Hopewell Junction, New Jersey, by the Philadelphia Association of Baptists, which schooled among others Samuel Stillman, Isaac Skillman and John Davis, all of Boston. Two of the most active figures in the promotion of the new school were the Rev. Morgan Edwards of Philadelphia and the Rev. John Gano of New York.[2]

Intercolonial influences were brought to bear upon local

---

[1] Montgomery, *op. cit.*, pp. 134-135; *History of Columbia University, 1754-1904* (N. Y., 1904), pp. 22, 40; C. K. Bolton and A. C. Potter, *The Librarians of Harvard College 1667-1877*, (*Harv. Univ. Library, Bibliog. Cont.*, no. 52), p. 23.

[2] R. A. Guild, *Early History of Brown University, including the Life, Times and Correspondence of President Manning* (Providence, 1897), pp. 7-9, 21.

institutions in diverse ways. To furnish better quarters for students at Philadelphia from other provinces and the West Indies, the suggestion was made to erect additional buildings, "as is done in the Jersey and New York Colleges." To get sums for these, collections were made in Great Britain where Dr. James Jay for King's College, and Dr. William Smith cooperated. Others who aided were Dr. John Morgan, famous in medical academic history, Mr. John Inglis, a trustee of the Philadelphia college and Moses Franks, a well known American Jew. Mr. Barlow Trecothick, an English political figure, and the Archbishop of Canterbury were of material assistance in making authorized collections for both colleges whose appeals to a sympathetic religious spirit netted profitable returns. Contributions were received from Oxford and Cambridge and from all the large commercial and manufacturing towns. David Garrick also came to the aid of the college with a benefit at the Drury Lane, so that collections amounting to £9000 in all were announced.[1] About the same time Harvard was likewise seeking the favor and patronage of King George III, but her efforts met with no response. Some of the successful appeals in the colonies themselves have already been noted, but in addition the Baptists of Rhode Island College and the Anglicans in Philadelphia went to the South for financial support which they readily found.[2]

There were reciprocal donations of another kind. Four

[1] Montgomery, pp. 354, 390, 410, 420; *Stirling Papers,* letter to Lord Romney, 1762; L. Hühner, "Jews (and) Colleges prior to 1800", *Am. Jew. Hist. Soc. Pub.,* vol. xix, pp. 116-17; C. M. Andrews and F. G. Davenport, *Guide to the Manuscript Materials for the History of the United States to 1783 in the British Museum in minor London Archives and in the Libraries of Oxford and Cambridge* (Wash., 1908), p. 72; *Pa. Mag. of Hist. and Biog.,* vol. 39, pp. 48-50; *N. Y. Mercury,* July 2, 1764, *Devoe's Index.*

[2] Josiah Quincy, *History of Harvard University* (Boston, 1840), vol. ii, p. 105; McCrady, pp. 499-500; Bronson, *History of Brown Univ.,* p. 39.

sons of Philip Livingston of New York studied at Yale, and in appreciation of their training he donated to the college a sum of money used later to support the "Livingston Professorship of Divinity." When Harvard's library was practically destroyed by fire in 1764, Franklin forwarded valuable instruments for electrical apparatus; he also sent a bust of Lord Chatham. From Philadelphia, Jonathan Smith sent the "Juvenile Poems" of Thomas Godfrey, one of America's earliest litterateurs.[1] Louis Langloiserie, formerly in New York attached to the family of Governor Burnet, was called to Harvard to teach French, in which he gave public instruction in Boston as well, where he formed a language club. Daniel Treadwell, it was mentioned, went to King's College to teach mathematics and philosophy, a chair later offered to Nathaniel Ward, Harvard librarian, who declined. Lewis Evans, the Philadelphia cartographer, was engaged to deliver twelve lectures at Princeton on the same plan he had adopted in New York and in his home town.[2]

There was a marked inheritance of college ideals and ideas. Yale transmitted the traditions and practises to Princeton which it had received from Harvard, whose academic customs had previously been modeled on those of Cambridge. The new Rhode Island College, in turn, followed the example of Princeton in many ways, including its entrance requirements and its curriculum. Horace, Vergil, the Greek Testament and mathematics comprised the larger part of the studies in the older schools. In the newer colleges

---

[1] F. B. Dexter, *A Selection from the Miscellaneous Historical Papers of Fifty Years* (New Haven, 1918), pp. 287-288; Quincy, *History of Harvard*, vol. ii, appendix, 491.

[2] Albert Mathews, "French at Harvard before 1750," *Col. Soc. of Mass., Trans.*, vol. 17, pp. 220-223; *Matricula of King's College*, p. 9, N. B.; Bolton and Potter, *op. cit.*, p. 29; McLean, *op. cit.*, vol. i, pp. 141-142.

the curriculum emphasized features indicating a broader preparation than that required for the ministerial office. King's College marked the new tendency, which included a comprehensive program of surveying, navigation, geography, history, husbandry and modern languages, although it was incompletely carried out by Dr. Johnson. Some years before in a correspondence with Franklin touching educational affairs, Colden heartily agreed with the suggestion that agriculture be taught as one of the sciences. Colden would not oblige all the students to learn Latin and Greek; English authors in prose and verse should be recommended. It is more than likely that these were matters under discussion between Colden and Johnson. The feeble start at King's College was made into an effective progress at Philadelphia under Dr. Smith who gave definite form to the American college course, directing it into the legitimate collegiate pathway. His curriculum, marked by the absence of any special aim toward theology as a profession encouraged the study of languages for their own sake and was much in advance of every other colonial college. He was more fortunate than some of his contemporaries in having a good part of his generous program actually carried out.[1]

On the boards of trustees and in the student bodies, mingled men of different religious affiliations and often of widely separated domiciles. Trustees who gathered at Princeton had studied at Harvard and Yale, while a few students from New England met those from New York and Philadelphia. As an educative factor these associations were perhaps as valuable as the course of study. Philip Vickers Fithian wrote his mother " I have an Oppertunity . . . . of acquainting myself with Mankind, by observing

[1] L. F. Snow, *The College Curriculum in the United States* (*Col. Univ., Cont. to Educa., Teachers College Series*, no. 10), pp. 37-39, 52, 56-73; Bronson, *op. cit.*, p. 104; *Colden Papers,* vol. iv, pp. 156-158, Nov. 1749.

the Conduct & Temper of the Students in this Seminary . . . . filled with Young Men . . . . from almost every Province, in this Continent," from the West Indies and Europe. Their early education being different makes our " Observations on them, both agreeable & profitable." [1] In James Madison's class 1771, were Gunning Bedford of Delaware, John Black of South Carolina, H. H. Brackenridge of Pennsylvania, Philip Freneau of New York and Samuel Spring of Massachusetts—a representative group. So widely scattered were its graduates, that Witherspoon on his tours in the South found "a Princeton tradition already sprung up, planted by alumni from the earliest classes." [2]

Among the extra-curricular activities at Princeton was a Cliosophic Society, a revival, in 1770 of an older " Well-Meaning Society," effected through the energy of Robert Stewart of New York, John Smith of Massachusetts, Isaac Smith of New Hampshire and others. It included in its membership men from Boston and Long Island and some Harvard graduates; many of its members left honorable memories in American history. King's College students formed a literary society for the advancement of learning, and youthful Thespians in several of the colleges exhibited their accomplishments publicly or privately, depending on the strength or weakness of local hostility to the theatre. Despite the antagonism of the college officials Yale students put on four performances in one week, which were attended by townspeople as well as nearly the whole student body. [3]

[1] Philip Vickers Fithian, *Journal and Letters*, Jan. 12, 1772; *Princeton University Catalogue, 1746-1906*, pp. 82-97.

[2] S. D. Alexander, *Princeton College during the Eighteenth Century*, pp. 139-146; Collins, *op. cit.*, vol. i, p. 130.

[3] G. M. Giger, *History of the Cliosophic Society, from 1765 to 1865* (Princeton, 1865) ; *History of Columbia University*, p. 45; Odell, *Annals of N. Y. Stage*, vol. i, p. 108; Dexter, *Historical Papers*, p. 271.

Over thirty southern students, mostly from Maryland, were graduated from the College of Philadelphia before 1775; Princeton had ten and Harvard listed a few. In its earliest days, Philadelphia had students from New York and New Jersey, even though local schools were a counter attraction.[1] Francis Hopkinson of Pennsylvania, a composer and a man of letters as well as an active politician in later years, wrote an elegy on the death of Josiah Martin, a New Yorker and former classmate at the college. John Johnston was in his third year at King's College when he went to Philadelphia; others on removal to the latter city transferred to the local school. On the other hand, there were a few registered at King's as from Philadelphia. Josiah Ogden and Isaac Ogden, formerly of Princeton, were graduated from the New York college. President Manning of Rhode Island College, educated at Princeton, adopted many of its customs in regulating a student body which included young men from New Jersey, Pennsylvania and Massachusetts; one student left Harvard for the new college. Among the first trustees of Queen's College were bearers of Dutch, British, French and German names in New York and New Jersey, the most prominent of whom were the Livingstons.[2]

Yale's influence in the life of other colonies as well as her own was very important. The biographies of its graduates largely tell the story, part of which reveals a lively interest in the early growth of the New Jersey college. In the first half-century of its history over one hundred students came from other provinces, mainly from Massachusetts and

[1] *William and Mary College Historical Quarterly,* vol. vi, pp. 217-219; southerners also went to European colleges; *University of Pennsylvania, Matriculates of the College,* pp. 5, 8.

[2] G. E. Hastings, *The Life and Works of Francis Hopkinson* (Chicago, 1926), pp. 96-97; *Matricula of King's College,* pp. 4, 5, 6, 8, 16; *Univ. of Penn., Matriculates,* p. 5, Guild, *op. cit.,* pp. 93-107; Demarest, *op. cit.,* pp. 61-64.

New York, with a scattering few from New Jersey and
Pennsylvania. Despite the new college facilities nearer
home during the next period, 1745-1763, students in about
the same number continued to come from distant colonies;
Rhode Island contributed some in these years. What is
even more significant, a larger proportion of graduates began to move away from their home colonies. Although
sixty-three registered from Massachusetts in this second
period, eighty-seven Yale graduates settled there; thirty-three
came from New York but forty-five located there, a situation that was paralleled for New Jersey and New Hampshire. Some of the leading lawyers and public personages in
local and intercolonial affairs, were either at college here
together or shared this common intellectual heritage. Joseph
Hawley of Massachusetts, Jared Ingersoll of Connecticut
and William Peartree Smith of New York and New Jersey,
all of whom were to be influential in law and politics, were
Yale classmates. The friendship begun at Yale between
William Livingston of New York and Noah Welles of New
England surely must have strengthened their common de-
termination to oppose the introduction into the colonies of
an Anglican bishop.[1]

The bestowal of honorary degrees, which incidentally is
an old American folkway with European precedents, indicates numerous intercollegiate contacts. Many of the
advanced degrees, it is only fair to state, were the rewards
of extended study, usually the preparation and defense of
a thesis. The large list of those whose efforts were recognized by colleges other than their own suggests a busy
academic inter-activity whose remains have vanished or are
difficult of access. Franklin's assistance secured European

---

[1] F. B. Dexter, *Biographical Sketches of the Graduates of Yale College with Annals of the College History* (N. Y., 1885-1912), vol. i, p. 773,
vol. ii, p. 783.

degrees for several Americans, including the Rev. Samuel Cooper and the Rev. Andrew Eliot of Boston, both of whom were granted D.D.s by Edinburgh. His aid was sought in getting an LL.D. for Professor John Winthrop. Yale made a Harvard man a doctor of divinity, Princeton did the same for two Yale bachelors and one Harvard graduate.[1]

Master's degrees from King's College were conferred on two students who had taken their bachelor's degrees at Philadelphia, and on one from Princeton; one student with a Yale A.B. got a like degree. Seven masters from Yale, three from Harvard and two from Princeton were similarly honored at King's. Four with a higher degree from Philadelphia, including Isaac Hunt father of Leigh Hunt, added to their names a King's M.A. Two who had M.A.s from Harvard and Yale received the same degree in New York; one was William Samuel Johnson. Francis Alison of Philadelphia, a graduate of Yale with a widespread reputation for classical scholarship, received an M.A. from Princeton. Two Harvard bachelors and one from Philadelphia took advanced degrees at Princeton. One, Jacob Green, Harvard 1744, was temporarily Vice-President of Princeton a few years later. Two M.A.s from Harvard, one from Yale and one from Philadelphia received the same degree at Princeton. One gentleman with degrees from Philadelphia and Rhode Island, bore an M.A. from New Jersey; two with higher Harvard and Yale degrees and one with King's and Yale degrees had master's conferred on them from Princeton. Harvard distributed several master's degrees to Yale bachelors and to some possessing higher degrees from Philadelphia, Princeton and King's

---

[1] " Price Letters," *Mass. Hist. Soc. Proc.*, ser., 2, vol. xvii, pp. 263, 264 and note 1; Franklin, *Cal. of Papers,* vol. ii, p. 90; *Catalogue of Officers and Graduates of Yale University, 1701-1924,* p. 573; *Princeton University Catalogue,* Ebenezer Pemberton, Naphtali Daggett, Noah Welles, (1774).

Colleges. Franklin was made an M.A. in 1753. A very surprising feature was the award of sixteen M.A.s to recent graduates of Princeton over a period extending from 1755 to 1773. A similarly detailed investigation of Yale degrees corroborates the statement that there was reciprocal recognition of scholarship throughout the colonies in the quarter century preceding the Revolution, and an added note of interest reveals the large number of its graduates whose fathers had Harvard degrees.[1]

Newspapers printed items concerning colleges beyond their immediate colonial boundary lines, paying especial attention to commencements. Boston newspapers informed their readers about such affairs in the middle colonies and when the new President Finley came to Princeton, the New England capital took note of the event.[2] College and preparatory school texts had a common patronage. Hammond's "Algebra," Ward's texts in mathematics and Watts' "Logic" were used in nearly all the higher institutions. For those intending to send their sons to the College of New Jersey, a New York paper advertised "A Complete Introduction to the Latin Tongue," published for the use of the grammar school at Newark.[3] Another "Introduction" for future Princeton students was available in New York and Philadelphia. "A Short Introduction to the Latin Tongue" appeared in Boston and was reprinted in Philadelphia for a New England customer. Cheever's "Latin Accidence," a very popular book, was requested of Jared Ingersoll by William Livingston; Andrew Stewart published for the

[1] *Matricula, King's College, Quinquennial Catalogue of Harvard; Univ. of Penn., Matriculates of the College, Princeton University Catalogue; Catalogue of Yale;* W. B. Bailey, " Statistical Study of Yale Graduates ", *Yale Review,* vol. xvi, pp. 424-425.

[2] *N. J. Archives,* ser. i, vol. xii, p. 503.

[3] *N. Y. Gaz. revived in the Weekly Post-Boy,* April 27, 1752, *loc. cit.,* pp. 150-151.

Philadelphia college "A Short Introduction to Grammar," which was also sold in New York.[1]

College administrators quickly appreciated the similarity of their problems, and exchanged views about them. Francis Alison of Philadelphia, in a discussion of entrance requirements, wrote Ezra Stiles that he had

seen proposals to unite the several Colleges on this continent, . . . in the same plan of Education, to govern them nearly by the same laws, & to admit none in one College that were expelld or denyd admittance in another, without previously consulting the heads of the College from whence the Student was expelld &c. . . . This proposal, [which had been made by President Clap of Yale, he added,] deserves a serious consideration.[2]

Moses Coit Tyler remarks that these youthful institutions, which so early revealed a consciousness of common interests, exerted a great influence upon American literary culture. More than that, they were

a means of colonial fellowship. Each college was itself, . . . a point of distinction for its own colony; at each college were gathered some students from other colonies; between all the colleges there grew a sense of fraternity in learning and letters, and this reenforced the general sense of fraternity in civic destinies.[3]

---

[1] Evans, 8728, 7567-68, 9309; *Ingersoll Letters,* Nov. 28, 1748.

[2] *Itineraries and Corr. of Ezra Stiles,* May 27, 1759.

[3] *Hist. of American Literature,* vol. ii, pp. 308-09.

CHAPTER VI

ARTS AND ARTISTS

In some of the schools native talent in the arts found some encouragement, while here and there a feeble poetic voice was lifted; but perhaps one should not expect many achievements in the rarer spheres of man's creative life from a pioneer society, which was further handicapped by Puritan opposition to the fine arts. The energy consumed in mastering elemental forces and wresting a livelihood in unfamiliar surroundings leaves little to be expended in the areas of more precious activity. And yet there were signs of a yearning for such fruits of a more advanced civilization, a yearning which still finds incomplete satisfaction in the American scene.

When sending some essays to Gronovius, the botanist at Leyden, Colden wrote,

No thing new & extraordinary in Literature from this part of the world is to be expected but as we are improving this Wilderness & have in Some Measure in Some places given it the appearance of the Cultivated grounds in Europe so we make some small attempts for improvement in learning.

In 1762 Copley wrote from Boston to a French painter Liotard,

You may perhaps be surprised that so remote a corner of the Globe as New England should have any demand for the necessary eutensils for practiceing the fine Arts, but I assure You Sir however feeble our efforts may be, it is not for want of inclination that they are not better, but the want of oppertunity to improve ourselves. however America . . . I would fain hope will one Day become the School of fine Arts.

The dream was rudely shattered, or was it a depression caused by an early utilitarian standard, characteristic of many more years in American development, which led the artist to complain that people looked upon painting as "any other useful trade?" In New York there was some agitation to establish a public academy for the study of architecture, sculpture and painting, but the plan died still-born.[1]

The most distinguished painters in the colonial period were Benjamin West and John Singleton Copley, although a few others, notably John Smibert of Boston, had established intercolonial reputations years before their more illustrious successors. West received his youthful education in Philadelphia where he began his more mature artistic efforts. He went to New York in 1758 to take advantage of the higher prices offered there and also to acquire funds to permit continued study. He stayed here for eleven months painting many portraits for which he was paid twice as much as he had received in Philadelphia. One of his patrons was a wealthy Mr. Kelly who took a personal interest in West's career. The latter was given an order to draw on Kelly's agents in Philadelphia for fifty guineas so that West might go to Italy.[2] Copley, whose home was in Boston, was known throughout the colonies. When the Rev. Alexander McWhorter of North Carolina visited

---

[1] *Colden Papers,* vol. iii, p. 97 (1745); *Copley-Pelham Letters, loc. cit.,* pp. 26, 65; Holt's *N. Y. Journal,* Jan. 17, 1767, in *Westervelt MS.,* No. 29, pt. I, p. 3.

[2] F. W. Bailey and C. E. Goodspeed, eds., *A History of the Rise and Progress of the Arts of Design in the United States by William Dunlap* (Boston, 1913), vol. i, p. 44; *Westervelt MS.,* pt. I, p. 22; J. T. Scharf and Thompson Westcott, *History of Philadelphia* (Phila., 1884), vol. ii, 1031-1032.

Boston with his wife they were painted by him.[1]   In 1768, Myles Cooper, President of King's College, sent the artist seven guineas for his portrait, and inquired about other pictures especially one called the "Nun with the Candle," which he wished to deposit in the college library as the beginning of a public collection.   Copley answered that he was willing to part with the "Nun with the Candle," "in consideration of the use You propose to make of it . . . . as it is my desire to see some publick collection begun in America."

Copley delayed sending the pictures and was reproved by Cooper who added that if he had gotten them he would have been able to secure more for the college library.   They were finally sent and attracted an admiring audience, which prompted the suggestion that the artist visit New York. "I am satisfied you would find an unparalleled Degree of Encouragement" wrote Cooper.   The painter was pleased over the welcome his work had received, but wrote he could not come then.   Two years later, Capt. Stephen Kemble and Copley conducted some correspondence relative to the latter's trip to New York.   The former sent a list of people who had subscribed to have their portraits painted, and in June, 1771, the artist arrived in the city where he entered upon a busy round of duties.   He wrote his cousin Pelham, also an artist,

there is so many that are impatient to sit that I am never at a loss to fill up all my time. . . . When we came here Capt. Richards's portrait . . . (was) so much admired that vast numbers went to see it. . . . People of the first Rank, who have seen Europe . . . say it is the best Picture they ever saw.

As a mark of honor Copley's picture of General Gage was hung "between Two of Lord and Lady Gages done by the Celebrated Reynolds."   The fame of Copley and West was

[1] Hill, *Old South Church, Boston*, vol. ii, p. 124, note 1.

not merely provincial; the former told Pelham he had heard " that the two great American Artists Mr. Copley and Mr. West almost entirely engaged the attention of the Coniseurs in Britain." On August 3, Copley wrote " I have began Painting to the amount of 3 hundred pounds Sterg." In November, he wished to return home; but he felt he could not hurry his work, for artistic taste was seemingly well develc ped in New York.

We Long much to see you all. . . . But it takes up much time to finish all the parts of a Picture when it is to be well finished, and the Gentry of this place distinguish very well, so I must slight nothing. . . . I have been obliged to refuse a great deal of Business here and in Philadelphia.

The next month, he wrote, "this week finishes all my Business . . . . 37 Busts." Dr. Ogilvie of Trinity Church, members of the Verplanck and De Peyster families, James Duane, Mrs. Roger Morris, John Taber Kempe, the Attorney General and Jared Ingersoll of Connecticut were among those painted by Copley. Another subject was William Plumstead, mayor of Philadelphia, in which city the painter was much impressed by the art collection of Chief Justice Allen.[1]

Copley and West were in a sense to art students, what Colden and Franklin were to those in medicine, acting as their guides in both the new and the old worlds. Charles Willson Peale of Maryland visited Boston where an introduction to Copley gained for him much encouragement. Peale, who was instructed also by John Hesselius, a Philadelphia painter, made his first attempt at a miniature, a portrait of himself. He traveled abroad where he studied with West, who had located in London to become in time

---

[1] *Copley-Pelham Letters*, pp. 70-74, 93-94, 127-128, 136, 163, 173-174, 179; *Ingersoll Letters*, 201; Scharf and Westcott, *op. cit.*, vol. ii. 1035; F. W. Bayley, *The Life and Works of John Singleton Copley* (Boston, 1915), *passim*.

the sympathetic adviser of many American students.   Peale
soon had a well established reputation in Philadelphia and
New York, where Abraham De Lanoy Jr., another student
of West, also worked.[1]

Robert Feke, a Newport artist, whom recent research
has accorded a high place in colonial art, painted in Boston,
New York and Philadelphia.   In the latter city he portrayed
Mrs. Charles Willing, the mayor's wife, Thomas Hopkinson
and Tench Francis.   When Dr. Alexander Hamilton visited
Newport he was taken to see "Feake," whom he classed
as an extraordinary artist; untutored, "he does pictures
tolerably well by the force of genius."[2]   Matthew Pratt,
born in Philadelphia, a distant relative and student of West,
painted occasionally in New York where he was commissioned by the Chamber of Commerce to do Gov. Colden's
portrait, which is still in existence.[3]   Joseph Blackburn was
in New York in 1754, recently from Bermuda, and the next
year was painting portraits in Boston, where his pastels
probably influenced Copley's medium of expression.   Du
Simitiere, a miniature painter who worked also in Philadelphia, advertised in a New York paper that he intended
to leave the city soon; so, should any one require his services,
prompt action must be taken.   There were a few pastel
portraits made, but these seem never to have been so popular
as those done in oil or miniature.   The portraits of heads
done in wax by Patience Wright were known not only in the

---

[1] A. H. Wharton, *Heirlooms in Miniatures* (Phila., 1898), p. 82;
Dunlap, *op. cit.*, vol. i, pp. 156-157; J. J. Foster, *Miniature Painters,
British and Foreign, with Some Account of Those Who Practiced in
America in the Eighteenth Century* (London, 1913), vol. ii, p. 3; William
Kelby, *Notes on American Artists, 1754-1820, Copied from Advertise-
ments Appearing in the Newspapers of the Day* (N. Y., 1922), pp. 7-8.

[2] W. C. Poland, *Robert Feke* (Providence, 1907); Wharton, p. 23;
Hastings, *Francis Hopkinson*, p. 29; *Itinerarium*, p. 124.

[3] *N. Y. Chamber of Commerce Records*, pp. 167, 169, 377-78 (1772).

colonies but also in England where she scored a tremendous success.[1]

Several engravers were at work in more than one colony. James Turner of Boston made a seal which was ordered from Philadelphia, and when sending it, added that he "would be glad of an opportunity to do any engraving." Maps which he engraved were published in New York by James Parker; book-plates for Boston and Philadelphia patrons were other creations by Turner. He also made an engraving of "Boston in 1746."[2] Philadelphia evidently afforded him the opportunity he sought, for he was living there a few years afterward. Lewis Evans' map of 1755, the seal for the Philadelphia college, a cut which he made and signed for the title page of the New England almanac of Nathaniel Ames, were among the products of Turner's workshop in his new home.[3] His work, writes the historian of American engraving, was of a comparatively high order of excellence.

Others were called upon to gratify the growing interprovincial interest in the arts. Henry Dawkins in New York engraved book-plates for local patrons, and in 1758 worked with Turner in Philadelphia where his engravings included

[1] Lawrence Park, "Joseph Blackburn," *Am. Antiq. Soc. Proc.*, vol. 32, p. 274; Theodore Bolton, *Early American Portrait Draughtsmen in Crayons* (N. Y., 1923), p. ix; Kelby, p. 7; E. S. Bolton, *Wax Portraits and Silhouettes* (Boston, 1914), pp. 12-14.

[2] Franklin, *Cal. of Papers*, vol. ii, p. 2; D. M. Stauffer, *American Engravers upon Copper and Steel* (N. Y., 1907), vol. i, pp. 278-279; C. D. Allen, *A Classified List of early American Book-plates* (N. Y., 1894), pp. 155-156; W. L. Andrews, *Fragments of American History Illustrated Solely by the Works . . . of Engravers in the XVIIIth Century* (N. Y., 1898).

[3] H. N. Stevens, *Lewis Evans: His Map of the Middle British Colonies in America* ... (London, 1920, 2nd ed.), p. 7; Montgomery, *Hist. of Univ. of Penn.*, p. 233; C. L. Nichols, "Justus Fox, German Printer of the Eighteenth Century," *Am. Antiq. Soc. Proc.*, vol. xxv, p. 66 (1760).

the music for a book of "Psalm Tunes;" he also did the frontispiece of "Father Abraham's Weatherwise" almanacs.[1] John A. Beau was another engraver who had worked in New York before removing to Philadelphia. The issue of "Father Abraham's Almanac" for 1759 contained a full-page copper plate engraving of Frederick III, King of Prussia, a Philadelphia creation which appeared in "Hutchin's Almanac and More's New York Pocket Almanac" for the same year. Paul Revere of Boston made the engravings for the two volume edition of Cook's "Voyages" printed by James Rivington in New York. For his prospective "Miscellany," Franklin wanted an engraving; he intended to take off some copies from a plate Colden had of the North American coast.[2]

Skilled workers in other fields were known in more than one of the principal cities. Several watchmakers moved from place to place; Daniel Dupuy of New York probably learned his goldsmithing from a relative in Philadelphia. The Wills family were well known pewterers with representatives in both these cities. The silversmiths in the larger urban centers had an intercolonial reputation, and some of their efforts reveal a common workmanship. American demand for pottery was satisfied by well trained workmen who had ordinarily learned their lessons in English establishments. Philadelphia pottery seems to have been a standard guiding the New York taste.[3] Philadelphia-made Windsor chairs were adopted by polite circles in New

---

[1] Kelby, p. 4; Allen, pp. 127-131; Stauffer, vol. i, pp. 60-62.

[2] Maurice Brix, *List of Philadelphia Silversmiths and Allied Artificers, from 1682 to 1852* (Phila., 1852), p. 117; Nichols, *loc. cit.*, p. 66; C. F. Gettemy, *The True Story of Paul Revere* (Boston, 1905), p. 32; *Colden Papers*, vol. iii pp. 273-276.

[3] Brix, *passim*; C. L. Avery, *American Silver of the XVII and XVIII Centuries* (N. Y., 1920), p. liii, pp. 78-79; L. G. Myers, *Some Notes on American Pewterers* (N. Y., 1926), pp. 69-73; John Spargo, *Early American Pottery and China* (N. Y., 1926), pp. 87-89.

York and Boston, but in some products the furniture makers of the middle colonies revealed a New England influence. On the other hand, the black walnut timber used by the Boston cabinet makers was brought from New Jersey and neighboring southern provinces. Stiegel glass, so eagerly sought now by collectors, was known nearly everywhere in colonial America through the efforts of numerous agencies. Boston was interested in wall paper designed in New York; a marble slab for a fireplace was advertised in the New England city, as from Philadelphia. There are indications of mutual influence in dress, and the anxiety with which the colonial aristocracy in all the seaboard towns followed the latest English models is well known.[1]

Knowledge of a larger America was gained through the medium of artistic offerings. Garrat Noel placed on sale "a curious Plan of the city of Philadelphia," followed in a few years by Michael De Bruls who advertised two land and two water views of New York City, four prospects in all, which were very elaborate affairs. De Bruls corresponded with towns in New England, New Jersey and Pennsylvania to deliver prints immediately after publication, notice of which was to be given in the local papers. An engraving of the "Cataract of Niagara" was announced with the promise of other American scenes. Revere made a copper-plate print of a view of part of Boston about the same time that Edes and Gill, prominent Boston publishers, were selling a plan of the city of New York.[2]

Contacts in architecture, as well, helped give a rather defi-

---

[1] W. A. Dyer, *Early American Craftsmen* (N. Y., 1915), pp. 75-79, 320-24; John Adams, *Works*, vol. ii, p. 357; Hunter, *Stiegel Glass*, pp. 239-40; Dow, *Arts & Crafts in New England*, pp. 152, 214; A. M. Earle, *Two Centuries of Costume in America* (N. Y., 1903).

[2] *N. Y. Mercury*, March 17, 1755; Weyman's *N. Y. Gaz.*, March 7, 1763, Kelby, pp. 4-6; *N. Y. Gaz. and Weekly Mercury*, Feb. 8, 1773; *Boston Gaz. and Co. Journal*, April 16, 1770; *ibid.*, Nov. 13, 1769.

nite impress to a more obvious feature of American civilization. Architecture of the type introduced into the colonies in the eighteenth century, where it became known as the Georgian style, had its roots in the English classical revival under Sir Christopher Wren. In the later years of colonial history a general similarity of building was preserved although variations are found in different localities. Christ Church, Philadelphia, was mainly designed by Dr. John Kearsley, a distinguished physician; the steeple, in part, by Franklin.[1] The architecture for Rhode Island College was copied from Nassau Hall, Princeton; when the new buildings were being erected, in which a Philadelphia architect took a hand, the Rhode Islanders sent observers to view the Harvard structures. Henry Caner, a Boston master carpenter whose work was evidently well known, superintended the construction of Yale's early building, and when a new structure was raised in the middle of the century, a chief mason from Philadelphia assisted by a New Yorker, took charge of operations.[2]

No original architectural work appeared in provincial America, but a number of builder's books recently printed in England are said to have been sold in large quantities in the colonies. Since nearly all builders followed the same texts a greater uniformity began to prevail in colonial architecture. "Rules for Drawing in Architecture" by James Gibbs of England, was the standard authority overseas, where Langley's books were also very popular. Peter Harrison, probably the leading architect among the colonists, was well acquainted with the work of Gibbs and may have been his pupil; McBean of New Jersey, who designed St.

---

[1] R. A. Douglas-Lithgow, "Andrew Oliver House," *Massachusetts Magazine,* vol. iii, pp. 57-58; Frank Cousins and P. M. Riley, *The Colonial Architecture of Philadelphia* (Boston, 1920), p. 219.

[2] Guild, *Brown Univ. and Manning,* pp. 139-140, 153-154; Dexter, *Yale Biog. and Annals,* 1701-1745, pp. 173, 296-97; vol. ii, 1745-1763, p. 227.

Paul's Chapel in New York, received his inspiration from the same source. Jefferson, an excellent architect, had a copy of Gibbs, as did the Library Company of Philadelphia, and the Virginian's visit to the middle colonial capitals revealed a similarity of architectural features which left an impression upon him. Harrison, who made his home in Newport, designed Christ Church, Cambridge; his services were also requested for the new King's Chapel, Boston.[1] Copley, who was also an architect, wrote from New York to Pelham, that "peazas" were so much in vogue he would add a "peazer" to his house on his return to Boston; they were "much practised here, very beautiful and convenient." [2]

Music played its part in forming a common cultural background, and the development in both its sacred and secular aspects was simultaneous throughout the colonies. Francis Hopkinson of Philadelphia was engaged as psalmodist and versifier to adapt the " Psalms of David " for the Reformed Protestant Dutch Church in New York; his handsome fee enabled him to go to England shortly after, where he heard the finest music. He made a "Collection of Psalm Tunes with a few anthems and Hymns" for the use of Christ Church and St. Peter's Church in Philadelphia, enhancing his already great reputation as a psalmodist. James Lyon, the other claimant to the honor of being the first composer among the colonials, was in Philadelphia in 1760 when he probably met Hopkinson. The

[1] A. J. Wall, " Books on Architecture Printed in America, 1775-1830," *Bibliog. Essays to W. Eames*, p. 299; W. R. Ware, ed; *The Georgian Period; being Photographs and Measured Drawings of Colonial Work with Text* (N. Y., 1923), vol. i, pp. 251-253; Fiske Kimball, *Thomas Jefferson, Architect* (Boston, 1916), pp. 25, 34 and note 2; F. W. P. Greenwood, *A History of King's Chapel in Boston* (Boston, 1833), pp. 118, 123.

[2] Fiske Kimball, *Domestic Architecture of the American Colonies and of the Early Republic* (N. Y., 1922), pp. 98-99, 275; " peazas " were low, wide porches.

next year, an anthem by Lyon and an ode by Hopkinson formed part of the Philadelphia commencement exercises. Two years earlier Lyon was a student at the New Jersey College, where an ode he had set to music was performed at the commencement.[1]

Lyon and Hopkinson wrote the first two secular American compositions in 1759. The former's psalm-tune collection, "Urania," was probably begun the year before. It appeared in Philadelphia in 1761 with a list of subscribers, including a number from New England and some from New York. A new edition was advertised in the "Pennsylvania Journal," to be sold in the middle colonies; a third edition was advertised in New York and a fourth was probably issued in New England, based upon the earlier printings. The "Urania," which gained a wide audience, has been characterized as the most carefully prepared attempt thus far to "spread the art of psalmody" throughout the colonies. The author, who was doubtless acquainted with the Rev. T. Walter's "Grounds and Rules of Music" issued in two editions in Boston, influenced Hopkinson in turn, when the latter made his "Collection of Psalm Tunes" in 1763. Josiah Flagg's "Collection of the best Psalm-Tunes" which appeared in Boston the next year, had an engraving by Paul Revere, taken from the title page of "Urania" done by Henry Dawkins. A little later Flagg advertised "A Collection of Anthems" which included those of Lyon; and a reprint of Williams' "American Harmony or Universal Psalmodist" contained an anthem by the same writer. Daniel Bayley's "New Universal Harmony or a Compendium of Church Musick," issued in Newburyport, printed Lyon's "Marriage Hymn."[2]   The most noted advance after

[1] O. G. Sonneck, *Francis Hopkinson and James Lyon* (Wash., 1905), pp. 10, 86, 94, 78-82, 77; Hastings, *Francis Hopkinson,* pp. 75-76, chap. iv.

[2] Sonneck, *op. cit.,* pp. 127, 134-147, 154, 164-165, 179-182, 187; see copy

"Urania" was made by the "New England Psalm Singer, or American Chorister," published in Boston by William Billings, a tanner, whose gift for musical expression earned for him the title of " Father of New England Psalmody." [1]

The "New York Mercury," in 1771, printed proposals for publishing by subscription, two pieces of church music by William Tuckey, who had introduced Handel's "Messiah," to America the year before, and had long been a powerful force in promoting good church singing.[2] Two years later, another proposal for printing church music was made and subscriptions were taken in by the printers in several of the larger towns, who were to forward them to their confréres in New York. David Propert, organist of Trinity Church, Boston, taught the boys Handel's oratorios; his music teaching was known in New York too. Josiah Flagg was instrumental in introducing to Boston some of the best music, including Handel and Bach. W. S. Morgan taught music in New York before 1770 when he moved to Boston to continue his work. John Rice, originally of London, was an organist in the Trinity Churches of New York and Boston. Others not so well remembered, through singing schools or by personal performances, endeavored to better the musical standards of the colonists.[3]

of *Urania* 1761, music room, N. Y. P. L.; F. J. Metcalf comp., *American Psalmody; or Titles of Books, Containing Tunes Printed in America from 1721-1820* (N. Y., 1917, *Heartman's Hist. Ser., no. 27*) has a 4th ed. in Phila., n. d., p. 37.

[1] George Hood, *History of Music in New England* (Boston, 1846), p. 166; James Warrington, *Short Titles of Books relating to . . . Psalmody in the United States 1620-1820* (Phila., 1898), p. 43; *Boston Gaz. and Co. Journal,* Dec. 10, 1770; Ninde, *American Hymn,* pp. 87-88.

[2] March 11; Sonneck, *Early Concert Life in America,* pp. 177-178, note 2; pp. 180-181; in 1753, Tuckey was giving two nights a week to teach his " Singing Scholars ", Odell, *Annals of N. Y. Stage,* vol. i, p. 69.

[3] Rivington's *N. Y. Gazetteer,* June 24, 1773; *N. Y. Hist. Soc. Coll.,*

John Gottlob Klemm (or Clemm), associated with Gustavus Hesselius in Philadelphia, built the first organ for Trinity Church in New York, whose vestry then engaged his son to play it.[1] Germans had introduced the organ into Philadelphia churches at the beginning of the century; by 1743 the Moravians had two such instruments, the high quality of whose music attracted the notice of John Adams when he visited the city years later. Hesselius built an organ for the Moravians at Bethlehem; others were placed in churches far removed from Pennsylvania. Before the end of the half century, the Catholics had installed one in Philadelphia. When the Continental Congress assembled in 1774, Adams, in company with Washington, made a visit to St. Mary's Church. To his wife Abigail, the former wrote, "The music, consisting of an organ and a choir of singers, went all the afternoon except sermon time, and the assembly chanted most sweetly and exquisitely. Here is everything which can . . . . charm and bewitch the simple and ignorant. I wonder how Luther ever broke the spell." [2] A few years before the Revolution the organ found its way into some Congregational churches which had formerly opposed its use in worship, and one instrument which had come from a Boston concert hall was set up in an Episcopal church in Providence.[3] When the Christ Church bells

1870, pp. 232-233; Sonneck, *op. cit.,* pp. 257, 261-63, 269, 159, note 1, p. 254; Odell, vol. i, p. 17; for Tuckey and Rice, see A. H. Messiter, *A History of the Choir and Music of Trinity Church New York from its Organization to the Year 1897* (N. Y., 1906), pp. 19-31.

[1] H. E. Krehbiel, "Early Music in New York," *N. Y. Tribune,* July 26, 1903; Sonneck, *op. cit.,* p. 169, note 5; Stokes, p. 570, quoting *Trinity Minutes.*

[2] R. R. Drummond, *Early German Music in Philadelphia* (N. Y., 1910, *Americana Germanica,* new ser., vol. 9), pp. 13-16; J. W. Jordan, "Early Colonial Organ-builders of Pennsylvania", *Pa. Mag. of Hist. and Biog.,* vol. xxii, p. 231; *Familiar Letters* Oct. 9, 1774; *American Catholic Hist. Researches,* vol. xv, pp. 174, 175.

[3] Stiles, *Diary,* July 10, 1770, Dec. 12, 1771.

were to be installed in 1745, their builder in England advised the Boston church officials to secure the services of a bell-hanger in Philadelphia. Twenty-five years later, with the assistance of a bell-founder from the latter city, a foundry was opened in Massachusetts which made bells for all purposes up to seven tons.[1]

To its most illustrious expatriate, his native province was indebted in this sphere also. Jonathan Williams of Boston sought Franklin's care for a son Josiah who was going to London to study music. Another son commissioned Franklin to get him a hand-organ similar to one he had sent to a previous correspondent and the office was duly performed. Franklin had a more direct interest in music. To Colden he wrote: "While in England . . . . I amus'd myself with contriving and bringing to a considerable Degree of Perfection, a new musical Instrument." He had a share in the development of the "Armonica," then attracting people in Europe and America. He perfected the "glassy-chord" so that it came into general use in the colonies, and London witnessed a performance with it. Franklin was a fair musician himself, dabbling with a few instruments, like the typical eighteenth-century dilettante.[2]

There was an increasing demand for musical instruments. Since Philadelphia had no music dealers, Anthony Lamb of New York, advertised his wares in the "Pennsylvania Gazette." The situation was remedied in that city by Michael Hillegas, who opened up the first real music store with a fine assortment. Rivington and Brown, booksellers, then succeeded to a preeminent position as a music house. Be-

[1] A. H. Nichols, "Christ Church Bells," *New Eng. Hist. and Genea. Reg.*, 1904, pp. 63-71; *Boston Gaz. and Co. Journal*, May 14, 1770.

[2] Franklin, *Calendar of Papers*, vol. iii, pp. 149, 154; *Colden Papers*, vol. vi, pp. 215-216; *N. Y. Gaz.* (Weyman's), 1762, no. 1007, *Devoe's Index;* O. G. Sonneck, *Suum Cuique* (N. Y., 1916), "Benjamin Franklin's Musical Side".

sides teaching music, Morgan also sold instruments in Boston.[1]

Before the close of our period, fairly large groups had grown up in the coastal cities, with sufficient worldly prosperity to support a natural craving for personal glorification. Severe competition ensued to secure the services of the most illustrious painters to perpetuate the family likenesses. Throughout the colonies were scattered portraits of varying standards of excellence, but issuing, more or less, from the same school. A spirit of mutual helpfulness among the artists was of value in the attainment of worthier standards. Engravers, silversmiths and other craftsmen, engaged in work entailing a high degree of skill, found an intercolonial market for their efforts. Additional wealth permitted the utilization of professional architects, acquainted with a common fund of information, to plan the housing of the colonial aristocracy. Music, more especially religious, brought many intercolonial contacts; psalm-tune collections in many colonies owed much to the work of James Lyon. Thus in many obscure ways experiences were commonly shared, which later gave a definite stamp to American esthetic tastes.

[1] Drummond, pp. 38, 40, 42; Sonneck, *Early Concert Life in America*, p. 269.

CHAPTER VII

Physic and Physicians

The development of medicine and the increasingly important position attained by physicians in the American colonies furnish us with many instances of cooperation which resulted in a heightened standard of medical practise. Obstacles erected by the difficulties of communication and traditional restraints were gradually overcome, and the knowledge of the latest advances in theory and practise rapidly became common professional property. Progress was halting, but alert individuals were stimulating more sluggish contemporaries to keep step in this scientific procession.

Eighteenth-century medicine and medical practise were very haphazard affairs; in America and Europe as well, apprenticeship for a comparatively short term to a doctor, who was also on occasion an apothecary, marked the extent of much of the education. The limits of the profession were hazy, and almost anyone with a little superior knowledge felt able to prescribe. The word "doctor" secured no general American usage it seems, until about the 1760's.[1] There were however, a considerable number of colonial physicians with formal medical educations which had been secured in European institutions, notably Edinburgh.

It was at Edinburgh during the period 1753-1773, that a number of American students met, and by the contacts gained here were enabled to assist one another in advanc-

[1] F. H. Garrison, *An Introduction to the History of Medicine* (Phila., 1914), pp. 317-333; A. C. Jacobson, "The Earliest Manhattan Practitioners", reprint, *The Medical Times*, May 1916.

ing medical education and medical practise in their own country. Samuel Bard of New York met John Morgan of Philadelphia there, an intimacy of great importance in the later annals of American medical history. Arthur Lee and Theodore Bland, of Virginia probably attended lectures with William Smibert of Massachusetts. Adam Kuhn and Benjamin Rush of Pennsylvania were also graduates of the university which was the nursery of American medicine.[1]

The more noted individuals, like Franklin and Colden, were liaison officers between the colonies and between the two continents. Colden, through his European acquaintances, made the path a little smoother for American students. He commended the young Samuel Bard to the notice of Dr. Robert Whytt, known for his studies of the nervous system, who promised to take care of him. The young student kept Colden informed as to the progress of his studies, and gratefully acknowledged the assistance which Colden's instruction in botany had afforded him. Franklin was always ready to assist the young learner and, when in England, the names of Rush and Jonathan Potts were recommended to him. Shippen, Morgan and Bard were also under obligations to him.[2] Dr. John Fothergill was the especial guardian of the American youngsters. Morgan was well known to him, Rush was taken under his protecting wing, and Benjamin Waterhouse of Rhode Island, later at Harvard, began to study in England under his supervision.[3]

---

[1] "American Graduates in Medicine at the University of Edinburgh to 1809", *New Eng. Hist. and Genea. Reg.*, vol. xli, pp. 391-92, vol. xlii, pp. 159-161; S. A. Green, *History of Medicine in Massachusetts* (Boston, 1881), p. 74.

[2] *Colden Papers*, vol. vi, p. 219; *Thomson Papers, N. Y. Hist. Soc. Coll.*, 1878, p. 17; William Pepper, *The Medical Side of Benjamin Franklin* (Phila., 1911), pp. 41-44.

[3] Fox, *Dr. John Fothergill and his Friends*, pp. 371, 375.

Complete dependence upon Europe was irksome in many ways; so native efforts were early directed to the establishment of societies for the dissemination of medical knowledge, and later there were successful attempts to found schools. While still in Philadelphia, Colden desired a systematic course of lectures on medical subjects, but the only thing approaching such an arrangement was possibly the education given by Dr. John Kearsley Sr., in his local office. Kearsley is justly known as a pioneer in this field and some of the most famous colonial doctors including William Shippen Sr., Cadwalader Evans, John Bard and John Kearsley Jr., learned their first lessons from the elder Kearsley. John Redman was another pupil who exercised great influence in the profession.[1] Again Colden sought to help fill a need and wrote to his friend Dr. Douglass in Massachusetts, urging the formation of a society of intellectuals from among the neighboring colonies. Though it had no immediate response of the kind desired, it may have been influential in the organization of a medical society in Boston in 1736. Douglass wrote that his friend Dr. Clark was on the way to Philadelphia; "You may remember that some years ago you proposed . . . . a . . . . Virtuoso Society or . . . . correspondence; We have lately in Boston form'd a Medical Society." He added that Clark was a member of this society and would give him further details. They designed to publish short pieces from time to time and a prospective publication was enclosed. This society had a successor in New York a few years later, and similar groups were organized in New Jersey, Connecticut and Charlestown, S. C.[2]

[1] F. R. Packard, *The History of Medicine in the United States* (Phila., 1901), p. 164; W. S. Middleton, " The John Kearsleys ", *Annals of Medical History*, vol. iii, p. 392; J. M. Toner, *Contributions to the Annals of Medical Progress, and Medical Education in the U. S. before and during the War of Independence* (Wash., 1874), p. 80.

[2] *Colden Papers,* vol. i, pp. 271-273; vol. ii, pp. 146-147; *American Medi-*

Despite early suggestions, it was not until some of the youngsters were engaged in their studies abroad that active steps were taken to erect American medical schools. It was from Edinburgh that Samuel Bard wrote his father about the proposals of Shippen, Morgan and others to start a school in Philadelphia. While he wished these students were in New York, he could also take the initiative, and suggested the advisability of a similar institution under the auspices of King's College.[1] Before these plans could be realized less pretentious programs were performing a much-needed service. Dr. William Shippen 2nd had been urged by Fothergill to give a course of anatomical lectures; this advice he followed on his return to Philadelphia. Anatomical drawings supplied by the English doctor were used in these lectures. Medical lectures were delivered in Rhode Island by Dr. William Hunter, a former associate of Dr. Peter Middleton in New York. In 1750, the latter with John Bard dissected the body of an executed criminal for the instruction of some students, but dissections had already been made in Boston years before.[2]

The real academic beginnings, however, must be sought in Philadelphia, where at the college commencement in 1765 John Morgan delivered "A Discourse upon the Institution of Medical Schools in America." It was asserted that the establishment of a school might encourage many students

cal and Phil. Register, vol. i, p. 409; Russell, Early Medicine and Medical Men in Conn., p. 148; McCrady, Royal Government in S. C., pp. 432-33.

[1] W. B. James, "Samuel Bard," Columbia Univ. Quarterly, vol. ix, p. 128 (1762).

[2] Fox, op. cit., p. 368; Toner, op. cit., pp. 73, 83; C. W. Parsons, "Early Votaries of Science in Rhode Island", R. I. Hist. Soc. Coll., vol. vii, pp. 251-252; Col. Soc. of Mass., Trans., 19, p. 279. An act 1752, in England provided that the bodies of all executed criminals might be used for dissecting purposes; W. B. Howell, "Some Humble Workers in the Cause of Anatomy a Hundred Years Ago", Annals of Med. Hist., March, 1926, p. 20.

from other colonies to come to Philadelphia and serve to stimulate a similar undertaking.[1] The school was fully organized that year with Drs. Morgan and Shippen on the faculty. New York quickly followed suit. In a letter written soon after, Morgan referred to the new school copied after his own, but he exhibited no apprehension over any possible rivalry.[2] In a " Medical Discourse", Dr. Peter Middleton acknowledged the debt owed " to the Medical Faculty of Philadelphia " for its priority in erecting an institution.[3] Samuel Bard, Middleton and John Jones were on the staff of the New York school; J. V. B. Tennent, a graduate of the College of New Jersey, was another of its professors.

Elsewhere there was a stir among the fraternity. A short time before, Dr. John Perkins had pleaded for the installation of a professor of medicine at Harvard, where there was some talk of establishing a medical school to be connected with the college.[4] In " An Essay on Physick," Nathaniel Ames bewailed the fact that Pennsylvania had gotten the start of Massachusetts in "the cultivation of this noble science . . . . Why," he continued, "has no one amongst us attempted to immortalize his name by making a donation to one of our colleges for a professor of physick? " And then as if in response to his urgent wish, the will of Dr. Ezekiel Hersey in the same year set aside £1000 for the support of a professor of anatomy and physic, but the fulfillment of this

---

[1] Pp. 28, 54.

[2] F. P. Henry, ed., *Standard History of the Medical Profession in Philadelphia* (Chicago, 1897), pp. 64-65; Joseph Carson, *A History of the Medical Department of the University of Pennsylvania from its Foundation in 1765* (Phila., 1869), pp. 67-68.

[3] (1769), p. 51.

[4] James, " Samuel Bard," *loc. cit.*; Toner, p. 101; S. F. Batchelder, *Bits of Harvard History* (Cambridge, 1924), p. 158 note 1; T. F. Harrington, *The Harvard Medical School* (N. Y., 1905), vol. i, p. 32.

program was delayed for some years.[1] In 1771, a number
of Harvard students had a secret anatomical society, a leading member of which was John Warren. It was the inspiration furnished by Morgan that led Warren to urge the
founding of the Harvard medical school in 1783.[2]

The reputations of medical men spread rapidly, so that
it was nothing unusual to see young students travel some
distance to be instructed by a distinguished doctor, especially
before the schools were founded. William Aspinwall of
Massachusetts, graduated at Harvard, studied with Dr.
Benjamin Gale in Connecticut, and completed his medical
education at Philadelphia to become a leading member of
the profession in his native province. His work in smallpox was particularly noteworthy. Gale, himself native to
Long Island, had studied with Jared Eliot in Connecticut.
Thomas Cadwallader of Philadelphia studied with Dr. Evan
Jones, and became a very famous surgeon attached to the
Pennsylvania Hospital. The son of Dr. Jones, in turn,
studied with Cadwallader and became professor of surgery
in the New York school. Dr. James Lloyd, originally of
Long Island, settled in Boston where he developed a lucra-
tive practise and became the mentor of local students.
Lloyd was a correspondent of William S. Johnson of
Connecticut, and became a member of the intellectual
aristocracy with election to the American Philosophical
Society. Dr. Barnabas Binney, whose father was a Boston
merchant, graduated from the Rhode Island College and
finished his education at Philadelphia and London.[3] An-

[1] Briggs, *Almanacs of Nathaniel Ames*, pp. 413-416; for 1770; Quincy,
Hist. of Harvard, vol. ii, appendix xxiv, pp. 524-525.

[2] Josiah Bartlett, *Mass. Hist. Soc. Coll.*, ser. 2, vol. i, pp. 109-110;
Batchelder, pp. 188, 157-158.

[3] Toner, pp. 23, 79, 29, 58, 31; Batchelder, pp. 168-169; Russell, pp. 80-
81; James Thacher, *American Medical Biography* (Boston, 1828), vol. i,
pp. 330, 324-327, 359; vol. ii, p. 162.

other student of Dr. Kearsley Sr. was Lloyd Zachary of Boston, an active figure in his chosen work. To Philadelphia, which was the medical center of the colonies, came David Ramsay, to study with Rush and Bond,[1] whence he left to practise in South Carolina.

Better opportunities beckoned to the members of this profession as it did to printers and teachers. Colden before his appointment as surveyor-general of New York had practised medicine in Philadelphia. The deaths of Drs. Dubois and Dupuy during the yellow fever epidemic in New York caused some citizens in that town to solicit the services of the Philadelphian Dr. John Bard. Franklin, who was friendly to Bard, advised Colden of the doctor's intended removal; would Colden encourage him? In his new home Bard became one of the leading physicians, exhibiting an energetic interest in all medical matters. When emigrants from Europe brought a "fever" with them, Bard suggested the erection of a hospital, and Bedloe's Island, of which he was named superintendent, was purchased for the purpose.[2]

Intercolonial efforts were directed to healing the ravages caused by some of the fatal diseases. The question of eliminating smallpox attracted the attention of European and colonial physicians. The disease held the eighteenth century in terror; its toll of human lives was tremendous. A New York paper in 1731 noticed that nearly every house in Philadelphia suffered from the pox. A later issue reported sixty-one deaths in New York. Gerard Beekman, a merchant in New York, alluded to the depressed conditions and

[1] G. W. Norris, *The Early History of Medicine in Philadelphia* (Phila., 1886), p. 20; T. G. Morton and F. Woodbury, *The History of the Pennsylvania Hospital* (Phila., 1895), p. 366; McCrady, *op. cit.,* pp. 420-21.

[2] Toner, p. 42; "Memoir of Dr. John Bard," *Amer. Med. and Phil. Reg..* vol. i, pp. 64-65; *Colonial Laws of N. Y.,* vol. iv, pp. 309-311, act for "pest-house" (hospital), Dec. 16, 1758; *Colden Papers,* vol. iii, pp. 180-183.

pointed to the smallpox as a cause, but added that a worse situation prevailed in Boston. When at a later date, the malady broke out again in Philadelphia, New York opened and aired incoming merchandise to cleanse it of infection. New Jersey followed its neighbor's lead. On other occasions, Boston took steps to protect itself against the importation of the dreaded disorder from the middle colonies.[1]

The first effective preventive measures were taken in Boston, at the insistence, strangely enough, of Cotton Mather and other clergymen against the judgment of all the local physicians, with the exception of Zabdiel Boylston.[2] Mather had read about inoculation against smallpox in a copy of the Royal Society's "Transactions" and immediately urged its adoption in the colonies. One of his most stout-hearted opponents was Dr. William Douglass who wrote to a professional friend, "The clergy spirited by Mather preached up inoculation." Douglass also corresponded with Colden about inoculation to which the latter was not immediately converted. The Boston doctor commented on the strength of Colden's reasons against the new treatment and then communicated the history of the epidemic of 1721 in his city. A subsequent letter displayed less violence in Douglass' opposition, with the information that two hundred and forty in New England had already been inoculated, and in his last years the doctor was willing to grant that this treatment was a " beneficial Improvement." [3]

---

[1] N. Y. Gaz., March 22, 1731; Oct. 11, 1731; Devoe's Index; Beekman's Letter Book, June 6, 1752 (or 1751); R. L. McClenahan, " N. J. Medical History in the Colonial Period ", N. J. Hist. Soc. Proc., Oct. 1925, pp. 369-370; Records of the Boston Selectmen 1743-1753, Dec. 4, 1745, Sept. 26, 1750.

[2] Toner, p. 22.

[3] Colden Papers, vol. i, pp. 141-145; Douglass to Dr. Alexander Stuart, Sept. 25, 1721, Andrews and Davenport, Guide to Materials for the History of the U. S. in Brit. Museum etc., p. 364; Green, Medicine in Mass., p. 68.

Inoculation then spread to other colonies, but like many innovations of this type had to overcome formidable obstacles. In New York, the criticism was especially strong; Governor Clinton issued a proclamation forbidding this medical treatment, but this was only a temporary reaction. As early as 1732, the success of inoculation was admitted in Long Island and the section around Amboy, and James Alexander, a lawyer of distinction, wrote Colden that the people began to inoculate themselves.[1] The " New York Gazette " stated that many had been inoculated, "not one, . . . died, but have had the distemper very easy." A year before, the same paper had printed a contribution from Philadelphia stating that inoculation was being favorably considered there.[2] Adam Thompson, a physician in the same city, published an article on the advantages of inoculation which was reprinted in New York. Charlestown, S. C., had already adopted the practise with some success, although here too, all the physicians at first opposed it.[3]

Franklin, who was intensely interested, corresponded with Bostonians and compared the reactions to smallpox of those inoculated and those who had not taken the treatment. Douglass was anxious to write on the subject again; John Perkins said that the proportion of deaths was much fewer than in 1730.[4] Franklin wrote an introduction to a pamphlet by Dr. William Heberden, the London scholar and physician, urging the benefits of inoculation. Frank-

[1] Packard, op. cit., p. 83 (1747) ; there was opposition in England also; Colden Papers, vol. ii, pp. 59-60.

[2] Jan. 18, 1732, quoted by McClenahan, loc. cit., p. 367; March 15-22, 1731, Stokes, p. 521.

[3] N. Y. Mercury, Dec. 13, 1756, " Items Relating to Medicine in N. Y.", Medical Reg. of N. Y., 1868-1869, p. 289; McCrady, pp. 180, 424.

[4] B. Franklin, Experiments and Observations on Electricity made at Philadelphia . . . (London, 1769), pp. 193-196; Franklin, Calendar of Papers, vol. ii, p. 6.

lin's composition, which traced the history of this treatment in the colonies was distributed in large numbers. Gale, of Connecticut, wrote on this engrossing subject and advocated the use of mercury as a preparative, a precaution that resulted in fewer fatalities. Others in New England were in favor of this treatment.[1] John Redman wrote a defense of inoculation, and likewise urged mercury as a preparative for small pox.

About the same time, Dr. William Barnet of New Jersey, who had achieved an intercolonial recognition, was invited to Philadelphia to inoculate and opened there the first hospital for this purpose. In 1764 Barnet conducted one of the two inoculating hospitals near Boston.[2] A hospital was opened in Elizabethtown, New Jersey, and Surgeon George Pugh advertised that he would also travel to perform inoculations; the poor were to be freely treated. A Mr. Latham, an army surgeon, at the request of some inhabitants of Massachusetts and Connecticut, opened an inoculating hospital in Claverack, New York. Individuals from five weeks of age to any number of years were accepted as inmates. Latham, who had accommodations for two hundred at a time, was also called to Salem to inoculate large groups. Dr. John Hill fitted up his place in Ulster County for such a purpose; Dr. Glentworth in Philadelphia, noting that other cities in America had hospitals, proposed to do likewise.[3] Dr. Gale in Con-

[1] Pepper, *Medical side of Franklin*, pp. 34-39, introduction reprinted; Russell, pp. 80-81; Ames's almanac for 1761.

[2] W. S. Middleton, " John Redman ", *Annals of Med. Hist.*, Sept., 1926, p. 219; Norris, *op. cit.*, p. 113; Stephen Wickes, *History of Medicine in New Jersey and of Its Medical Men from the Settlement of the Province to 1800* (Newark, 1879), pp. 31-32; Packard, p. 87; Benjamin Rush, *Medical Inquiries and Observations* (Phila., 1809), vol. iv, p. 394.

[3] *N. Y. Journal*, July 12, 1770; *N. Y. Gaz. and Weekly Mercury*, Nov. 18, 1771; *Boston Gaz. and Co. Journal*, Nov. 25, 1771; Felt, *Annals of Salem*, (ed., 1827), p. 485; *Pa. Packet and General Advertiser*, Jan. 4, 1773.

necticut, who mistrusted his own ability sent for a New Jersey doctor to inoculate a "class", and sometimes Newport groups went to Long Island to receive treatment.[1]

Giant strides were made in the conquest of this infection. The "Pennsylvania Journal" stated that of seven hundred inoculated only one died of the smallpox, whereas in the ordinary way of infection one out of every five died. In the hospitals near Boston, about four thousand were treated in a few weeks in 1764, "with a mortality of one in a thousand." [2] This method of fighting the disease, which the cautious Colden informed Dr. Fothergill had long been practised by negroes in the colonies, was succeeded at the end of the century by the more effective measure of vaccination.[3]

The "sore throat distemper," which was in many cases diphtheria, was another disease that caused much apprehension. The New York and Boston papers made references to cures during 1735 and 1736. Douglass and Colden corresponded on the subject, its prevalence in Massachusetts, the symptoms, etc. The Boston doctor suggested that "mercurials especially Calomel" were very valuable[4] in treating inflammatory complaints, a practise which probably originated with Douglass and then was widely adopted. Dr. Jacob Ogden, of Long Island, was known to practise it extensively about 1749, and it soon came into common use in pleurisy, pneumonia and rheumatism. Dr. Thomas Bond introduced it generally in Philadelphia. Thirteen years before, Douglass had published a tract on the "sore throat

---

[1] *Itineraries and Corr. of Ezra Stiles,* pp. 486-487; Stiles, *Diary,* Nov. 26, 1772.

[2] June 26, 1760, quoted by McClenahan, *loc. cit.,* p. 367; Harrington, *op. cit.,* vol. i, p. 33.

[3] Fox, *op. cit.,* p. 79, note 1.

[4] Packard, p. 98; *Colden Papers,* vol. ii, pp. 196-200; vol. vii, pp. 363, 368, also *ibid.,* vol. vii, pp. 337, 338.

distemper " noting its prevalence throughout the colonies.[1] This tract was quoted in the "American Magazine and Historical Chronicle" soon afterwards. Colden also wrote on the disease, and in a letter to Dr. Fothergill, describing its spread and treatment, he acknowledged his debt to Douglass.[2]

Dr. Ogden, who was well acquainted with Colden and Bard, wrote some letters on the distemper. Jared Ingersoll of Connecticut conversed with Ogden about the " sore throat " when the former was temporarily located in Newark in 1769. The next year, Ogden wrote to Ingersoll that at the request of some doctors he would publish a treatise on the "said disorder," and he inquired about the statistics of mortality in Connecticut and Massachusetts. Would Ingersoll send Dr. Douglass' paper on the disease? Ogden's copy was lost.[3] John Kearsley Jr. wrote some notes on "Angina Maligna" (sore throat) which were forwarded to the "American Magazine" of 1769, but the most prominent effort was the " Enquiry into the Nature, Cause and Cure of the Angina Suffocativa," written by Dr. Samuel Bard, in which the previous activity of Dr. Douglass was duly recognized.[4] This discourse, praised by Jacobi "as our best colonial tract on diphtheria," was communicated by Dr. John Morgan to the American Philosophical Society.[5]

[1] J. B. Beck, *An Historical Sketch of the State of Medicine in the American Colonies* (Albany, 1850), pp. 15, 24-27; Rush, *op. cit.*, vol. iv, p. 398.

[2] Vol. ii, 1745, p. 145; Beck, pp. 38-39.

[3] Thacher, vol. i, p. 410; see Ogden's Letters in *Hutchin's Almanack*, 1775; *Rivington's New Almanack*, 1774; *Ingersoll Letters*, pp. 430-431; the proposed treatise, it seems, never appeared.

[4] Middleton, " The John Kearsleys," *loc. cit.*, vol. iii, p. 398; Bard's work printed 1771, p. 19, 22, 27.

[5] F. H. Garrison, " Samuel Bard," *N. Y. Academy of Medicine Bull.*, 2nd ser., vol. i, p. 90; *Transactions of American Philosophical Society* (Phila., 1769-1771), vol. i, p. 322.

The treatment of other ailments also enlisted cooperative endeavor. A Newport member contributed to the New Jersey Medical Society a copy of one of Dr. Jared Eliot's nostrums. The correspondent Dr. Ayres, a former student of Eliot, had seen it given, and had himself prescribed it successfully in "dropsies and hysteric cases." With a reserve more characteristic of nineteenth than eighteenth-century medicine, the society replied, "taking the above medicine into consideration [we] were greatly surprised at the accounts but judged it not prudent to recommend the use of it without more authentic proof of its success."[1]

Some aspects of medicine in this period illustrate the perennial credulity of both the initiate and the uninitiate. The discovery of "cures" and the rushing into print of the discoverers are known to many ages. "Tar water" was a favorite eighteenth-century panacea. In 1746, the "American Magazine and Historical Chronicle" printed an article on the "Effect of Tar Water in the Cure of Smallpox," a Liverpool contribution. Bishop Berkeley wrote on "Tar Water" occasioning some "Reflexions" in the same magazine.[2] In Boston it was tried as a preventive against small pox and many other ailments.[3] Colden sent the famous Dr. Gronovius of Leyden his essay on "Tar Water" as a cure for gout, etc. Samuel Johnson, the future college president, had a few words to say on the subject to Colden. Franklin received the latter's medical essay, and answered that there was much discussion about it, and that wide publication might enhance its usefulness.[4]

---

[1] Russell, *op. cit.*, pp. 65-66.

[2] Vol. iii, vol. ii, p. 145.

[3] Franklin, *Calendar of Papers,* vol. ii, p. 5; adv't of " Tar Water " in *Boston Gaz. and Co. Journal,* July 14, 1760.

[4] *Colden Papers,* vol. iii, pp. 97-98, 1745; *ibid.,* pp. 148-149, 139-143, 180-183; Parker published it for Colden, *ibid.,* pp. 102, 200.

"Cancer cures' are an old story. The "Gentleman's
Magazine" in England carried an article on the "Cure of
Cancers" by the pokeweed, which Colden supposed Franklin
had already seen. The former, a little incautiously this
time, was certain it would make a perfect cure. Johnson
had described years before a similar use of pokeweed.
Franklin lauded Colden on the success of the new discovery and informed him that Boston did not know the
right plant, for in one of its papers appeared a request
that an accurate description be given of the weed, its
habitat, etc. Despite much quackery, this period contributed at least one paper, on yellow fever, by Dr. John
Mitchell of Virginia, which was to prove of great service.
Franklin transmitted the article to Colden for additions or
criticisms, and many years later it was to furnish Benjamin
Rush with the ideas to fight the yellow fever epidemic in
Philadelphia.[1]

To Pennsylvania one turns again to note further progress,
for it was the first colony to establish a real hospital,
later intimately associated with the medical school. The
will of Daniel Denormandie in New York bequeathed
£50 to the Philadelphia institution. Fothergill sent drawings and contributed the first medical book to the library
begun in 1763.[2] Six years later Samuel Bard published
"A Discourse . . . . on the necessity . . . . of a Public
Hospital," which bore fruit in 1771 with the organization of the "Society of the New York Hospital." Fothergill,
who aided Dr. John Jones in collecting English subscriptions, was made one of the first governors. Andrew Elliot,

---

[1] *Colden Papers*, vol. iii, pp. 148-149, 77-78; vol. iv, pp. 317, 323; Lyman
Carrier, " Dr. John Mitchell ", *Amer. Hist. Assn. Annual Rep.*, 1918,
vol. i; *Amer. Med. and Phil. Reg.*, vol. iv, pp. 181-215, 378, 383.

[2] *N. Y. Hist. Soc.*, Abstracts of Wills, vol. vi, p. 2, March 16, 1760;
Fox, pp. 368-370.

formerly a trustee of the College of Philadelphia, was a charter member and governor of the New York hospital.[1]

There are a few instances of consulting physicians and wandering "medicine men," the latter very untrustworthy. Dr. John Kearsley Sr. and Dr. Thomas Graeme, both of Philadelphia, were treating a case of "stomach trouble" and wished Colden's advice. The latter suggested the latest treatment as practised in Europe, and offered to send the medicines from New York if unavailable in Philadelphia.[2] Dr. Adam Thompson, of Philadelphia and New York, was frequently sent for to superintend operations in various sections of the country. Jared Eliot of Connecticut, an exceedingly interesting personality, was especially "distinguished for . . . . successful treatment of chronic complaints," and was often called to Boston and Newport. Philip Turner of the same colony had an extensive reputation as a surgeon, which won him the coveted praise of Dr. Shippen, as well as calls from the larger cities.[3] Jerry Shea advertised in the "New York Mercury" a cure for rheumatism, " offering to exhibit ' certificates from those he cured at Philadelphia.' " He was followed a few years later by Dr. Graham, "Oculist and Aurist," who evidently exhausted the local field before moving to New York. Doctor Dubuke, "Oculist and Dentist," who cured almost everything, was in New York, having just arrived from Boston.[4]

[1] E. W. Sheldon, *The Society of the New York Hospital; Historical Address at the Celebration of the 150th Anniversary* (N. Y., 1921), p. 71; the hospital burnt down just when completed.

[2] *Colden Papers*, vol. i, pp. 148-157; the combined efforts were fruitless for the patient died.

[3] Morrison, *History of St. Andrew's Society in N. Y.*, p. 43; Russell, pp. 63-68, 113.

[4] Oct. 5, 1767, quoted by M. J. O'Brien in *Amer. Irish Hist. Soc. Journ.*, 1916, p. 249; "Items Relating to Medicine in N. Y.", *loc. cit.*, pp. 302, 303.

In the latter town, Paul Revere, along with other activities, made artificial teeth which he promised to fix "as well as any Surgeon-Dentist who ever came from London." Patent medicines attained a popularity that has scarcely waned to this day, and some of the more famous ones like "The Great and Learned Doctor Sanxay's Imperial Golden Drops" were widely distributed, finding markets in Boston and Philadelphia.[1]

Although there was much buncombe in this, as well as in later periods of medical history, some very definite advances were recorded. Dr. John Morgan was among the first to urge doctors to restrict themselves to prescriptions, and to leave to apothecaries the compounding of medicines, a suggestion that gradually found adoption elsewhere in America. The practise of midwifery in the hands of females who knew little or nothing of medicine was slowly taken over by the profession. Dr. James Lloyd of Boston and Dr. William Shippen Jr. of Philadelphia, probably known to each other, commenced the practise about the same time in their respective cities. Dr. Tennent of the New York school was likewise interested in obstetrics. Franklin invented a flexible catheter, and treated patients with electricity.[2]

To raise the standards of the profession and safeguard society, William Livingston, in his "Independent Reflector," urged the strict regulation of medical practise, and seven years later a law with that end in view was enacted in New York. Influenced by her neighbor, New Jersey also passed such an act. Skilled physicians and surgeons of other colonies, called upon to practise in New Jersey, were not to be barred by this law; but there were severe fines for traveling medicine

---

[1] *Boston Gaz. and Co. Journal*, July 30, 1770; in this period of animosity towards things English, everything "home made" was favored; *ibid.*, June 3, 1771.

[2] Toner, p. 58; Beck, pp. 10-11; Wickes, p. 59, note 2; Pepper, pp. 28-30.

men and " Mountebank Doctor(s)." [1] Long before, in 1741, a candidate for the Harvard M. A. had debated the question, "Should any one practise medicine before he has been approved by some competent persons?" Again in 1768, it was argued that to tolerate quacks would be fatal to society.[2] Strict regulation of inoculating hospitals was provided for in Massachusetts. Dr. Ames in his vigorous way, when pleading for a medical school, drew attention to the safeguards that protected the pulpit and the bar, "while the important art of preserving health . . . . lies open to the intrusion of every ignorant drone that assume[s] the title of doctor, to rob his Majesty's good subjects of New England not only of their estates, but of joints and limbs, and even life itself." [3]

The latter half of the century saw a great increase in the number of medical practitioners, and medical literature was enriched through importations and American contributions. Boerhave, the continental authority, was read in many of the colonial cities. The famous Scotch Professor Cullen's lectures on the "Materia Medica," which superseded Boerhave, were sold in New York and Philadelphia.[4] Dr. John Jones in his "Plain Remarks upon Wounds and Fractures," dedicated to his preceptor Cadwallader, indicated the absence of provincial boundaries in the domain of science when he

---

[1] No. xxiv, May 10, 1753; *Colonial Laws of N. Y.,* vol. iv, p. 455; Samuel Allinson, *Acts of the General Assembly of New Jersey* (Burlington, 1776), pp. 376-377 (Sept. 26, 1772).

[2] *Mass. Hist. Soc. Proc.,* I, vol. xviii, pp. 133, 134.

[3] *Acts and Resolves, Public and Private of the Province of Massachusetts Bay,* vol. iv, pp. 728-729, June 15, 1764; Briggs, *Almanacs of Nathaniel Ames,* pp. 413-416 (1770).

[4] Boerhave for sale, *Boston Gaz. and Co. Journal,* Jan. 14, 1760; *Constitutional Gazette,* Nov. 18, 1775, in *Med. Reg. of N. Y.,* 1868-1869, p. 303.

addressed his work to "students and young practitioners of surgery through all America." [1]

With the end of the colonial period the educated physician was in a position of great importance. He was often a distinguished member of colonial society, a man of sufficient means and culture to play an enviable role in politics and society. His rise to this state of acknowledged prestige was rapid. At the opening of the eighteenth century, one could hardly speak of a medical profession, for its members rarely had a formal training, and were usually associated with many other activities, not always related. In the course of the century specialization set in, particularly among the better known physicians and technical advances of significant proportions were also recorded. Finally, by professional organizations and the institution of schools, a community of interests was established whose intercolonial ramifications augured well for scientific achievement.

[1] Beck, pp. 41-42; Thacher, vol. i, p. 330.

CHAPTER VIII

SCIENCE AND CURIOSITY

THE intercolonial contacts so valuable to the doctors, are only one illustration of a larger community of scientific spirits who were, like Colden, anxious to give the colonies something of the appearance of the " Cultivated grounds in Europe." When Edward Bromfield Jr. of Boston died, Thomas Prince wrote a short biography depicting his interest in cartography and mathematics, the rather elaborate organ which he had built on English models and the optical and mechanical instruments which he had invented. Andrew Oliver Jr., son of the secretary of Massachusetts, was a student of music, had a taste for poetry, was very proficient in mathematics and dabbled much in scientific questions.[1] These are but two of a large number in Europe and America who were fired by the inquisitive spirit of the age, sometimes only to amateurish efforts but sometimes to work of a more enduring quality.

Before and after the establishment of an American philosophical society, colonials interested in science contributed papers to the Royal Society in London; it was in fact the central scientific organization for the colonies. Its " Transactions " included papers by Dr. Kearsley and Joseph Breitnall of Philadelphia, by James Alexander, Gov. Burnet, and Colden of New York, and Paul Dudley of Boston.[2] When

---

[1] *Amer. Mag. and Hist. Chronicle*, vol. iii, pp. 548-551 (1746) ; *Two Lectures on Comets, also an Essay on Comets by A. Oliver Jun. Esq., with Sketches of the Lives of Professor Winthrop and Mr. Oliver . . .* (Boston, 1811).

[2] Samuel Miller, *A Brief Retrospect of the Eighteenth Century* (N. Y., 1803), vol. ii, pp. 355-368.

in London, Franklin transmitted to the Society the scientific observations of the Harvard scholar, John Winthrop.[1]   This long-distance correspondence was however unsatisfactory, and early in the eighteenth century attempts were made to organize an American society which was to transcend provincial barriers.

Cadwallader Colden proposed to his friend Dr. William Douglass the formation of a " Society for the advancing of Knowledge."   Interested persons in the neighboring provinces were to be invited, but Boston should take the lead "because the greatest number of proper persons are . . . . to be found in your Colony."   Each member was to contribute a paper once in six months to be sent to an editorial board in Boston and then published for the other members.   Nothong of an intercolonial nature [2] came of this suggestion until Franklin, aware of Colden's interest, took a hand in the proceedings.   Late in 1743, Franklin wrote Colden that he had " had no Leisure to forward the Scheme of the Society," but would " proceed in the affair very soon." [3]   In the same year he issued a circular " Proposal for promoting useful knowledge " by an " American Philosophical Society ", " of virtuosi or ingenious men . . . . in the several colonies." [4]

Early the next spring it was announced that the organization so far as related to Philadelphia, had been formed and had already met; a list of members followed including a new addition, James Alexander of New York.[5]   The latter

---

[1] " Winthrop-Franklin Letters," *Mass. Hist. Soc. Proc.,* i, xv, 11-12, June 6, 1770.

[2] *Colden Papers,* vol. i, pp. 271-273, n. d.; a medical society formed in Boston has been mentioned.

[3] *Ibid.,* vol. iii, p. 34, Nov. 4, 1743.

[4] G. B. Goode, *Papers of the Amer. Hist. Assn.,* vol. iv, pt. 2, p. 6; A. H. Smyth, *The Writings of Benjamin Franklin* (N. Y., 1905-07), vol. ii, pp. 228-29.

[5] *Proceedings of the Amer. Phil. Soc.,* bound in vol. xxii, pp. 1-2.

had written Colden of the usefulness of Franklin's proposal and promised his encouragement. Colden wrote to Peter Collinson, a Londoner very much interested in colonial intellectual activities, " No doubt You will hear of a Philosophical Society now forming at Philadelphia " and added that he and some others from neighboring colonies had been invited to join. An " American Philosophical Miscellany, Monthly or Quarterly " was projected on which Colden's advice was requested.[1]

To be asked into this organization was the highest honor that could be paid intellectual achievement, and there were heartburnings indeed when an election was in doubt.[2] Prof. John Winthrop and Dr. Edward Holyoke of Harvard, and Dr. Ezra Stiles, later president of Yale, were among the early corresponding members. Dr. Samuel Bard of King's College, originally a member of the American Society of Philadelphia which amalgamated with the American Philosophical Society, was also of the elect. Another was the first professional American architect, Peter Harrison of Newport and Boston.[3] The presidents of King's College and Princeton, Dr. Myles Cooper and Dr. John Witherspoon respectively, were also members. Before 1775 scarcely a colonial of note in any of the professional fields was unconnected with the Philadelphia Society, which included on its roster distinguished European names as well. In 1771 the Society had a large enrolment, 157 in Pennsylvania, ten in Massachusetts, two in Rhode Island, four in Connecticut, eleven in New York, eleven in New Jersey, three in Dela-

[1] *Colden Papers*, vol. iii, pp. 82-83, 93-94, 60-61, 180-183.

[2] Smith, *Life and Corr. of the Rev. William Smith*, vol. i, pp. 485-487, Andrew Oliver to Smith anent a certain election, Dec. 6, 1773.

[3] *Proc. of A. P. S.*, vol. xxii, pp. 4, 6, 8, 9; laws and regulations, p. 30; also abstract from " Junto Minute Book ", *History of A. P. S.*; for Harrison see C. H. Hart in *Mass. Hist. Soc. Proc.*, vol. xlix, p. 267.

ware, five in Maryland, four from Virginia, five in South
Carolina, one in Georgia, ten from the West Indies and
twenty-five members living in Europe.[1]

Contributions were read by the local members, and papers
were sent by the correspondents which were presented to
the society by a sponsor. Cadwallader Colden's " Some Remarks on Some Obvious Phenomena of Light " made reference to the work of Rittenhouse, whose accomplishments inspired much respect among his contemporaries. The Society
promoted the temporary enthusiasm for silk culture, and an
offering by Andrew Oliver on a solar shadow was highly
praised. Mr. Bernard Romans whose " Natural History of
East and West Florida " was published in New York 1774,
was an attendant at one of the meetings, and promised to
leave a drawing of two Florida plants. Christopher Colles
received encouragement from a committee appointed to in-
vestigate a steam engine which he had erected to raise water.
Dr. John Perkins of Boston sent a paper " On Tornadoes,
Hurricanes and Waterspouts " (1773), which won him election the next year. Furnishing a precedent for its innumerable successors in the next century, the Society published in
Philadelphia a volume of " Transactions," of which Boston
took ten copies and New York seven.[2]

The contents of this volume show a decided interrelation
of intellectual currents. In volume two of the " Transactions," not printed until 1786, are papers contributed by
Andrew Oliver on " Lightening and Thunder Storms " and
" Waterspouts " (1774) which reveal the author's acquaintance with the writings of Ebenezer Kinnersley, Franklin and
others. The Rev. Samuel Williams from New England was

[1] Proc. of the A. P. S., 1770, pp. 6, 35, 48; Miller, op. cit., vol. ii, p. 372,
note g; Transactions of A. P. S., vol. i, for list of members in 1770.

[2] Proc. of A. P. S., 1771, pp. 64, 65, 68; 1773, pp. 82-84, 87; Transactions,
1769-1771, passim.

an active investigator, transmitting " Experiments . . . .
and Meteorological Observations," remarks on the transits of
Venus and Mercury in 1769 and an eclipse of the sun at
Bradford, Massachusetts, two years later.[1]

The methods of popularizing novelties in eighteenth-century thought reveal the preparation of the American mind
for the nineteenth-century Chautauqua. Lecturing, often
arranged in tours, was a common means of awakening interest in new ideas at a time when books were printed comparatively infrequently. Audiences in New York and Philadelphia attended the lecture series of a Dr. Spencer.[2] Ebenezer Kinnersley of the College of Philadelphia, who was
responsible for much of value in Franklin's thought, was a
well known lecturer in the middle and New England colonies,
where his arrival was heralded by newspapers and broadsides.[3] Franklin used his good offices to secure Kinnersley
a favorable reception and gave him a letter of introduction
to James Bowdoin when he left for Boston Bowdoin wrote
Franklin that Kinnersley's experiments had pleased many,
and hoped the lecturer's tour would be turned to good
account. The spirit of the times led Professor Winthrop to
lecture on electricity at Harvard.[4] When Kinnersley came
to New York, James Alexander spoke highly of his experiments which Colden was unable to see. About the same time
James Trotter was advertising local exhibitions and a course

[1] Vol. ii, pp. 74-101, 101-118, 118-141, 246-249, 249-250, 250-251.

[2] *Hamilton's Itinerarium*, pp. 232-233; *N. Y. Post-Boy*, Jan. 16, 1744,
Stokes, p. 578.

[3] *Rhode Island Imprints, 1727-1800*, p. 13; Franklin, *Experiments and
Observations*, pp. 99-101, 103-106, in which Kinnersley suggests experiments to Franklin.

[4] Montgomery, *Hist. of Univ. of Penn.*, p. 173; Franklin, *op. cit.*, pp.
166-177; John Perkins also wrote that Kinnersley was well received;
Feb. 17, 1752, Franklin, *Calendar of Papers*, vol. ii, p. 5; *Col. Soc. of
Mass., Trans.*, vol. xviii, p. 9.

of experiments on "newly discovered Electrical Fire."[1] Other individuals, for a consideration, kept Boston and Salem posted on the latest in science.[2]

Lectures on electricity were but a single aspect of this fad which patronized in America and Europe all the latest expositions, especially in the field of physical science. Christopher Colles gave a series of lectures in New York on " Geography, the Globe, Eclipses and Tides . . . ." which he had previously given in Philadelphia the same year.[3] He was but one of many in the cities of both continents, who attracted both the merely curious and those who came to learn. Of Paris, where the democratization of science helped prepare the French mind for revolution, Buckle has written that " the assemblages were crowded to overflowing "; all classes of society listened to discussions in botany, zoology and electricity, a study to which Franklin had given a marked impetus.[4]

Franklin and Cadwallader Colden were looked upon as the savants to whose criticism all matters pertaining to science should be submitted. Did a gentleman in New York observe meteorological conditions, Franklin must be informed so that his suggestions might be received. James Bowdoin was intellectually knighted when his explanation of the " crooked direction of lightening " met with the master's approbation. He was a close student of Franklin's works, an interest that was appreciated, for the latter sent Bowdoin a paper on magnetism. Water spouts and shooting stars were troubling a Boston doctor; so letters were dispatched

[1] *Colden Papers*, vol. iv, pp. 336, 343-344; Stokes, p. 633, May 18, 1752.

[2] Felt, *Annals of Salem* (ed. 1827), pp. 476, 479; *Boston Rec. Comm. Reports, Selectmen's Minutes, 1764-1768*, Wm. Johnson, Aug. 7, 1765.

[3] *N. Y. Gaz. and Weekly Mercury*, supplement, April 25, 1774; *Pa. Packet or General Advertiser*, Jan. 31, 1774.

[4] H. T. Buckle, *History of Civilization in England* (London, 1882), vol. ii, pp. 406, 407 and note 193.

to and from Philadelphia. Was Alexander in New York proposing an experiment to measure the time taken by an electric spark to move through space? Franklin must hear about it and find time to answer critically. From Charlestown, the leading cultural center in the South, came the similar correspondence of Dr. John Lining, an illustrious Scottish physician. Even the learned Winthrop, the Harvard professor, could write to this amazing layman, seeking a possible explanation for a novel electrical phenomenon.[1] Evan Jones sent some observations on the bite of a rattlesnake to Colden, who was to revise the paper and forward it if he saw fit, to the Philosophical Society.[2]

Franklin was also the source of much of the colonial electrical apparatus. Colden wrote that some New Yorkers were desirous of continuing their experiments and had heard that Franklin had received the necessary apparatus from England; could a copy be made by Philadelphia artisans and sent to New York? Franklin judged that it could; in fact he would oversee the work that was to begin immediately. He had already sent a glass tube and a part of his " Electrical Journal," the rest to follow soon, which papers were also accessible to others in New York.[3] Ezra Stiles while a tutor at Yale experimented on apparatus sent by Franklin. William Clagget of Newport, who was known to the latter, constructed a large electrical machine on which he gave public exhibitions for the Boston poor. Joseph Brown of Providence had an elaborate outfit for experimentation. In fact, all fields of intellectual life in the eighteenth century attracted Rhode Islanders who kept in touch with like-minded colonials of other provinces.[4]

---

[1] Franklin, *Experiments and Observations*, pp. 254-261, 166-181, 207-237, 280-283, 434; McCrady, *Royal Government in S. C.,* p. 415.

[2] *Colden Papers*, vol. iii, pp. 64-66.

[3] *Ibid.,* pp. 397-398, 409-410, 414-415, 418; vol. iv, pp. 218-219.

[4] C. W. Parsons, *loc. cit.,* pp. 245-248; W. E. Foster, " Rhode Island Contributions to the Intellectual Life of the Eighteenth Century ", *Am. Antiq. Soc. Proc.,* vol. viii, pp. 103-133.

When the Philadelphia Academy was building, Franklin informed Colden of his proposal to have an observatory at the top. In a discussion of the prospective transits of Mercury (1753) and Venus (1761), Alexander suggested to Franklin that the colleges be induced to set up apparatus to make them expert in taking observations by the later date. Urging that he was the man best fitted for the task, Alexander added that the institutions merely needed to be " put in mind of it." [1] Evidently the colleges were mindful of the demands of the age; for this period witnessed the collection of apparatus for physical and astronomical work at Harvard, to which James Bowdoin added an orrery.[2] King's College vied with the latter school in its collections. President Johnson wrote to a Boston correspondent, " We have an apparatus of instruments, which [with additions already ordered] will . . . . be at least equal to that at Cambridge." [3] The scientific machines at Princeton, which included an orrery made by Rittenhouse, elicited favorable comment from the observant John Adams. The new Rhode Island College received electrical apparatus, microscopes and a telescope as part of the foreign and domestic contributions.[4]

Franklin's lightning rods, although widely known, were not accepted without opposition. David Colden and Sir William Johnson had some correspondence on electrical phenomena, in which the former wrote that the Trinity Church steeple had been struck by lightning, but he hastened to add that such an occurrence did not invalidate Franklin's

[1] *Colden Papers,* vol. iv, pp. 218-219, 363-368.

[2] Snow, *College Curriculum in U. S.,* p. 52 (1760); apparatus from London and elsewhere, *Harvard College Records, Col. Soc. of Mass., Coll.,* vol. xvi, pp. 732, 813.

[3] *Johnson Papers,* to Rev. East Apthorp, Dec. 1, 1759.

[4] Woods, *John Witherspoon,* p. 107; M. J. Babb, " David Rittenhouse," *Univ. of Penn., Lectures Delivered by Members of the Faculty,* 1914-1915, p. 600; Bronson, *Brown University,* pp. 106-107.

theory of protecting houses by means of such conductors. John Winthrop early believed in their efficacy, and when he read in the Royal Society's " Transactions " of the effects of lightning on a church steeple, he expressed amazement at the idea of repairing the edifice without these conductors. The Harvard professor, who did his utmost to encourage the use of lightning rods, wrote a newspaper article which induced the people of Waltham, Massachusetts to adopt them, and he informed the inventor that they " are now becoming pretty common among us." [1]

Other questions kindled an intellectual curiosity which cooperative effort sought to satisfy. Franklin was always interested in the problem of heating and ventilation, and he advised Bowdoin how to keep rooms warmer in cold weather with less fire. Colden approved of Franklin's notions on " cold and heat conductors " and urged him " to pursue the scent." His " fire-places " attracted immediate attention. Alexander wrote to Colden that Franklin's new stove chimneys were much approved in New York, adding " theres one . . . . for you." The " American Magazine and Historical Chronicle " in the issue for December, 1744, included an extract from a Philadelphia pamphlet, " An Account of the New Invented Pennsylvania Fire Places," and one contributor could only express his enthusiasm by leaping into verse. From Boston, Benjamin Mecom priced a small fire-place he needed for his printing office. Parker needed a sliding iron for his fire-place and also a bake-stone from Philadelphia, as none could be obtained in New York. [2]

[1] *Colden Papers*, vol. vi, pp. 306-307; Franklin, *Experiments and Observations*, p. 485; " Winthrop-Franklin Letters ", *loc. cit.*, pp. 12-13, Oct. 26, 1770; Dr. Holyoke's Diary, Aug. 19, 1768, noted probably the earliest lightning rods in Salem, Felt (1849), vol. ii, p. 123.

[2] Franklin, *Experiments and Observations*, pp. 276-279, 369-374; *Colden Papers*, vol. iii, pp. 82-83; Franklin, *Calendar of Papers*, vol. v, pp. 180, 197-198.

Astronomical observations occupied much of the attention of the colonial *philosophes*. Thomas Robie, a Harvard teacher, sent a New Yorker some notes on the eclipse of the sun (Nov. 1722), and hoped that observations of a similar nature might be made in his correspondent's locality. Douglass thought Colden's communications on "Jupiters Moons", observed at New York, were "very acceptable." Dr. Nathaniel Ames of Massachusetts had many correspondents interested in astronomy. The approaching transit of Mercury over the sun in 1753 hurried along preparations in which the restless Franklin took a leading part. He struck off fifty copies of letters on the "Transit of Mercury" and sent them to distant colonials with instructions for the proper observation of this phenomenon.[1] The transit of Venus in 1769 was the occasion for the greatest excitement, and elaborate plans were laid to secure observations in widely separated localities. It was really a cooperative scientific enterprise, whose results attracted the notice of European students. Among those participating were Benjamin West at the Rhode Island College, Winthrop at Cambridge, Rittenhouse and Shippen of Philadelphia.[2] Boston published at the express desire of the college students, "Two Lectures on the Transit of Venus," by Professor Winthrop, and a local newspaper called popular attention to "one of the most entertaining spectacles in the heavens, a Transit of Mercury over the sun."[3]

The correspondence between Franklin and Cadwallader

[1] *Colden Papers*, vol. i, pp. 157-159, 164-167; vol. iv, pp. 371-376; *Harvard College Records, loc. cit.,* index, under Thomas Robie; Briggs, *Almanacs of Nathaniel Ames*, p. 223.

[2] Simon Newcomb, *U. S. Nautical Almanac Office; Astronomical Papers,* vol. ii; "Discussions of Observations of the Transits of Venus in 1761 and 1769" (Wash., 1891), pp. 320-324; *Transactions of the A. P. S.,* vol. i.

[3] *Boston Gaz. and Co. Journal,* May 22, 1769; *Boston Eve. Post,* Nov. 6, 1769.

Colden and the latter's son David, reached into all the by-ways of eighteenth century accomplishment. Franklin was very generous in permitting others to read and make use of his papers which he transcribed for them. In the field of electricity Colden acknowledged his indebtedness to him; " The oftener I read over [your electrical experiments] the more I am pleased with them & every time discover some thing new." In 1754, Franklin was awarded the gold medal of the Royal Society for his discoveries, and his theories, though modified in more recent times, long held a respected place in the highest scientific circles.[1] His work was also favorably known in France, although Abbé Nollet passed some severe strictures upon it. These moved the younger Colden to make a comparison of the Abbé's efforts with those of Franklin, which pleased the latter so much that he wished to send the notes to England for publication. Franklin would write the Abbé a civil yet critical note, but wished the elder Colden to revise it first. " It is not without Reluctance," wrote Colden, " that the Europeans will allow that they can possibly receive any Instruction from us Americans . . . . I think it behooves us all to join Hands for the Honour of the American Philosophy." [2] Certainly these two did all they could to further that end by assisting each other and lending aid to less advanced disciples of these new ideas.

Colden sent his selection " On Gravitation &c." to Frank-lin who promised to print it. A list of those who had read his " First Causes of Action in Matter, and Cause of Gravi-tation," was forwarded from Philadelphia. It included provincial officials and merchants, none of whom could make

[1] *Colden Papers,* vol. iv, pp. 227, 314-317, 379; Franklin, *Calendar of Papers,* vol. i, Prof. Ernest Rutherford. " Modern Theories of Electricity and Their Relation to the Franklinian Theory ".

[2] Franklin, *Experiments and Observations,* pp. 130-142; *Colden Papers,* vol. iv, pp. 385-359, 382-384.

much of Colden's philosophy; Franklin himself, uncertain about parts of the treatise, nevertheless testified to its stimulating qualities. " Some of our Gentlemen to render themselves more capable of comprehending your Doctrine, have been mustering up and reading whatever else they could find on Subjects . . . . akin to yours." Praising Colden for his " Principles," Franklin inquired as to a spare copy to be sent to James Bowdoin in Boston, who was apparently unknown to the author, and to save postage, proffered his services as the " Medium of (the) literary Commerce," which he felt was certain to ensue. Busy as he was in England, Franklin could find time to correspond with David Colden about the latter's paper on electricity to be published as a supplement to his father's "Principles ". In answer to a previous message, the elder Colden was pleased to note that Franklin's theory of light confirmed his own, which had just been published.[1] His kite experiment, recorded in the New York and Philadelphia papers, drew some remarks from Colden, while a discussion of the increase of mankind and a theory of universal magnetism provided additional correspondence. The younger Colden engaged in a spirited correspondence with Kinnersley because of the Philadelphia professor's criticism of some of the conclusions he had advanced.[2]

Partly romantic, partly scientific was the zeal for agriculture whose development, writes a leading authority, " entered a new phase " in the quarter century preceding the Revolution.[3] William Franklin wrote from New Jersey to his father, " I have entered into the spirit of Farming," and

---

[1] *Ibid.*, vol. iii, pp. 180-183, 273-276; vol. iv, pp. 371-372, 382-384, 325-328; vol. v, p. 260.

[2] " Franklin's Kite Experiment," *Am. Antiq. Soc. Proc.*, Oct., 1924, p. 188-205; *Colden Papers,* vol. iv, p. 431, vol. vi, pp. 213-216; *Colden Scientific Corr.*, March 9, 1759, Jan. 26, 1759.

[3] Lyman Carrier, *Beginnings of Agriculture in America*, p. 229.

asked that some implements be sent.[1]   Many aspirants for
the master's degree at Harvard wrote on agriculture, but
others made more definite contributions.   The " Essays on
Field Husbandry " by Jared Eliot, printed in New York,
New London and Boston, are by far the most considerable
agricultural writings in this period, and indicate an acquaintance with the work of Jethro Tull in England, which he
sought to improve.[2]   Eliot's " Essays " stimulated others to
keep records of observations and experiments, while agriculture generally became more and more " an important subject for discussion," writes Carrier.   " Meager remnants of
an extensive correspondence among the leading planters of
the various colonies have been preserved," and nearly everywhere in America the " most intelligent minds . . . . were
awakening to the fact that agricultural improvement offered
a field for study."   Nathaniel Ames appealed to his large
public to keep abreast of agricultural progress, on the ground
that it was a necessary foundation for a prosperous commonwealth.[3]

Contemporary almanacs made frequent reference to the
latest improvements and the " American Magazine " in
February 1758, contained essays in which colonial legislatures were urged to encourage agriculture.   " Agricola "
quoted Jared Eliot to advise sowing grass seed with crops
to improve old worn fields.   Eliot was again referred to as
the source of the recommendation that cattle be penned and
the pens be ploughed up for dung.   A Boston newspaper
essayist praised Eliot, whose writings he wished " were in
every Farmers Hands and Head."[4]   The purchaser of

---

[1] *N. J. Hist. Soc. Proc.*, vol. i, p. 107, May 11, 1769.

[2] R. H. True, "Beginnings of Agricultural Literature in America,"
Am. Lib. Assn. Bul., no. 14, 1920, p. 189 and note 15; Evans, 6999, 8847.

[3] Carrier, *op. cit.*, p. 229; Briggs, p. 355 (1764).

[4] P. 234; July, 1758, pp. 491-492; *Boston Gaz. and Co. Journal*,
Feb. 11, 1760.

a farm in Pennsylvania found the accumulated manure of many years unused. He carted it to the fields and his crops of wheat, rye and Indian corn were made the richer thereby.[1]   In the same colony, a local diarist mentioned a seed which was sent from " Jared Elliot in New England." Timothy hay as a forage crop was introduced to New York from New Hampshire by one Timothy Hanson, and other provinces, near by and further south, likewise gave it a popular reception.   The " New American Magazine," 1758, made a feature of publishing pieces on the improvement of agriculture.   David Colden invented a machine for sowing seeds in rows, which received the commendation of Franklin.[2]   In the " Pennsylvania Magazine or American Monthly " for February, 1775, is a description of a new threshing machine, modifying an English model, and the writer asserts that he has heard of such machines having been erected in America. A Swiss invention for " pulling up trees by the roots " was made known to frontier America through a London intermediary.[3]

New York had an agricultural society before 1765 which advocated better breeding of sheep; premiums were given for the greatest quantities of flax, hemp, seed and barley raised off one acre.   Sir William Johnson who had sent contributions to the organization from the Mohawk Valley was asked to spread the news of the society and its work among the farmers in his neighborhood.[4]   Societies of this nature had of course, a background in Europe, where

---

[1] R. W. Kelsey, " Materials for the History of Early Agriculture in Pennsylvania ", *Ann. Rep. of Amer. Hist. Assn.*, 1920, p. 287.

[2] Carrier, pp. 241-243, quoting William Logan's diary about 1755; *Colden Papers,* vol. vii, pp. 183-186.

[3] *Schuyler Papers,* 1761-1767, from Thomas Brand, March 10, 1763.

[4] Walter Rutherford and Wm. Smith for committee of correspondence, Feb. 5, 1765; *Myers Collection,* " Prominent Civilians and Officers in the Colonial Period ", p. 332.

they had been in existence in England and elsewhere for some years.[1] At a meeting of the American Philosophical Society a discussion of the injury to wheat caused by flies, and the consequent loss of trade in Pennsylvania and the other colonies prompted remedial suggestions.[2] The almanacs kept their readers informed about fairs to be held throughout the country at which livestock, home manufactures and produce were sold and exhibited. Closer attention was paid to the better breeding of horses, not only in the southern and middle colonies where an interest in racing would provide an impetus, but also in New England. Stallions were brought from other sections or even imported from abroad at the request of the more progressive to develop a finer stock.[3]

The immensity of the continent with its scenic wonders provoked attempts to map its extent, in which political and economic, as well as scientific considerations were involved. The search for a northwest passage around America was still going on. While the commercial motive may have been uppermost, there was a scientific interest attached to several expeditions that were fitted out. In 1753, Capt. Charles Swaine was in command of a venture subscribed to by merchants of Maryland, Pennsylvania, New York and Boston. Franklin, who raised a large sum for it in Philadelphia, kept Colden and Jared Eliot of Connecticut in touch with the undertaking. In the same year Rhode Island fitted out an expedition, aware of the one setting out from Philadelphia.[4]

[1] R. H. True, "Early Development of Agricultural Societies in the U. S.", *Ann. Rep. Am. Hist. Assn.*, 1920, p. 295.

[2] *American Magazine*, 1769; appendix, *Trans. of A. P. S.*, p. 32.

[3] *Boston Gaz. and Co. Journal*, April 30, 1770; June 16, 1760; ("Shakespare" imported).

[4] E. S. Balch, "Arctic Expeditions sent from the American Colonies," *Pa. Mag. of Hist. and Biog.*, vol. xxxi, pp. 419-428; *Colden Papers*, vol. iv, pp. 371-372.

More fruitful studies in cartography claimed some of the time of these intellectuals.   In 1724, Colden was planning a map of North America which Douglass hoped to assist by sending some information about New England.   The latter was acquainted with the work of Thomas Robie in fixing the latitude and longitude of Boston.[1]   The " American Magazine and Historical Chronicle " printed a contribution by Joseph Morgan on a method for finding the longitude, which had previously appeared in the " Pennsylvania Gazette." [2] John Bartram, the botanist, sent Collinson a beautiful map of the falls of " Mohocks River " (Mohawk) made on the spot.   Another map of the middle colonial area was also forwarded to Collinson about the same time.[3]

Lewis Evans of Philadelphia, the leading cartographer in the colonies, collected a vast amount of information which he incorporated in his map issued in 1749.   To Colden, who had been very helpful he wrote, " My Map is finisht at last, & now waits upon . . . . Mr. Alexander's & your Revisal " before going to press; additional geographical information was requested.   The map of 1755 was the leading model for North American cartography, and left its impress on other maps throughout the remainder of the century.[4]   A controversy arose over its accuracy, with especial regard to the French claims, and Evans defended himself in a number of essays, obtainable in Philadelphia and New York.   By reason of the wide knowledge gained during his travels collecting materials for his maps, Evans included with them geographical, historical, political and philosophical essays (special references on the middle colonies), which went into two editions.   The map of 1755 had subscribers in the three most important

[1] *Colden Papers*, vol. i, pp. 164-167.

[2] Vol. ii, pp. 263-264, May 30, 1745.

[3] *Colden Papers*, vol. ii, p. 247.

[4] *Ibid.*, vol. iv, pp. 107-108; Henry N. Stevens, *Lewis Evans, His Maps*.

cities in the north.[1] John Mitchell's map, done the same year, was to be useful in settling territorial disputes.[2] The intercolonial reputation of David Rittenhouse caused the New York Chamber of Commerce to request his services in determining the latitude of the flag bastion in the local Fort George. He and McLean, also of Philadelphia, assisted in the settlement of the boundary line between New York and New Jersey, and on various other occasions Rittenhouse was drafted for this work in the middle colonies.[3]

Bernard Romans, while engaged in his work on Florida cartography, made some investigations on the compass, which were communicated to the American Philosophical Society. Abel Buell, of Connecticut, a man of much ingenuity, assisted Romans in constructing the map. The New York Chamber of Commerce subscribed for twelve sets of the " Natural History of East and West Florida " which included the maps. To satisfy popular interest in the subject, Alexander Miller at the request of several gentlemen in New York, announced the formation of three clubs of eight female scholars each to teach them geography.[4]

Botany was another field in which the curious could exercise their fancy. The most distinguished colonial botanist was John Bartram, of Pennsylvania, who traveled in many parts of America, collecting seeds and curiosities for himself and for European noblemen. Peter Collinson described Bartram to Colden, and asked the latter to give him any information that might be requested. Colden was very much impressed by Bartrám's knowledge and industry when they

[1] Evans, *Amer. Bibliog.*, 7411-12, 7652; Stevens, pp. 11-13; Stokes, 672; Dow, *Arts & Crafts in New England*, p. 30.

[2] Lyman Carrier, " John Mitchell," *loc. cit.*, pp. 206-207.

[3] *N. Y. Chamber of Commerce Records*, pp. 61-62, 63; Stokes, p. 872; Babb, " David Rittenhouse ", *loc. cit.*, p. 602.

[4] *Chamber of Commerce Records*, pp. 191, 338, note 111, 378 note cc.; *N. Y. Gaz. or Weekly Post-Boy*, Nov. 29, 1764.

met shortly after. The latter advised Colden how and when to gather certain roots for medicine; they discussed natural phenomena and the use of plants in curing cancer. The New Yorker sent some information about a new edition of Linnaeus' "Characteres Plantarum," and in return, was rewarded with Bartram's latest findings. The botanist was known throughout the colonies, and many lent him their assistance. The Boston medical society sent him a description of eleven hundred plants growing near the city, while John Mitchell, the Virginia doctor, informed Bartram about the plants in his colony. Mitchell in fact, carried on a large correspondence with prominent colonists throughout America. He and Colden learned of each other's accomplishments through Bartram, and were fellow members of the Philosophical Society. Dr. Alexander Garden of South Carolina, was another who wrote glowingly of Bartram's hospitality and his botanical collections. With himself as the leading spirit guiding these collective efforts, Bartram intended gathering materials to enable him to write a description of American plants.[1] Colden and his daughter, Jane, were botanists with international reputations. The father's observations, transmitted to Gronovius and known to Linnaeus who published them, have been described by Asa Gray, as "an extraordinary performance." Jane awakened a decided taste for botany in young Samuel Bard, later the prominent physician. Interest in natural history in Europe and America was quickened by the discovery of animal remains near the Ohio.[2]

[1] *Colden Papers*, vol. ii, pp. 207-208, 280, 272-277, vol. iii, pp. 3-6, 78-79; vol. iv, pp. 471-473; *cf.* William Darlington, *Memorials of John Bartram and Humphry Marshall* (Phila., 1849).

[2] H. W. Ducachet, *A Biographical Memoir of Samuel Bard* (Phila., 1821), p. 4; Asa Gray, *Selections from the Scientific Correspondence of Cadwallader Colden with Gronovius, Linnaeus, Collinson and Other Naturalists* (New Haven, 1843), p. 4; *Colden Papers*, vol. iii, pp. 273-276, vol. v, pp. 202-205, vol. vii, pp. 132-133.

Following the prevailing fashion in England, whose botanical collections were greatly enriched by American contributions, colonials had their gardens as well, to beautify domestic surroundings and add variety to the diet. Wealthy citizens, like John Hancock, had their own private gardeners who raised specimens for public sale. In one issue of a Boston paper there were seven advertisements of sales of garden seeds, an activity largely in the hands of women.[1] An advertisement in a New York paper revealed very clearly the international aspect of this scientific curiosity:

All persons employed in botany or gardening, and such who want to supply their european friends with seeds or plants . . . produced by America . . . may be supplied with . . . every species (worthy a place in good collections) to be found in the Carolinas, Pennsylvania, Jerseys, New York, and Canada by applying to Thomas Vallentine.[2]

The latter part of this century saw a rapidly increasing demand for books on natural sciences, so that Priestley, the English scientist, turned to writing on these subjects in a popular style, an early precedent for a modern fashion. His experimental efforts were known in America through Franklin, who sent to Winthrop Priestley's article on the impregnation of water with "fixed air"—it was warmly praised by the Harvard professor. To David Colden, Franklin wrote from London, " Priestley's Experiments on Fix'd Air is the Subject of much Conversation here at present." [3] Dr. Benjamin Rush also made some observations on this experiment. The

[1] *Boston Gaz. and Co. Journal*, supplement, Feb. 26, 1770; *ibid.*, March 6, 1769; Feb. 27, 1769.

[2] *N. Y. Gaz. and Weekly Mercury*, Sept. 9, 1771; J. B. Botsford, *English Society in the Eighteenth Century as Influenced from Oversea* (N. Y., 1924), pp. 230-232.

[3] Buckle, *op. cit.*, vol. i, p. 432, note 223; Franklin, *Calendar of Papers*, vol. ii, pp. 145, 147; *Colden Papers*, vol. vii, pp. 185-186.

knowledge of this, like other fields of science, was quickly prepared for popular comprehension. Priestley's works, which were sold in Boston in 1772, doubtlessly through the efforts of Franklin, had already been preceded by public lectures on " Pneumatics," the nature and properties of air.[1]

The frequent announcements of lectures and the variety of subjects presented indicate the emergence of a group genuinely curious, and provided with the funds to gratify that curiosity. Inclination and greater opportunities for indulging scientific propensities resulted in the production of some work of great merit, along with much of minor importance. Colonial Americans kept in touch with European intellectual movements, but in several instances asserted an independence of spirit that produced superior achievements. It was an age when man was seeking a more reasoned basis for his existence, when more and more phenomena provoked an insatiable curiosity. In the satisfaction of that curiosity, widely scattered individuals escaped provincialism by joining together in an active organization, and through a busy correspondence became fellow citizens in the world of ideas. That citizenry was further enlarged by an early popularization of science, a practise that was to receive a tremendous impetus in the early decades of the nineteenth century.

[1] Franklin, *Calendar of Papers*, vol. ii, p. 133; *Boston Gaz. and Co. Journal*, June 11, 1770 (advertisement by Eccleston).

CHAPTER IX

THE SECULARIZATION OF AMERICAN LIFE

THE growing intercolonial interest in the various fields of science does not mean that religion had sunk to a negligible position in American life; in fact the " Great Awakening " was contemporaneous with much of this activity. Nor does it mean that interest in the supernatural with mysterious explanations of natural phenomena had disappeared. And yet, while colonial and even European thought still exhibited many of these features supposedly more characteristic of the seventeenth century, certain influences were effecting a gradual change which we may conveniently term the secularization of American life.

A hardy tradition in American letters has buried the colonists under such a mass of theology, neglecting their secular thinking except on politics, that perhaps it is advisable to consider for a moment the religious and worldly aspects of civilization. The influence of writers like Voltaire, and in more recent times Buckle, has undoubtedly served to strengthen the belief that in an age when religion seems the central interest, there can be little progress in other activities. This statement may be true of certain periods of history, but such stagnation may perhaps have been due to other causes than a theologically choked atmosphere; e. g., artificial governmental restrictions, wars, pestilence and economic depression, or what is known as a psychological dead level. On the other hand there were definite achievements of such magnificence in an age looked upon as marking the apogee of the medieval Catholic Church, that it has earned the appellation, too enthusiastically, of the " Greatest of All Centuries." [1]   It is not too much to suppose that theological writings, be they controversial, historical or homiletic, may provoke an accelerated general intellectual curiosity, or probably these writings themselves are merely symptomatic of a renewed mental activity.

It is not impossible that some better equipped explorer may do for the " Glacial period " [2] in New England history what Vilhjalmur Stefansson has done for the icy regions of the Arctic, revealing an unsuspected greenery; but I dare say that no luxuriant growth will be discovered.   Infertile soil as the colonies have been considered, seeds were sown in some areas whose promise slowly unfolded, until the twentieth century is witnessing their quickened maturity. It is not to be expected that this western portion of the world, with political, economic, cultural and ecclesiastical ties, joining it to a rapidly changing Europe could be immune to such an influence.   The vast stirrings in its religious life; the scientific and political speculations suggested by Descartes, Newton, Hobbes, Sidney and Locke; the agricultural revolution in England sponsored by Charles (Turnip) Townshend, Jethro Tull and others; the advance of skepticism and deism; the increasing output of secular literature; all these are features of the shifting scene which were reproduced on a less grandiose scale in America. " Linked as he was with the movement of thought in Europe," writes J. T. Adams, the colonist " was to duplicate in the movement of his own thought that rationalizing tendency " so characteristic of the continent.[3]

[1] J. J. Walsh, *The Thirteenth, Greatest of All Centuries* (N. Y., 1924). The sixteenth century full of theological speculation, witnessed much secular intellectual activity.

[2] C. F. Adams, *Massachusetts, Its Historians and Its History* (Boston, 1893), called the period up to about 1740 the " Glacial period " in Massachusetts.

[3] *Provincial Society,* p. 119.

In 1752, Franklin wrote to Colden in New York,

It is well we are not, as poor Galileo was, subject to the Inquisition for Philosophical Heresy. My whispers against the orthodox doctrine, in private letters, would be dangerous; but your writing and printing would be highly criminal. As it is, you must expect some censure, but one Heretic will surely excuse another.[1]

These correspondents were members of a small group, whose contact with continental thought left a marked impress on early American philosophy, traceable in deeper strains in later deistic pronouncements. " The drift of the English mind away from the supernatural, as evinced in the success of natural philosophy through the impulse given by Bacon and the Royal Society, is paralleled in America by the popularity of Newton and by the foundation . . . . of the American Philosophical Society." [2]

The process by which a change came over many intellects can be seen in the career of Samuel Johnson. When he entered Yale College the content of his prescribed studies introduced him to a medieval scholastic atmosphere. The young scholar thought he was fairly learned, till, to quote his autobiography, " accidentally lighting on Lord Bacon's . . . . Advancement of Learning . . . . he immediately bought it, and greedily fell to studying it." To quote further,

About this time 1714 when he was turned of 18 came over from England a well chosen library. . . . He had then all at once the vast pleasure of reading the works of our best English poets philosophers, and divines Shakespeare and Milton &c. and Norris

[1] B. Franklin, *Experiments and Observations on Electricity*, 1769, p. 267.

[2] I. W. Riley, *American Philosophy. Early Schools* (New York, 1907), p. 44; V. L. Parrington, *Main Currents in American Thought* (New York, 1927), vol. i, p. 148.

&c. Boyle and Newton &c. . . . . All this was like a flood of day to his low state of mind.[1]

Although Bacon fired the imagination of the young American, and revealed to him the deep abyss of human ignorance, Johnson's philosophy was indebted rather to " Locke and his contemporaries," writes Professor Schneider. To appreciate Newton and " Natural Philosophy," Johnson, now a tutor at his alma mater, began to study higher mathematics, and learned more about physics and astronomy. His new learning was made part of the curriculum and Johnson's conversation soon included references to " natural religion," while his reading embraced " the milder deists, such as Locke and Wollaston."

Johnson was soon forced to take stock of surrounding conditions, and the " intellectual backwardness of his colony . . . . the controversial temper and lack of order among the congregational churches " to which he belonged, disheartened him. After serious consideration, he determined, with a few likeminded friends in 1722 to take orders in the Anglican Church. His European visit brought him in contact with rationalists who stimulated his own thinking, and it also revealed to him that the colonies were really nothing but frontier settlements, which Johnson thought should be sown with the seeds of England's fruitful civilization. Professor Schneider, the editor of Johnson's manuscripts, writes, " The admirable harmony and laws of nature which [Locke, Newton and the milder deists] emphasized delighted him as being reason's witness to God. It never occurred to him that there was the least conflict between the latest science of nature and the oldest truths of revelation."

It was Dean George Berkeley, the English philosopher

---

[1] *Memoirs*, paragraphs 7 and 8. Most of this on Johnson comes from Prof. H. W. Schneider's essay in the forthcoming edition of Johnson's writings, to be issued by the Columbia Univ. Press.

temporarily residing in Rhode Island, who caused Johnson to reconsider his position, by pointing out to him whither Newton's philosophy was leading. Berkeley showed him how, starting from the deistic position, one might prove the " doctrine of fate and the impossibility of the existence of God; " and when " the deterministic implications of Locke and the tendency toward freethinking in Wollaston, Shaftesbury and others " were made clear to him, Johnson drew back alarmed. In later years Johnson's position was not much different from that of the Calvinists emphasizing the " dominant power and even the special providence of God," but he could not completely escape his earlier deism. Like a man between two worlds, he was trying to reconcile the old orthodox theology with the new scientific thought. With others in the mid-century, the King's College President stressed the humane aspects of God and the benevolence of both human and divine character. The basis of morals was shifted for many from " the sense of sin [where Jonathan Edwards fixed it] to the desire for happiness " and it can truly be said that " Johnson opened the door to human nature."

Although Johnson failed to follow through his premises to their logical conclusions, there were many who did. In Boston, Jonathan Mayhew and Charles Chauncy were but two of a number subject to the same intellectual influences as Johnson, which led them to critical treatment of a harsh Calvinism. To a minister like Chauncy, God was a rational Being " who does not communicate being or happiness to his creatures by an immediate act of power, but by concurring with an established course of Nature." [1] Some, including Cadwallader Colden and his frequent correspondent Franklin, went beyond the usual eighteenth-century deism. The former, who was educated in what he once called the " Mechanic phylosophy," is classed as the earliest of the

[1] Riley, *op. cit.*, pp. 199, 201.

colonial materialists, and his system like Franklin's "issued in a movement essentially modern,—the resolution of matter into the mechanics of energy."[1] Colden's ideas were known in Boston, where Thomas Prince was anxious to compare them with those of Berkeley;[2] they were known to Benjamin Rush and other members of the Philadelphia circle, called the most modern examples of thought in the colonial era.[3]

While the English philosophers were better known than their continental contemporaries, there were many colonists familiar with the latter, more especially Voltaire, who reached a popular audience very early through the almanacs.[4] The intellectual fermentation attributable to the international Frenchman is evidenced in an interesting letter to Thomas Hollis, the generous Londoner, from Jonathan Mayhew.

In the last parcel came also a very ingenious sensible book, *A comparative view of the State & faculties of man with those of the Animal World,* which I have read with much satisfaction & for which I return you hearty thanks. I am not certain whether I heretofore expressed my sentiments to you about Voltaire's two last books, *The Philosophy of History,* & the *Philosophical Dictionary.* Tho I cannot agree with him in some of his notions relative to religion, or rather in what appears to be a great part of his design, viz., the entire subversion of *revelation;* yet I cannot but think, these, as compositions, to be very fine performances. I have read them with delight, as containing much useful learning, many fine observations on antiquity, & written throughout in a most spirited, entertaining & masterly way; so that I would not be long without them for twice their value.[5]

[1] *Colden Papers,* vol. v, p. 240, July 5, 1758 to John Bard; Riley, pp. 330-335.

[2] *Ibid.;* Johnson to Colden, Oct. 20, 1744, *Colden Papers,* vol. iii.

[3] Riley, p. 21.

[4] E. g., Poor Roger, *The American Country Almanac* for 1758.

[5] *Bancroft Transcripts;* J. M. to Hollis, Boston, Jan. 7, 1766, Andrew Eliot, Jonathan Mayhew, Thomas Hollis, correspondence, 1761-1776.

Another student of the new light, Ezra Stiles, soon to be President of Yale College, read the " Philosophical Dictionary " twice within a few months, and noted in his diary that Voltaire " has some instructive Remarks." [1]

Much has been written of Locke's political influence in America and Europe.   Ames wrote in his almanac " As it is unpardonable for a Navigator to be without his charts so it is for a Senator to be without His which is Lock(e)'s ' Essay on Government.' " [2]   Yet it is careless to overlook the wide attention given to his work " On the Human Understanding," which was included in the college curriculum.[3] At Philadelphia, seniors studied Harrington and Algernon Sidney, who seem to have had a larger audience than has been generally recognized, nor was Milton's influence restricted to the domain of belles-lettres.   Andrew Eliot in Boston wrote of Sidney, " I am perhaps prejudiced in favor of that great man, because he was the first who taught me to form any just sentiments in government."   A few months later he wrote again to Hollis, " Harrington, Sydney, Locke almost any man may study his whole life to advantage.   I am particularly obliged to you for Milton's prose works.   They who consider that very great man only as a poet of the first rank, know less than half his character." [4]

Changing ideas found expression elsewhere.   In 1752, Parker indiscreetly published in his paper a little piece on freethinking, which created something of a flurry in official

[1] *Diary*, vol. i, May 29, Oct. 30, 1771.

[2] Briggs, p. 450 (1774).

[3] Benjamin Pierce, *A Hist. of Harvard Univ.* (Cambridge, 1833), p. 237; Montgomery, *Hist. of Univ. of Penn.,* p. 257.   " On the Human Understanding " was used more frequently than the "Essay on Government ", in Dartmouth College library (1774-77), H. D. Foster, *Dartmouth Alumni Mag.* (April, May, 1921), p. 14 (reprint).

[4] To Thomas Hollis, May 13, December 10, 1767, *Mass. Hist. Soc. Coll.,* ser., 4, vol. iv.

circles.   Franklin came to the printer's aid with a letter to
Colden of New York and urged his intercession, writing
that the cause of religion could best be served by stopping
the prosecution, for publicity could only make the article
more effective.   It was added that the selection was an old
one, originally printed in England and then in Philadelphia,
but had died from inattention.[1]   Theophilus Cossart was a
Newport printer and freethinker, who in his travels through
all the principal colonial cities was in a favorable position to
spread many unorthodox ideas.[2]   Nathaniel Ames gave
wide circulation to opinions like " True Religion is True
Reason," " To defend the Christian religion is one thing,
and to knock a man on the head for being of a different religion is another," an idea which William Livingston had
expressed in identical language some years before in his New
York paper.[3]   A large body of the population even outside
of the main colonial centers of culture was affected by these
new ideas.   John Adams was informed that deistic literature
" circulated with some freedom " in Worcester, and that
the " principles of Deism had made considerable progress
among the persons in that town and other towns in the
county." [4]

A few years before Parker's indiscretion, " The New
York Post-Boy " had printed a letter telling of the expulsion
of two students from Yale for attending a " New Light "
meeting.   The writer asked that a college be established in
another colony in which there should be freedom of religion
without endangering the civil power, a college of liberal arts
and sciences; students to be taught music, dancing and

[1] *Colden Papers*, vol. iv, May 14, 1752.

[2] Stiles, *Diary*, Oct. 25, Oct. 29, 1771.

[3] Briggs, pp. 387, 402; Tyler, *Amer. Lit.*, vol. ii, p. 221.

[4] *Works*, vol. ii, p. 3, note (1755).

fencing among other subjects.[1] President Clap in his defense stated that " New Lights " were tolerated at the college but the lay exhorters to whom the expelled students had listened were particularly obnoxious. It is perhaps of some significance to note that, although unable to get their degrees then, both students were awarded them some years later.[2] The " American Magazine and Historical Chronicle " printed a paper on the unreasonableness of persecution; it was opposed however to Catholicism.[3]

In some remarks on a proposed college in New York, William Livingston, who was contending against Anglican control of such an institution, pointed to Harvard and Yale as being free from Episcopalian influence. He asserted that students were molded by the religious principles of a college, and these affected public administration; therefore these institutions should be established by acts of legislatures, making them subject to civil authority in order to avoid sectarian control.[4] Livingston and his group were alleged, not quite accurately, to be seeking the erection of " a free thinking or latitudinarian Seminary." [5] At the very time he was upholding the Anglican control of King's College, Johnson was complaining to President Clap about the control of education by dissenters. " I must think it sufficient," he wrote, " to raise our passions to be denied a public education for our children unless we will in direct violation of our consciences enjoin them to go to dissenting meeting." Thus,

---

[1] Letter reprinted in *Amer. Mag. and Hist. Chronicle,* vol. ii, pp. 122-123. " New Lights " were religious dissenters of the eighteenth century who supported the evangelical movement.

[2] F. B. Dexter, *Doc. History of Yale,* 1701-1745 (New Haven, 1916), pp. 368-372.

[3] Vol. ii, pp. 255, 257.

[4] *Ecclesiastical Records of N. Y.,* vol. v, 3338-3339; 3359-3362.

[5] W. W. Kemp, *Support of Schools in Colonial N. Y.,* pp. 41-42; see S. Johnson to Bishop Secker, Oct. 25, 1764, *N. Y. Col. Doc.,* vol. vi, pp. 912-913.

even through partisan efforts, as in this instance, the objective of a more inclusive toleration might be gradually approached.[1]

In 1755, New England suffered one of its infrequent earthquakes. This occasioned a lecture by Prof. John Winthrop of Harvard, followed by a controversy carried on in the Boston newspapers with the Rev. Dr. Thomas Prince, a learned man, who opposed natural explanations as being detrimental to religion. Prince held that electrical disturbances and earthquakes were manifestations of God's displeasure. Winthrop replied defending philosophical discussion from " imputations of impiety or irreverence," a position supported by Andrew Oliver Jr., with an advocacy of free inquiry in religion and politics.[2] Other colonists watching this controversy came to the aid of Winthrop. A Connecticut clergyman wrote Ezra Stiles in Newport that " Mr. Winthrop has laid Mr. Prince flat on his back " and added, since " an Error in Philosophy is neither Heresy nor Treason it would have been most for Mr. Princes honour to have acknowledged the mistake." Professor Winthrop, whom Moses Coit Tyler has called " the most symmetrical example both of scientific and of literary culture produced in America during the colonial period," was keenly appreciative of this support. He wrote a generous note of thanks to Stiles, with the information that local clergymen were losing their heads over the situation. " One rev. Gentleman . . . . was pleased lately to observe to his audience, that not one Protestant place had suffered in the late European earthquake. What a narrow spirit of party do such observations discover? How unworthy of ministers of that God

" Who sees with equal eye, as God of all." [3]

---

[1] *Johnson Papers*, letter to Pres. Clap, Feb. 19, 1754.

[2] *Two Lectures on Comets*, pp. vi, vii, xxiv; *Col. Soc. Mass., Trans.*, vol. xviii, p. 7, note 1.

[3] *Hist. of Amer. Lit.*, vol. ii, p. 315; *Itineraries of Ezra Stiles*, John Devotion to Stiles, March 24, 1756; Winthrop to Stiles, April 17, 1756.

A few years before, Franklin had written Colden: " Surely
the Thunder of Heaven is no more supernatural than the
Rain Hail or Sunshine of Heaven, against the Incon-
veniences of which we guard by Roofs and Shades without
Scruple." [1]   In 1768 Hollis Hall was damaged and Winthrop was called upon to defend the erection of lightning
rods, probably thinking then what he had written to Franklin some months before, " How astonishing is the force of
prejudice even in an age of so much knowledge and free
enquiry! "   To which the worldy-wise Franklin replied,
that it was not unusual for even learned people to oppose
innovations.[2]

How far some of the minds of New England and elsewhere had drifted from seventeenth-century concern with
the supernatural, is revealed in this delightful bit from
Nathaniel Ames.

Many Persons in their Study of Nature have div'd so far above
the Apprehension of the Vulgar, that they have been believed to
be Necromancers, Magicians, &c.   But the Mistake lays in the
People's Ignorance, and not in the other's Studies.   That human Creatures should have actual Society and Communion with
spiritual Daemons is a strange Thing . . . But we are not to
believe such Reports, unless the Evidence of the Fact be equal
to the Strangeness of the Thing.   If there be an old Woman
. . . prodigious ugly, her Eyes hollow and red, her Face shrivel'd
up, that goes double, and her Voice trembles, she is a Witch
forsooth; but the handsome young Girls are never suspected;
as tho' Satan took a Delight in the Dry Sticks of Humane
Nature, and would select the most neglected Creature in the
humane Species to be his Privy Counsellor.[3]

[1] *Colden Papers*, vol. iv, April 12, 1753.

[2] *Amer. Antiq. Soc. Proc.*, Oct., 1924, p. 205; B. Franklin, *Exp. and
Obs. on Elect. at Phila.*, 1769, p. 485; *ibid.*, pp. 486-492.

[3] Briggs, pp. 198-199, *Almanack for 1747*, " An Essay on Conjuration
and Witchcraft."

The literary interests of the colonists reveal a steady growth in the secularization of thought. Too long has it been repeated that the American colonials had a literary fare with practically one course alone, a steady diet of religious works. Perhaps the great interest later in political questions is attributable in slight measure to literary indigestion. To those who think there is little interest in religious writings today, it would probably be surprising information that despite the diversified character of modern publications more religious books are published yearly than any other group with the exception of fiction.

To satisfy a curiosity of long standing, a count was made in Evans' "American Bibliography," through the years 1751 to 1775, of publications that were printed or reprinted contemporaneously in two or three colonial cities; in some cases there were imprints of other towns besides those under consideration, New York, Philadelphia and Boston. In the religious category were placed books of a doubtful character, that is, not definitely secular; the enumeration showed 39 under " religion " and 92 under " secular." In the period 1751-1760, there were 21 " religious " and 33 " secular," a relationship which became disproportionate with the following years, troubled by political controversies. A survey of Rhode Island imprints reveals a similar situation. The count showed between 1727 and 1750, 30 under "religion" and 41 under "secular". In the period, 1751-1774, there were 88 "religious" and 160 "secular" issues from the press.[1] But a study of press issues is insufficient to indicate the scope of reading material, for it has been pointed out conclusively that, although the New England presses printed a great deal of religious literature, especially in the early years, there was a

---

[1] *Rhode Island Imprints, 1727-1800.* Not a strictly exact count; greater exactness would have favored the secular balance. Then too, many New England sermons were really political tracts.

wide acquaintance with secular literature imported from London.[1]   In 1760 a Boston bookseller advertised a list of books of which 26 could be classed as "religious" and 46 as "secular".   Ten years later another in the same city inventoried 8 of a religious nature and 41 that were listed under the secular classification.[2]

The shifting emphasis in reading material from generation to generation occurred frequently through the guidance of elders who had only met this secular literature as mature individuals, but were anxious to feed it very early to their younger contemporaries.   Samuel Johnson was about twenty when he came in contact with a wealth of such literature including Milton's " Paradise Lost " and Locke's " On the Human Understanding."   His son, William Samuel, knew this literature along with his religious reading, when only a young boy.   At the age of eight he had read " A History of the Lives of the Pirates ; " he was nine when he met " Robinson Crusoe " and the " History of Don Quixote," and fourteen when he reread Milton and Addison.   A year earlier he had gone through Voltaire's " History of Charles XII, King of Sweden," which his father, it seems, had as yet not read.[3]

The most familiar book to colonial children, the " New England Primer ", gave rise to a rival in the mid-century, with which it has frequently been confused, " The Royal Primer."   This Primer which came from Newbery, the children's bookmaker in London, writes a student, " represents the more liberal Anglican standpoint as contrasted with the rigid Puritanical background of the New England

---

[1] C. A. Herrick, *The Library*, 1918, pp. 1-18.

[2] Phillip Freeman, *Bos. Gaz. and Country Jour.*, Jan. 14, 1760; John Langdon, *ibid.*, Dec. 24, 1770.

[3] *Books read by Samuel Johnson from Year to Year since I left Yale College; Catalogue of Books read from Year to Year by Wm. Samuel Johnson.*

Primer." The difference between the two primers from a theological standpoint, he continues, is the " fact that youthful readers of the Royal Primer are promised as the result of the practise of virtue, a mundane and not a celestial reward," a general characteristic of Newbery's juvenile books, which were well known in the colonies. In contrast " with the austerities of the New England Primer," the " humanity, interest and diversity of the Royal Primer . . . . must have made a strong appeal to normal and healthy-minded children." First announced in Philadelphia, it secured an immediate popularity and the earliest American edition appeared in 1753. Three reprints were issued in Boston within five years, a competition which influenced the New England Primer and " to some extent humanized it." A Boston issue of the latter in 1781 contained verses, cuts, pictures of animals and a secular alphabet drawn directly from the Royal Primer.[1]

The education of youth generally, was compelling an abandonment of older ideas. In the " Noetica " which includes one of the first pleas for a better treatment of the child, Johnson wrote, " We ought to think little Children to be Persons of much more Importance than we usually apprehend them to be "; to be " indulgent . . . . to their inquisitive Curiosity; . . . with how much Candour, Patience and Care, we ought to bear with them and instruct them."[2] A Boston correspondent, the Rev. East Apthorp, forwarded to Johnson a comprehensive plan of education to prepare youths for college. After passing through

---

[1] This paragraph is based on " The Royal Primer," E. P. Merritt, in *Bibliog. Essays to W. Eames,* pp. 35-60.

[2] Johnson, *Elementa Philosophica,* . . . *Noetica* (Phila., 1752), p. 79, written years before Rousseau's *Emile* (1762), often supposed to be the earliest articulate recognition of the child as different from the adult.

nine years of this curriculum, the student at sixteen was ready to take up a program whose catholicity and secular emphasis probably placed it far in advance of most colleges of the early nineteenth century.[1] Others too, were discussing educational problems, for the " Pennsylvania Magazine or American Monthly Museum " ran a series of letters devoted mainly to the consideration of children, and written in a very liberal spirit.[2]

Readers of colonial newspapers were familiar with Addison, Pope and Swift, either directly or in imitation. These papers influenced one another. Bradford's " New York Gazette " looked to the " Boston News Letter " as a model.[3] Parker wrote Franklin he was intending to publish a " New York Chronicle " after the style of Goddard's paper. He did so but it lasted only a short time.[4] James Franklin's '" New England Courant " was patterned after Addison's " Spectator," and the " New England Weekly Journal " likewise had contributions influenced by Pope, Addison and also Milton. Benjamin Franklin's " Education of Youth in Pennsylvania " suggested instruction in English grammar by reading Addison, Pope, Algernon Sidney, etc. Franklin's earliest essays in Philadelphia were modeled after Addison, but his native contribution could not be submerged.[5]

In the various magazines published during the century, hardly any having any great life span, writers found an inter-colonial audience. Franklin, and Rogers and Fowle, were among the first with the " General Magazine " and " The American Magazine." The latter was said to compare favorably in execution with contemporary English periodi-

[1] *Johnson Papers,* June 20, 1760.
[2] Beginning in April issue, 1775.
[3] E. C. Cook, *Lit. Influences in Col. Newspapers,* p. 121.
[4] *Cal. of Franklin Papers,* vol. ii, March 29, 1769.
[5] Cook, pp. 15-18, 37-39, 58-64.

cals.[1] " The Christian History," intimately associated with the religious movement known as the " Great Awakening," begun in 1743, was the first to live beyond a few issues.[2] In the " American Magazine and Historical Chronicle," of Boston, sold also in New York and Philadelphia, was an account of the wonderful discoveries made in Germany and elsewhere, in electricity; in this and in the next volume were a description of electrical apparatus at Paris and a paper on the " Art of Acting." [3] " The American Magazine " published by William Bradford in Philadelphia 1757, was conducted by Provost William Smith with distinction.[4] Francis Alison wrote to his friend Ezra Stiles asking for literary and financial contributions to the magazine, suggesting " that it may promote a friendly intercourse among men of Learning in our different Colonies." [5] Francis Hopkinson contributed two poems to the November issue whose origins are obvious, " L'Allegro " and " Il Penseroso." To the December issue Professor Winthrop contributed a paper on the cause of earthquakes, in answer to a previous article.[6] " The New American Magazine " was edited by Sylvanus Americanus (Samuel Nevil) and carried contributions from New York, Philadelphia and Boston.[7] It printed an ode in

---

[1] Buckingham, *Specimens of Newspaper Literature*, vol. i, p. 158; Thomas, *Hist. of Printing*, vol. ii, p. 343; vol. i, p. 324.

[2] Wm. Beer, "Check List of Amer. Periodicals," *Amer. Ant. Soc. Proc.* 1922, p. 335.

[3] Vol. ii, p. 530, Oct. 1745; vol. iii, p. 461, vol. ii, pp. 548-549; *N. J. Archives,* ser. 1, vol. xii, Wm. Nelson, " Hist. of Amer. Newspapers," p. cxliii.

[4] A. H. Smyth, *Phila. Magazines and Their Contributors, 1741-1850* (Phila., 1892), p. 46.

[5] *Itineraries of Ezra Stiles,* Sept. 17, 1757; for subscribers in other colonies, Wallace, *Sketches of Col. Wm. Bradford,* pp. 65-70.

[6] Hastings, *Francis Hopkinson,* p. 100.

[7] 1758, sold in N. Y. and Phila.

Latin by a gentleman in New England to his friend in Boston. John Beveridge, who resided for five years in New England on terms of friendship with Jonathan Mayhew and others, and then became a professor of languages in the college at Philadelphia, was also a contributor of Latin verses.[1] A comparatively early romantic view of nature is seen in several of the verses. Another " American Magazine " (1769) which printed an article by David Colden on natural history, was edited and owned by Lewis Nicola, Philadelphia, a member of the American Philosophical Society, of which the publication was, in a sense, the mouthpiece.[2] The "Pennsylvania Magazine or American Monthly" under the " List of New Books," noted in a review, that Lord Chesterfield's " Letters to his Son " were being reprinted at New York.[3]

The native contributions to pure literature apart from those appearing in the magazines and newspapers were meagre; greater achievements were scored in the political essay. The poems of Nathaniel Evans of Philadelphia were edited by Provost William Smith, and fifty copies were sent to New York.[4] In the former city, Francis Hopkinson published " Science, a Poem," which Rivington sold in his New York and Boston stores. Evidently it was fairly popular, for a third edition appeared from Hugh Gaine's press in New York.[5] When William Livingston wrote his " Philosophic Solitude; or the Choice of a Rural Life," his good friend Jared Ingersoll circulated a subscription paper at Yale, the poet's alma mater. Of about 110 students, 58

[1] Fisher, " Early Poets and Poetry of Pa.," *Hist. Soc. of Pa., Memoirs,* vol. ii, pp. 2, 80.

[2] Pp. 6-9; *Phila. Mag. and Their Contributors,* pp. 46, 47.

[3] Jan. 24, 1775, p. 40.

[4] E. P. Oberholtzer, *Literary Hist. of Phila.,* p. 72.

[5] Hastings, *Hopkinson,* pp. 83-85.

subscribed for 83 copies.[1]   The poem which had been published in New York was reprinted in Boston.[2]   Phyllis Wheatley (Peters), a slave girl in the Wheatley family, of the latter city wrote "An Elegiac Poem on the Death of Rev. George Whitefield," which was also published in New York and Philadelphia.[3]   Philip Freneau's poetry was known in Philadelphia and New York shortly before Mercy Warren's " The Group " appeared in the latter city and Boston.[4] Narratives of adventures with the Indians were always popular, and one published in Philadelphia in 1756 was immediately reprinted in Lancaster, New York and Boston.[5]

Importations were reprinted.   Frederick the Great of Prussia was a popular figure in the colonies through his alliance with England in the Seven Years War, which probably accounts for his poem " The Relaxation of War, or the Hero's Philosophy," being printed at New York and Phila-delphia in 1758.[6]   Two years later, the second edition of the " Life and Heroic Actions " of the Prussian King appeared in Boston.   Oliver Goldsmith's " Vicar of Wakefield " was reprinted in Philadelphia (1772) and sold by most of the booksellers of America.   " She Stoops to Conquer " was issued in Philadelphia and New York the next year.   The " Deserted Village " was reprinted in part in a New York newspaper, and the " Irish Widow " by David Garrick, came from one New York and three Philadelphia presses in 1773.[7]

---

[1] *Ingersoll Letters, loc. cit.*, pp 225-226 and note.

[2] Evans, 1762, no. 9160.

[3] *Ibid.*, 1770, nos. 11812-15.

[4] *Ibid.*, nos. 12397-98; Oscar Wegelin, *Early American Plays*, pp. 77-78.

[5] Evans, nos. 7658-62.

[6] Evans, 1758, nos. 8133-34.

[7] Fowle and Draper in *Boston Gaz. and Country Journal*, March 10, 1760; Evans, 12405, 12794-95; *N. Y. Journal*, Nov. 1, 1770; Evans, 12780.

The private libraries and the booksellers' stores indicate a diversity of interests. Bradford's store in Philadelphia, had between 1765 and 1769, a wide selection in history, biography, "general and elegant literature," Greek and Roman classics, jurisprudence, medicine, voyages and travels, architecture, gardening, grammars, and in much smaller number than in earlier years, books on theology.[1] " General and elegant literature " included novels of a distinctly sensational interest; memoirs of virtuous ladies confronted with villainous intentions were sold in such abundance as to wring a cry of protest strangely similar to modern compositions. One complaint ran:

When one reflects how easy . . . it is to give a wrong bias to the minds of youth, it is impossible to help being astonished at the remissness of those parents and guardians who suffer their daughters and wards to read indiscriminately the multiplicity of novels which are daily published. Novels not only pollute the imaginations of young women, but likewise give them false ideas of life.[2]

The Boston readers who bought books at an auction attended by Dr. Alexander Hamilton were especially interested in this type of literature.[3] Franklin's advertisements of books represent a wide array of secular literature; Rabelais, Locke's " On the Human Understanding," Bacon, Congreve's " Works," are some of the titles. His own private library reveals a remarkable breadth, wandering into all the fields of human knowledge.[4]

Phillip Freeman in Boston had for sale Milton's " Paradise Lost," Smollett's "History of England" and many other

[1] Wallace, *An Old Philadelphian, Col. Wm. Bradford,* pp. 90-93.

[2] *Pa. Packet and Gen'l Advertiser,* supplement, Sept. 13, 1773.

[3] *Itinerarium,* p. 137.

[4] Cook, *Lit. Inf. in Col. Newspapers,* pp. 113-115; G. S. Eddy, " The Franklin Library ", *Am. Ant. Soc. Proc.,* Oct. 1924, pp. 206-226.

books of geography, travel and medicine, with some on religion. Gray's "Elegy in a Country Churchyard" was advertised by another.[1] Lewis Morris, a governor of New Jersey and well known in New York, sent to England for his books, including Milton's "Works," in a two-volume edition.[2] The English poet was known to America in the beautiful issues of John Baskerville, the English printer. Henry Pelham, a Boston artist, made a gift of the two volumes printed in 1759 to Miss Sally Bromfield.[3] Samuel Loudon in New York imported a Baskerville folio Bible with cuts,[4] and in the same province several Baskervilles were owned by Samuel Provost, a King's College graduate and early bibliophile. Milton was in the Harvard library; and in Philadelphia, Robert Bell had printed the poet's "An old looking glass for the laity and Clergy of all denominations."[5]

Franklin was accustomed to make presentations of books. A gift copy of "Cato Major" from his press was inscribed to President Clap of Yale. Professor Winthrop was the recipient of Franklin's "Some thoughts on Education," and his "Account of the new invented Pennsylvania Fireplaces."[6] He sent books to Samuel Johnson in his home at Stratford, Connecticut.[7] Sometimes Franklin was presented with books in return, as when among many others, he received a compilation of "Devotional Offices" from Robert

[1] *Bos. Gaz. and Country Journal*, Jan. 14, 1760; Nov. 23, 1772.

[2] *N. J. Hist. Soc. Coll.*, vol. iv, 47, letter to John Clarke, May 25, 1739.

[3] D. R. Slade, "Henry Pelham," *Col. Soc. Mass., Trans.*, v, p. 199.

[4] *N. Y. Gaz. and Weekly Mercury*, Jan. 18, 1773.

[5] "King's College Alumni," *Col. Univ. Quar.*, Sept., 1907, pp. 479-480; *Mass. His. Soc. Proc.*, ser. 3, vol. ii, p. 154 *et seq.*

[6] *Am. Ant. Soc. Proc.*, Oct., 1924, p. 178.

[7] Bancroft's *Transcripts of Samuel and W. S. Johnson's Letters*, 1737-1769.

Elliston, comptroller of the customs in New York.[1] Franklin's advice on books and bookselling was frequently sought. A Miss Hubbart of Boston enclosed a catalog of her father's library, and wrote that the books were not to be sold until Franklin decided whether he wanted any or all of them.[2] He and Colden corresponded about books and prices; the latter thought of setting up a son in the business in New York.[3] Colden's " Indian History," a second issue, was printed in London by Thomas Osborne, who was anxious to send some copies to New York, Boston and Charlestown. S. C. Fifty copies were sent to James Read at Philadelphia, which were taken over by Franklin, who felt that he could distribute them more easily.   Franklin wrote that the " History " was an instructive and well written book and " must be exceedingly useful to all those Colonies who have anything to do with Indian Affairs."   He sent Colden a copy in which Osborne had inserted the charters etc., of Pennsylvania.[4]   Gov. Thomas Hutchinson's " History of Massachusetts Bay " was soon known to the southward, where William Franklin wrote from New Jersey to his father that he had just received it from New York.   Thomas Prince's " Chronological History of New England " had distant subscribers; Constant King who settled on Long Island was down for three copies, the Rev. Ebenezer Pemberton of New York and Jonas Green of Philadelphia were also purchasers.[5]

To lend a book in the eighteenth century seemed to be attended with as much risk as accompanies such an offer in the twentieth.   John Pintard, a prominent citizen placed a notice in a New York paper of the books that were to be

[1] *Col. Soc. Mass., Trans.,* vol. xxiv, pp. 71-80.

[2] *Cal. of Franklin Papers,* vol. ii, Feb. 16, 1756.

[3] *Colden Papers,* vol. vii, pp. 344-346; vol. iv, pp. 64-66.

[4] *Ibid.,* vol. iii, pp. 369-370, 402-403, 424-425; vol. iv, pp. 6, 78-80.

[5] *N. J. Hist. Soc. Proc.,* vol. i, p. 107, Oct. 23, 1767; *New Eng. Hist. and Genea. Reg.,* vol. vi, pp. 193-196.

returned to him. But already were functioning, or soon to function, libraries throughout the colonies for the convenience of the public. They were not really free, but were subscription affairs supported by a permanent membership, or else by borrower's fees, in the manner of some modern systems.[1]

Capt. Robert Keayne began the public Boston library in 1656 which lasted to its latest fire in mid-eighteenth century. The Library Company of Philadelphia was an outgrowth of Franklin's group called the " Junto," organized there in his early years. The minutes of the meetings in 1774 stated that visiting members of the Continental Congress might borrow books. The Library Society in Charlestown, South Carolina, was contemporaneous with the Philadelphia group.[2] A complete plan for a subscription library was forwarded by Franklin to Thomas Hancock, a wealthy Boston merchant, and although nothing materialized the suggestion probably influenced John Hancock, nephew and heir of Thomas, to donate later to Harvard a collection of over one thousand volumes largely gathered abroad.[3] Franklin himself made many contributions to the Harvard and Yale libraries, as well as to the Library Company in Philadelphia and to the college there. In 1774 he sent Harvard a French translation of his philosophical works.[4] Forty years before, a library

[1] *N. Y. Gaz. revived in the Weekly Post-Boy*, Nov. 2, 1747, *Devoe's Index;* about the same time Englishmen began to form societies to purchase books, and even the industrial classes had their reading clubs; Buckle, *op. cit.,* vol. i, p. 433.

[2] *Col. Soc. of Mass., Trans.,* vol. xii, " Old Boston Public Library 1656-1747 "; G. M. Abbot, *Short History of the Library Company of Philadelphia* (Phila., 1913) ; McCrady, *op. cit.,* p. 510.

[3] *Mass. Hist. Soc. Proc.,* i, vol. vi, pp. 354-356; Brown, *John Hancock, His Book,* pp. 92-93.

[4] A. C. Potter, *The Library of Harvard University; descriptive and historical notes* (Cambridge, 1915, *Bibliog. Contrib.,* 55), p. 27; Oswald, *Franklin, Printer,* p. 224; *Franklin, Calendar of Papers,* vol. ii, p. 161.

was founded in New York under the inspiration of the S. P. G., but controlled by the city, from which clergy and gentlemen of the neighboring provinces might borrow books. Like many libraries ancient and modern, it led a quiet existence.[1]

The New York Society Library, organized by local gentlemen with intercolonial affiliations, and still operating, opened its doors in 1754, a fact of interest to Philadelphia.[2] The library and King's College, founded the same year, had intimate associations. The college library was enlarged by gifts from abroad and at home; from England came the large collection of a Dr. Bristowe and a valuable gift from Oxford.[3] On the fly leaf of a copy of Hutchinson's " History of Massachusetts Bay " in the Columbia University library, is inscribed " The Gift of the Revd. Mr. Jeremy Condy, of Boston . . . . Nov[r] 1766." That the library had more than local recognition is shown by the preface to a " Catalogue of the Juliana Library Company of Lancaster," which took note of the King's College collections and its " elegant Building." [4]   New York also had a Union Library Society which boasted one thousand volumes and one hundred and forty members.[5]

The colonists undoubtedly got their idea of circulating libraries from London, where they had been set up by the middle of the eighteenth century.   As early as 1754 David Rittenhouse and Thomas Barton, a tutor in the Phila-

---

[1] A. B. Keep, *History of the New York Society Library* (N. Y., 1908), p. 66.

[2] *Penn. Gaz.*, April 11, 1754.

[3] W. A. Duer, *The Life of William Alexander, Earl of Stirling* (N. Y., 1847), p. 64, note.

[4] Condy was a pastor of the First Baptist Church. Keep, " Library of King's College ", *Col. Univ. Quarterly*, June 1911, p. 280; C. I. Landis, " Juliana Library Company in Lancaster ", *Pa. Mag. of Hist. and Biog.*, vol. 43.

[5] *N. Y. Journal or General Advertiser*, Jan. 14, 1773, *Devoe's Index*.

delphia college, had opened a circulating library in Norriton.
Garrat Noel, the New York bookseller, had such a library in
1763, which lasted for two years.[1]   In the latter year John
Mein, at the request of a number of Bostonians, established
a circulating library of twelve hundred volumes, whose catalog is still in existence.[2]   His example was followed in
Philadelphia by Lewis Nicola and Thomas Bradford, whence
Goddard carried the idea to Baltimore.   " Between 1745
and 1763," writes J. T. Adams, " there were no less than
seventeen (subscription libraries) founded . . . . in small
villages " as well as in large towns.[3]

The increasing interest in secular matters may be traced
in the subjects chosen for master's degrees at Harvard.   A
recent tabulation by Professor E. J. Young of subjects debated in the negative or the affirmative exhibits some interesting information, at least as to what the respective candidates
were thinking about.   There may be a question as to the
justice of Young's classification, but it seems sufficiently
accurate to warrant drawing some conclusions.[4]

Up to 1740, sixteen papers were offered on " Society and
the State," while from 1740 to 1772, a period less than one
half as long, there were thirty-eight on this topic.   Of
questions relating to " Philosophy " there were nineteen up to
1740 and ten from this date to 1781.   In 1690, Descartes' influence is seen in the affirmative of the question, " Is doubt

---

[1] Babb, " David Rittenhouse," *loc. cit.*, p. 597; *N. Y. Gaz.*, June 20,
1763, *Devoe's Index;* Keep, *op. cit.*, p. 101, *et seq.*, for circulating libraries
in N. Y.

[2] Justin Winsor, *The Memorial History of Boston* (Boston, 1880-81),
vol. ii, p. 433; Evans, 10069.

[3] *Pa. Mag. of Hist. and Biog.*, vol. xlii, pp. 213-216; Evans, *Amer.
Bibliog.*, vol. iv, preface x; *Provincial Society,* p. 305, with list of
libraries.

[4] " Subjects for Master's Degrees at Harvard, 1655-1791," *Mass. Hist.
Soc. Proc.*, 1, vol. xviii.

the beginning of all indubitable philosophy?" In the earlier period there were seventeen offerings on "Science," many however with an unscientific approach. From 1740 to 1773, there were nineteen on this subject. "Physiology and Medicine" were of absorbing interest to eighteenth-century folk. To 1740 nineteen candidates offered these subjects but from 1740 to 1791 there were thirty-seven. The chronology shows what is probably a more scientific viewpoint. "Is there a universal remedy?" was argued in the affirmative in 1698, and in the negative in 1761. In an age when insanity was widely thought to be a divine affliction, it is worth while noting that in 1770 the negative of the question, "Does insanity exist without bodily disease?" was proposed. There are references again to the influence of bodily organs on intelligence in 1773 and in 1786.

There were seven questions in each period on "Law." "Ethics" attracted a large number of students, forty-seven to 1740 and thirty-two from thence to 1787. An early discussion of capital punishment took the negative of "Is capital punishment as effective in deterring men from crime as sentence to hard labor for life?" John Adams quoted from Beccaria's "On Crimes and Punishments," in his effective legal defense of the British soldiers on trial for their part in the Boston massacre.[1] Not all those included in the list of theses grouped by Young under "Scriptures," of which there were eighteen to 1740 and fifteen from 1740 to 1773, were really "Religious;" "Has the confusion of tongues been a curse to the human race?" was argued affirmatively twice. There were twenty-three questions on the "Church and the Ministry" between 1700 and 1740, and twenty in the next forty years. They included an interesting reversal of judgments. In 1730 it was denied that "Organs excite a devotional spirit" in divine worship, whereas in 1762 the

[1] *Works*, vol. ii, p. 238, note 1.

positive view was given in the question, " Does music promote salvation? " In nearby Salem a few years later, a
pamphlet appeared upholding the " lawfulness and advantages
of instrumental music in the public worship of God." [1] The
decline in number of those questions cataloged under " Theology " most certainly indicates the growing secularization of
thought. From 1668 to 1740 there were seventy-two; in the
remaining period there were but twenty, and the advancing
years bear witness to a progressively increasing enlightenment. There was, wrote Professor Young, who classified
the essays, " a larger spirit of tolerance and catholicity in the
religious questions that were propounded. Even when the
doctrine remained unchanged, theological asperities were
softened."

The secularization of American life may be noted by the
shifting interest in professional callings and vocations generally. Of the Harvard graduates between 1706 and 1728
about one-half became ministers. Over one-half of the Yale
graduates between 1701 and 1745 selected the ministry, but
the proportion steadily diminished until less than one-third
entered this field in the years 1763-1778. [2] On the other hand,
while only 8.7 per cent of the early Yale graduates became
lawyers, 32.6 per cent of the later students, 1778-1791, took
to law. A distracted parent complained to Dr. Johnson that
his son preferred the law and refused to follow the paternal
command to study for the ministry. The King's College
president expressed his sympathy, writing of his own son who
had turned to law; but he wisely added, " Scarce any ever
succeed well in a calling they do not like, . . . therefore it

---

[1] Felt, *Annals of Salem* (ed., 1827), p. 480.

[2] W. B. Bailey, " Statistical Study of Yale Graduates," *Yale Review,*
vol. xvi, pp. 407, 409; Dexter, *Yale Biog. and Annals, 1763-1778,* p. 715;
S. A. Eliot, *A Sketch of the History of Harvard College and of its Present State* (Boston, 1848).

is best to let every one . . . . judge for himself." [1]   The Yale students who adopted teaching and medicine showed a decided increase, while the number who chose farming remained fairly constant.   An interesting comparison showed that over one-half the graduates who chose law or trade followed in their fathers' footsteps, whereas only about four-tenths followed their fathers in the ministry and but one-fourth in agriculture.

Of a group of Princeton graduates between 1751 and 1771 having some intercolonial contacts, at least nine became lawyers, about six went into the ministry, five became doctors and a few merchants.   King's College graduates selected a wide range of vocations and avocations.   Four went into the administrative service, one became a doctor, another ran a military school, seven were merchants who mingled in politics with the five gentlemen land-owners, nine chose the ministry and twelve became lawyers, including the distinguished John Jay, Robert R. Livingston and Peter Van Schaack.[2]

Although theological influences extended markedly into the nineteenth century and are yet with us, their position as dominating factors in human society was already being seriously questioned in the early decades of the eighteenth. Greater familiarity with the European rationalists served to weaken orthodox theology, and at the same time prompted a search for less miraculous explanations of natural phenomena.   Stripped somewhat of fearful characteristics, God became to many a gentler, more humane and lovable figure, and strong emphasis was now placed upon good works, which

---

[1] *Johnson Papers*, letter from Edward Antill (1762?).

[2] Alexander, *Princeton College during the Eighteenth Century*; L. M. Fuld, " Graduates from 1758-1769 ", *Col. Univ. Quarterly*, Sept. 1907, Dec. 1907, June and Sept. 1908, March and June, 1910.

resulted in the establishment of many benevolent institutions. Progressive personalities here and there were battling for a more unfettered expression of opinion, and the tide of publications favored their cause.   As the century aged, an ever larger group was accumulating the wherewithal to buy and read books, whose secular character became increasingly noticeable.   Surely it would be uncritical to overemphasize this colonial activity, yet to minimize it as has frequently been done, is equally unwise.   This comparatively small group, whose members treasured one another's support in unconventional speculations, was gradually being enlarged.   Within a short time the impact of this newer thought shook to its foundations well established religious structures like the Puritan churches of New England, and suggested new paths for the American intellect.

CHAPTER X

A New Nation In Embryo

Samuel Johnson's son, William S., who turned to law, was only one of many who, by their choice, indicated the stronger attraction of this profession over that of the ministry for the youth of America. This group which was rapidly growing in number after the turn of the half century, was to be a powerful influence, in conjunction with the merchants, in local and intercolonial politics in the succeeding years. The low esteem in which lawyers were held in the early colonial period is well known. This antagonism lasted well into the eighteenth century when ministers as well as merchants continued to qualify as attorneys, and judges were still chosen without legal training. Not until higher standards began to prevail within the profession itself, whose members were yearly increasing because of the expansion of American business, did lawyers begin to play a significant part in community life. These higher standards were the result of the return of young colonials educated in the London Inns of Court, and the efforts of local groups to reform themselves as described, for instance, by John Adams in Massachusetts.

In the case of the lawyers, as in that of the doctors and merchants, a group consciousness quickly asserted itself, and local organizations were formed whose members were well acquainted with their professional contemporaries in other colonies. The Rhode Island lawyers signed a " Bar Compact of 1745 " which regulated practise and fixed fees.[1] The

[1] Wilkins Updike, *Memoirs of the Rhode Island Bar*, pp. 294-295.

New York group, although small at first, was well known elsewhere, for it included the names of William Smith, the elder, and James Alexander who formed the local "Bar Association" in 1748.[1] Less than twenty years later "The Sodality" met in Boston to discuss legal topics, and in 1770 "The Moot" was founded in New York for a similar purpose.[2] The latter group permitted the introduction of non-resident "Gentlemen of the Law" as visitors; less formal organizations of lawyers in other provinces as well, date from the same period.[3]

The common background of legal training, both abroad and at home, must have promoted a sympathetic understanding among many members of the bar. "Coke on Littleton," "was the universal elementary book of law students," wrote Thomas Jefferson, and he added, "a sounder Whig never wrote." Blackstone's "Commentaries," which were thought to have encouraged Loyalism, had a tremendous sale in America; a thousand imported copies of the English edition were succeeded by an advance sale of 1400 copies of the American edition (1771-1772), which found their way to booksellers and private subscribers throughout the colonies. Many laymen were interested, for there were probably no more than a few hundred lawyers in all the colonies at the time. A leading English bookseller told Edmund Burke that "in no branch of his business, after tracts of popular devotion, were so many books as those of the law exported to the plantations," and it was said that the American colonies bought nearly as many copies of the "Commentaries" as England herself. Blackstone's work was of great significance, writes Warren, for it

[1] Charles Warren, *A History of the American Bar* (Boston, 1911), p. 98.

[2] Adams, *Works,* vol. ii, p. 146; *Copy of Moot Cases* (N. Y. H. S.).

[3] E. Q. Keasbey, *The Courts and Lawyers of New Jersey, 1661-1912* (N. Y., 1912), vol. i, p. 370.

opened the eyes of American scholars to the broader field of learning in the law. [It] taught them, for the first time, the continuity, the unity, and the reason of the Common Law and just at a time when the need of a unified system both in law and politics was beginning to be felt in the colonies.[1]

Throughout the century, Americans attended the London Inns of Court, but they were more numerous in the period from 1750 to 1775. Here many young men from various sections of the American colonies went through the same training and sometimes studied together.[2] Living mainly with Whig families whose political ideas stimulated their own thinking, these Americans at the Inns of Court formed the habit "of solving all legal questions by the standards of English liberties and of rights of the English subject," a valuable practise for many who returned to take leading parts in the Revolutionary controversies.[3] Among the earlier group of lawyers educated in England, were three who came to the defense of John Peter Zenger, the New York printer, in the famous trial for libel; Andrew Hamilton, James Alexander and William Smith had all learned their law at Gray's Inn.[4] The New England lawyers seem to have known one another quite intimately; following the circuit meant that many opportunities were presented for personal contacts, and in the second volume of John Adams' "Works," we can see how an inquisitive mind kept posted on the progress of his profession, locally and distantly. In a letter to his wife Abigail, Adams pointed out the speed with which lawyers outside of Boston were accumulating

[1] Warren, pp. 174-180.

[2] E. Alfred Jones, *American Members of the Inns of Court* (London, 1924) ; C. E. A. Bedwell, "American Middle Templars", *Amer. Hist. Rev.*, vol. 25, pp. 680-689.

[3] Warren, p. 188.

[4] Jones, *op. cit.*

wealth, frequently by real estate speculation.[1]   On an earlier
occasion, Robert Auchmuty, a leader of the Boston bar, at
one of its meetings had " railed about the lowness of the
fees."   " In Jamaica, Barbadoes, South Carolina and New
York," he said, " a lawyer will make an independent fortune
in ten years." [2]

In more direct ways lawyers developed intercolonial connections.   Andrew Hamilton, the hero of the Zenger trial,
was employed in several colonies and provincial governors
often sought his advice.[3]   James Alexander, who had been
associated in practise with Hamilton before the trial, was,
with William Smith, a member of both the Philadelphia and
New York bars.[4]   John Read, with a great reputation in his
own day, had a practise which took him through nearly all
of New England, and his name was not unknown in the
middle colonies.[5]   In the latter territory, Richard Stockton,
a New Jersey signer of the Declaration of Independence, had
a flourishing practice.[6]

At a time when a sound legal education could often
be obtained only by apprenticeship in the offices of noted
lawyers, individuals like Stockton and Judge Trowbridge
in Massachusetts were frequently the teachers of youngsters who traveled from other provinces for instruction.[7]
Sometimes lawyers turned cases over to local practition-

[1] *Familiar Letters of John Adams and His Wife, Abigail Adams,* June
29, 1774.

[2] Adams, *Works*, vol. ii, p. 197.

[3] F. M. Eastman, *Courts and Lawyers of Pennsylvania, A History*
(N. Y., 1922), vol. i, pp. 252-253.

[4] J. H. Martin, *Martin's Bench and Bar of Philadelphia* (Philadelphia,
1883), pp. 244, 313; Livingston Rutherford, *J. P. Zenger,* pp. 57-59.

[5] W. A. Beers, " John Read, the Colonial Lawyer," *Fairfield Co.
Hist. Soc.* (1886).

[6] W. A. Whitehead, " Memoir," *N. J. Hist. Soc. Proc.*, sec. ser., vol. iv.

[7] Warren, p. 114; Updike, pp. 82-83.

ers, when the distance from the scene of action made it
inexpedient to involve themselves, as when William Livingston asked Ingersoll to start legal action against a debtor in
Connecticut.[1] John Taber Kempe in New York had
clients in Philadelphia, and Jared Ingersoll, when he made his
headquarters in the Quaker capital as Judge of the Vice-
Admiralty Court, kept in close touch with his New Haven
office now being conducted by his nephew.[2] Benjamin Pratt
and John Gardner, both originally of Boston, became Chief
Justices of New York where their reputations had preceded
them.[3] Intercolonial legal actions were becoming fairly frequent, and the settlement of the estates of deceased individuals was often entrusted to executors located in different
cities. A Philadelphia correspondent wrote to Kempe that
he was carrying on several actions against " sundry persons
in New York," a process that was reversed when the Van
Cortlandts asked their associates in the former city to institute a suit against an agent whose bill was long overdue.[4]
In the year 1761, twenty-six suits for debts were brought
against inhabitants of New Haven by parties in New York,
Massachusetts, Pennsylvania, and New Jersey.[5]

The lawyers rapidly became an important force in local
and intercolonial politics. The " triumvirate " in New York,
William Livingston, John Morin Scott and William Smith
the younger, were very active against the spread of Anglican
influence, especially in education.[6] With the merchants,

[1] *Ingersoll Letters*, May 26, 1762.

[2] *J. T. Kempe, Papers;* L. H. Gipson, *Jared Ingersoll.*

[3] *Colden Letter Books*, vol. i, pp. 154-155; Emory Washburn, *Judicial
History of Massachusetts, 1630-1775* (Boston, 1840), pp. 225-226.

[4] George Spencer to Kempe, Aug. 23, 1765, *Papers;* "Abstracts of
Wills," *N. Y. H. S. Coll.,* vols. iv, v, vi, vii, *John and Stephen Van
Cortlandt Letter Book, 1771-1792,* to Taylor and Willing, Nov. 9, 1772.

[5] Gipson, *Ingersoll*, pp. 252-253.

[6] *Independent Reflector*, N. Y., 1752.

doctors and ministers, the lawyers assisted the development of the colleges during this period. Over half the delegates to the Albany Congress in 1754 were lawyers; about the same proportion attended the Stamp Act Congress in 1765 and the Continental Congress nine years later. In the many intercolonial conferences to discuss questions of defense against the French and trade with the Indians, and in the congresses which preceded that of 1774, many individuals met to examine matters of common interest. In the correspondence of a man like Governor William Shirley of Massachusetts, one can see how these questions were agitating minds with an imperial outlook, and the intercolonial contacts which resulted from an effort to solve these problems smoothed the way for cooperation among loyalist or radical groups in later years.[1]

Historians have too often stressed the fact that participants in these meetings were previously unknown to one another, and even contemporaries like John Adams were sometimes unaware of the ties that held some of them together.[2] Many of the commissioners who attended the Albany Congress had intercolonial associations of one kind or another. The Pennsylvania group included Benjamin Franklin who was known everywhere, and Isaac Norris, a wealthy merchant in Philadelphia, whose business kept him in touch with affairs beyond his provincial boundaries. Nine years earlier he had been one of the commissioners to treat with the Indians at Albany.[3] Three of the New Hampshire representatives were Harvard graduates,[4] and every one of

[1] C. H. Lincoln, *The Correspondence of William Shirley* (N. Y., 1912).

[2] *Familiar Letters*, Sept. 25, 1774.

[3] *The Nat. Cyc. of Amer. Biog.* (1893-1926), vol. v, p. 88.

[4] Theodore Atkinson (1718), Richard Wibird (1722), Meshech Weare (1735).

New York's delegation was known beyond the local limits.[1] All of the Massachusetts members had Connecticut associations; John Chandler was born there, and had been employed as surveyor to run a boundary line between his native colony and Massachusetts, his adopted home, where he took an active part in politics; [2] Oliver Partridge, John Worthington and Samuel Welles, a correspondent of Cadwallader Colden, were Yale graduates.[3] From Rhode Island, came Stephen Hopkins, who had previously attended an Albany meeting in 1746, and for whom a long political career lay ahead.[4] Connecticut sent three men who, through one or more channels, were known outside their colony.[5] It is important to note these relationships because in any discussions of colonial union, individuals who by their personal experiences had gained an intimacy with intercolonial affairs would naturally take leading parts.

The Stamp Act Congress of 1765 brought together lawyers and merchants from nine colonies, a number of whom had long been acquainted with one another, while some knew of each other indirectly. Philip Livingston of New York and Oliver Partridge of Massachusetts, besides having a common collegiate background at Yale, had attended the Albany Congress together. All the large merchants in Philadelphia and

[1] John Chambers and Wm. Smith (Yale 1719), connected with the Zenger case; Philip Livingston (Yale 1737) merchant; James De Lancey, through politics and social connections; Sir Wm. Johnson, Indian agent; Joseph Murray, a leader of the bar, had attended a conference in 1744.

[2] *Nat. Cyc. of Amer. Biog.*, vol. xiii, p. 557.

[3] Dexter, *Yale Biog. and Annals*, vol. i, p. 417; *Colden Papers*, vol. iii, pp. 267-268.

[4] S. G. Arnold, *History of the State of Rhode Island and Providence Plantations* (N. Y., 1859-1860), vol. ii, p. 152.

[5] William Pitkin, *Pitkin Papers, Conn. Hist. Soc. Coll.*, vol. xix, p. xxiii; Roger Wolcott, *Papers, loc. cit.*, vol. xvi; Elisha Williams, Harvard, 1711, chaplain of Conn. forces to Louisburg 1745, *Nat. Cyc. of Amer. Biog.*, vol. i, p. 165.

New York were well known to each other. George Bryan, a Pennsylvania representative at the Congress had commercial relations with New York; John Dickinson, through family relationships in Massachusetts and New Jersey and his prominence as a lawyer, was another with interprovincial associations.[1]   The three New Jersey delegates were acquainted with New Yorkers and Philadelphians through common participation in building up the college at Princeton, or, as in the case of Joseph Borden, through a large transportation business which joined the two cities.[2]   Philip Livingston was at Yale with Eliphalet Dyer, who represented Connecticut, whence also came William Samuel Johnson (Yale 1744), a familiar figure in New York.   From South Carolina came Christopher Gadsden, who at one time had worked in Philadelphia as a clerk.[3]   Thomas McKean and Caesar Rodney from Delaware were very well known among the lawyers in Philadelphia, where the former resided in after years.[4]   The activity of James Otis against the writs of assistance, four years earlier, had given him an intercolonial reputation, and a fellow Massachusetts delegate, Timothy Ruggles, by participation in the conflicts with the French, had gained some knowledge of colonial cooperation.

The reputations of the leading members of the Continental Congress in 1774 were so widely extended that Stiles in his Newport diary, could list " The Cardinals of this Body or the men of greatest Abilities and Influence," with especial significance attaching to the names of Samuel Adams, Samuel

[1] B. A. Konkle, *George Bryan and the Constitution of Pennsylvania 1731-1791* (Phila., 1922) ; C. J. Stillé, *The Life and Times of John Dickinson 1732-1808* (Phila., 1891).

[2] Hendrick Fisher, *N. J. Archives*, ser. i, vol. xix, pp. 390-91, note; Robert Ogden, *loc. cit.*, vol. xxiv, p. 295.

[3] Gadsden, *Southern Hist. Assn. Pub.*, vol. ii.

[4] J. T. Scharf, *History of Delaware* (Phila., 1888), vol. i, p. 568.

Ward of Rhode Island, Peyton Randolph and Col. Richard Bland of Virginia, Gadsden and Edward Rutledge of South Carolina.[1] Eight members of this Congress had met before at the previous gathering in New York in 1765. Philip Livingston and Stephen Hopkins renewed an old acquaintance, for they had been at the Albany Congress twenty years earlier. Washington was well known through social contacts in many places, and also by his military career.[2] William Livingston represented New Jersey, but had many intimate ties with other colonies; at the Congress he met a fellow student from Yale, Eliphalet Dyer, delegate from Connecticut. Silas Deane, the latter's colleague, a lawyer and a merchant, was " intimately acquainted and closely connected with people at New York," wrote John Adams. A year before, the Pennsylvania delegate Thomas Mifflin was visiting relatives in Boston, where this " very sensible and agreeable man " became acquainted with the future Massachusetts representative John Adams, over the tea-cups. At another social gathering the next month, Adams met Thomas Lynch of South Carolina, " a hearty friend to America," whom he was soon to meet again at Philadelphia.[3] John Sullivan, the New Hampshire lawyer, was well known by the profession in New England, and his compatriot, Nathaniel Folsom, had been in the colonial militia during the French war twenty years before.[4]

In the Congress that met the next year, most of the old faces turned up and, although a few new ones were present, in nearly every instance they were men who had already learned to cooperate with one another. North Carolina sent

---

[1] *Diary*, vol. i, p. 459; Sept. 26, 1774.

[2] Stokes, p. 678, Feb. 15, 1756.

[3] Dexter, *Yale Biog. and Annals*, vol. i, pp. 644-47, 682-84; Adams, *Works*, vol. ii, pp. 341-42, 321, 323.

[4] Folsom, *New Hamp. Hist. Soc. Coll.*, vol. v, p. 217.

three individuals whose personal associations might easily stimulate an intercolonial interest. William Hooper (Harvard 1760) came from Boston where his sympathy was counted as an important asset; Hewes, born in New Jersey, was much concerned in his mercantile firm at Philadelphia, while Caswell's old home was in Maryland.[1] Franklin was again greeting old friends, including Stephen Hopkins and Philip Livingston, with whom he had attended the Albany Congress. The signers of the Declaration of Independence were either old friends and acquaintances, or men whose experiences had fitted them for cooperative activity. Among the less well-remembered signers was Lyman Hall of Georgia, a native of Connecticut, Yale 1747, and a temporary resident of South Carolina, which he left in company with the descendants of an earlier New England settlement for the colony which sent him to the Continental Congress. Roger Sherman was known outside of Connecticut through his almanacs and his Massachusetts family relationships, while his share in the Susquehanna Company for the development of property in Pennsylvania indicated an interest not limited by provincial boundaries.[2] The signatures of John Witherspoon from New Jersey and Benjamin Rush from Pennsylvania, were merely the political expressions of lives already associated in cooperative endeavor in education and medicine, with individuals throughout America. It would be tedious to press the point, but previous neglect of these intercolonial relationships with their political implications justifies attention to such details.

In addition to these meetings which were building up

[1] S. A. Ashe, *History of North Carolina* (Greensboro, N. C., 1908-1925), vol. i, p. 422; Josiah Quincy, *Memoir of the Life of Josiah Quincy Jun. of Massachusetts* (Boston, 1874), p. 392.

[2] John Sanderson, *Biographies of the Signers to the Declaration of Independence* (Phila., 1823-1827), vol. iii, pp. 52-56, 201 *et seq.*

groups of Loyalists or Revolutionaries, other forces were tending in the same direction. In the newspapers, then growing in number, the lawyers who were frequent contributors found ready organs for the expression of their views. Although having a comparatively small circulation, these newspapers were very important in the political controversies of the Revolutionary period. In times of popular excitement the speed with which news flew from town to town and was reprinted in the local sheets was truly amazing. A false report of a movement by the British troops in September, 1774, " flew like Lightning," wrote Ezra Stiles in his diary. " In . . . . five or six days the Alarm spread thro' above a Million of People." [1] The reforms in the Post Office which had been instituted by Franklin and Hunter increased intercolonial correspondence and the letters were frequently published in the local papers. The latter, writes a historian of American journalism, " were placed on a better subscription basis, and the exchange papers, being more regular in their receipt, not only improved the news service, but also aroused a news interest in what was going on in all the colonies." [2] Even though weak and halting,

early American journalism, [in the opinion of Moses Coit Tyler], began to lift the people of each colony to a plane somewhat higher than its own boundaries, and to enable them by looking abroad, . . . to correct the pettiness and the selfishness of mere localism in thought. Colonial journalism was a necessary and a great factor in the slow process of colonial union.[3]

The unanimity that prevailed among nearly all of the papers was strikingly exemplified during three crises. The

[1] *Diary,* vol. i, p. 485.

[2] J. M. Lee, *History of American Journalism,* p. 77.

[3] Tyler, *History of Amer. Lit.,* vol. ii, p. 304.

appeal for concerted action against the French in 1754 was enforced by a design of a snake in eight parts, the head of which was New England, while the other seven colonies, omitting Georgia, were the rest of the serpent. Underneath the snake was the legend " Join, or Die "; this device was reprinted in nearly all the colonial newspapers in connection with news of the Albany Congress, and was probably suggested by Franklin whose wide acquaintance among the printers, aside from the general interest of the topic itself, may have had something to do with the adoption of this slogan. In the excitement over the Stamp Act eleven years later, the " Constitutional Courant " appeared with the snake device. It was printed by William Goddard, a journalistic radical in New Jersey, circulated in New York by hawkers hired for the occasion, and probably reprinted in Boston and Philadelphia, in all of which places it gained a wide notoriety. The newspapers made a united stand against the Stamp Act, for not a single one appeared on stamped paper.[1] The union device did not appear again until June 1774, when John Holt's paper, the New York mouthpiece for the " Sons of Liberty " used it, and Georgia now formed the tail of the snake, with the motto " Unite or Die." Others followed Holt's lead, and a touch of originality was added by the " Massachusetts Spy " which adopted the design of a snake and dragon, the latter being Great Britain.[2]

In a less spectacular way, personal contacts among the colonists were also promoting a community feeling. It has already been observed that traveling became more frequent in the second half of the century, and the mutual enlightenment resulting from meetings on the road helped to clear

[1] Lee, *op. cit.*, pp. 83-84.

[2] Albert Mathews, " The Snake Devices " (1754-1776), *Col. Soc. of Mass., Trans.,* vol. xi; for Goddard, see Wroth, *A History of Printing in Colonial Maryland,* chap. x; Stokes, p. 649.

away existing prejudices. In one company on a trip to Cambridge, John Adams found Massachusetts men traveling with visitors from Virginia and South Carolina, who were " taking the Northern tour for their health." " The Virginia Gentleman," wrote the diarist, " are very full and zealous in the cause of American liberty." [1] Josiah Quincy Jr. made a tour through the colonies in 1773, beginning in South Carolina where he dined with political leaders. Passing through North Carolina, he met among others an old Boston neighbor, William Hooper; he went on to Philadelphia, where he had a letter of introduction to Joseph Reed. Reed wrote to Thomas Cushing of Boston that Quincy's travels were of great value;

His observations of the Provinces thro which he has passed ... his perfect knowledge of yours . . . and the intelligent, sensible accounts he gives us of your public affairs have opened a host of new scenes to us. Such men travelling through the different colonies, will admirably cement them in the common interests. The new and intimate intercourse which during his tour he had laboured to establish, [added Reed,] resulted in a correspondence with several . . . eminent men.[2]

George Clymer, a Pennsylvania signer of the Declaration of Independence, had visited Quincy in Boston, and by personal association had learned to know more intimately other political leaders. On Clymer's return to Philadelphia, Quincy wrote him a letter, observing that " a mutual exchange of sentiments will give us as men, a knowledge of each other; that knowledge naturally creates esteem, and that esteem will, in the end, cement us as colonists. As men, and as brethren then, in one common cause, let us think, converse, and act." [3] Looking forward to the approaching Congress,

[1] *Works*, vol. ii, pp. 249-250 (1770).
[2] *Joseph Reed Papers*, 1773; *Memoir of Josiah Quincy Jun.*, pp. 56-114.
[3] *Ibid.*, pp. 119-120.

John Adams thought of the opportunities it would provide to " see a little more of the world than I have seen before," and he later wrote to his wife, that he and his companions had formed " acquaintances with the most eminent and famous men in the several colonies we have passed through." [1]   Meeting with colonials of a similar mind at New York in the Stamp Act Congress resulted in a correspondence between Christopher Gadsden and Samuel Adams. Hooper, in the North Carolina delegation at a later gathering, wrote James Duane that personal contact with the New Yorkers had pleasantly surprised himself and others, so that many conventional notions respecting the northern province underwent a revision.[2]   This correspondence of a rather personal nature was, of course, only a part of the vast mass dealing more directly with the political controversies of the 1760's and 1770's.   The local committees in charge of this correspondence were usually composed of men who, like Dr. Thomas Young and Isaac Sears of the " Sons of Liberty," had through professional or trade channels, made the acquaintance of their compatriots in other colonies.[3]

Other straws indicated the direction of the winds of political doctrine.   Historians in greater number were taking for their subjects the whole range of colonial America. Ezra Stiles for many years corresponded with individuals in diverse places, collecting materials for an " Ecclesiastical History of New England & British America," which was never published.   John Comer, it will be remembered, was interested in a history of the Baptist churches wherever they were located.   Morgan Edwards wrote a " History of the

[1] *Familiar Letters*, July 6, Aug. 28, 1774.

[2] *Southern Hist. Assn. Pub.*, vol. ii, p. 249, note; *Duane Papers*, Nov. 22, 1774.

[3] " Memoir of Thomas Young," *Col. Soc. of Mass., Trans.*, vol. xi; Gipson, *Jared Ingersoll*, p. 342.

American Baptists " with which Stiles was acquainted.[1] A writer in a New York paper proposed to publish by subscription a work dealing with most of the American provinces.[2] Ames' almanac for the next year included " An account of the several Provinces in North America " which was copied and expanded by a New York almanac. Samuel Nevill began a history of North America in his " New American Magazine." To prepare a vast citizenry for participation in politics to the end that popular control might be insured, Nathaniel Ames recommended the study of geography and history, adding the true nationalistic note: " it is proper to begin with the history of your own nation." [3]

The trend of thought suggested by this historiography was further emphasized when, as a recent writer says, perhaps a little too confidently,

Americans began to feel that their mother tongue was something near and intimate, the speech which gave to them a unity upon their own American soil. The special history of American English as something consciously separate and distinguishable began therefore, with the realization of the existence of an American nation.[4]

Though a more acute consciousness of the existence of differences in language between England and America did not come till later, it was noted long before the Revolution that New York had adopted New England tricks of speech, and an " American dialect " was already acknowledged.[5] A

[1] *Diary,* vol. i, p. 5; June 4, 1772, p. 241.

[2] *N. Y. Post-Boy,* May 5, 1755, Stokes, p. 668.

[3] Evans, no. 8939; Briggs, *Almanacs of Nathaniel Ames,* pp. 269-270, 381-383.

[4] G. P. Krapp, *The English Language in America* (N. Y., 1925), vol. i, p. 5.

[5] *Hamilton's Itinerarium,* p. xxii; H. P. Johnston, *The Correspondence and Public Papers of John Jay* (N. Y., 1890-93), vol. i, p. 4; Adams, *Provincial Society,* pp. 288-90.

magazine article addressed to the "Literati of America" asked for an "American Society of Language" with members in all the colleges, a subject in which John Adams was likewise interested.[1] At the same time this curiosity about themselves, which revealed a growing self-consciousness, was seen in the contemporary newspaper discussions of the origins of the word "Yankee."[2]

This feeling of expansiveness and self-sufficiency was expressed in a natural desire to see the control of colonial affairs lodged in the hands of natives. In the 1750's, one member in eight of the Connecticut General Assembly was a Yale graduate. In the early years of the next decade the proportion had increased to one in six.[3] These college graduates were looked upon as future political leaders; for, as Richard Stockton, the New Jersey lawyer, wrote to his pupil Joseph Reed, "after our Colleges shall have thrown into the lower Houses of Assembly men of more foresight and understanding than they now can boast of, perhaps the time may come" when great changes will occur.[4] Ambitious colonials were angered by the nepotism of some of the royal governors, and complained that they were discriminated against in political and military appointments.[5]

An irrepressible sense of growth not primarily connected with politics pervaded American life. Under date of Aug. 23, 1773, Stiles wrote, "We have an Account of above Seventeen Thousand Settlers embarked for America from Europe

---

[1] *Col. Soc. of Mass., Trans.,* vol. xiv, pp. 263-264.

[2] *Conn. Gaz. and Universal Intelligencer,* June 3, 1775; *Penn. Journal or Weekly Advertiser,* May 24, 1775; Stokes, p. 892, for *Va. Gaz.,* June 10, 1775.

[3] Dexter, *Yale Biog. and Annals, 1745-1763,* pp. 399, 780.

[4] *Reed Papers,* Oct. 8, 1764; see also Woods, *John Witherspoon,* pp. 148-149.

[5] McCrady, p. 538; Adams, *Works,* vol. ii, p. 151.

this year, chiefly from Ireland. A grand Accession this!"
The next day his attention was attracted to the wanderings
of the people nearer home. " I find by the Prints that
Settlements are making on the Mississippi with great Rapid-
ity." " The wilderness of America is all alive with the
Travels of Settlers." [1] Years earlier, plans had been drawn
for a combination of forces to encourage immigration.
Archibald Kennedy, receiver-general in New York, in his
plan of union for the colonies provided that joint payments
be made for the importation of immigrants. Franklin, who
knew of Kennedy's plan, included a provision for settling
new colonies in his own more famous document. He wrote,
" The power of settling new colonies is therefore thought a
valuable part of the plan, and what cannot so well be executed by two unions as by one." [2]

The American tradition of mechanical ingenuity and
" natural genius " had already been firmly established. A
correspondent wrote to Stiles, " I am convinced that America
abounds in Natural Genius as hardly a town but has its
Genius." [3] John Trumbull, the young Connecticut poet,
went even further in a commencement address at Yale when
he said " It is universally allowed that we excel in the force
of natural genius," adding, " perhaps there is no nation in
which a larger portion of learning is diffused through all
ranks of the people." [4] This interest in education and a
greater diffusion of knowledge resulted in the establishment
of Dartmouth College and agitation for such institutions in

---

[1] *Diary*, p. 409.

[2] Stokes, p. 625 (1751); A. H. Smyth, *The Writings of Benjamin
Franklin*, vol. iii, pp. 219-220.

[3] *Itineraries and Corr. of Ezra Stiles*, from John Devotion, April 22,
1767.

[4] M. C. Tyler, *The Literary History of the American Revolution*, 1763-
1783 (stud. ed., N. Y., 1897), vol. i, pp. 208-209.

Georgia, South Carolina, North Carolina, and for a second college in Rhode Island; " College Enthusiasm," wrote Stiles in his diary, was contagious, spreading through all the land.[1]

A long tradition had stimulated colonial ideas of imperial grandeur. Long before Bishop Berkeley, the sentiment that the course of empire was taking its way westward had found expression. An invitation to settle in the new world promised that

> . . . Virginia may in time,
> Be made like England now;
> Where long-lov'd peace and plenty both
> Sits smiling on her brow.[2]

Sir Thomas Browne had spoken of the time

> When the new world shall the old invade,
> Nor count them their lords, but their fellows in trade.

A local " booster " had prophesied great things for the Pennsylvania capital when it was yet a small town in 1730.

> Europe shall mourn her ancient fame declined,
> And Philadelphia be the Athens of Mankind.[3]

In the almanacs of Nathaniel Ames, which it will be remembered were widely circulated, this ebullient sentiment was frequently uttered, but never so extravagantly as in his issue for 1758.

The Curious have observ'd, that the Progress of Humane Literature (like the Sun) is from the East to the West; thus has it

---

[1] *Diary*, April 5, 1770.

[2] C. H. Firth, ed., *An American Garland; Being a Collection of Ballads relating to America 1563-1759* (Oxford, 1915), p. xxiii.

[3] Richard Frothingham, *The Rise of the Republic of the United States* (Boston, 1872), pp. 99-100; Tyler, *History of Amer. Lit.*, vol. ii, p. 239.

travell'd thro' Asia and Europe, and now is arrived at the Eastern Shore of America. . . . Arts and Sciences will change the
Face of Nature in their Tour from Hence over the Appalachian
Mountains to the Western Ocean; And as they march thro' the
vast Desert the Residence of Wild Beasts will be broken up . . .
and the inestimable Treasures of Gold & Silver (will) be broken
up. Huge Mountains of Iron Ore are already discovered; and
vast Stores are reserved for future Generations; This metal
more useful than Gold and Silver, will imploy Millions of
Hands, not only to form the martial Sword and peaceful Share
alternately, but an Infinity of Utensils improved in the Exercise of Art, and Handicraft amongst Men. Stone from the
vast quarries will be piled into great Cities. O! Ye unborn
Inhabitants of America, [Ames concluded with a dramatic burst
of language], When your Eyes behold the Sun after he has
rolled the Seasons round for two or three Centuries more, you
will know that in Anno Domini 1758, we dream'd of your
Times.[1]

Radicals and conservatives alike felt the surge of this life.
William Smith Jr., who took the Loyalist side at the outbreak of military hostilities, had written a few years before:
" What a disjointed Empire is this! I am afraid it is too
complex for so vast an Extent. At all Events America
must rise." [2]

Often during this decade and the following years, leaders
in colonial life and obscure students in college orations were
to pen similar phrases, or enchant commencement audiences
with glowing pictures of the present and future greatness of
America. Orators were to break down colonial barriers
with fervent phrases. Gadsden swept them away at the
Stamp Act Congress: " There ought to be no New England
man; no New Yorker, known on the Continent; but all of

---

[1] Briggs, pp. 285-286.
[2] *Schuyler Papers*, May 17, 1767.

us Americans," a sentiment echoed by Patrick Henry ten years later. " I am not a Virginian," he said, " but an American." [1] Thus rhetoric was creating a fictitious maturity for an embryonic state; but in more sober ways, these same individuals, who had come to grips with the realities of intercolonial life in all its varied aspects, were painfully and haltingly, yet more surely, laying the foundations of a new nation.

[1] Frothingham, p. 188; Adams, *Works*, vol. ii, p. 367.

LIST OF AUTHORITIES

A much wider range of authorities was consulted but for the most part, only those actually cited in the text are listed. I have divided the list into those authorities which have proved useful generally, and those which had a more restricted use.

MANUSCRIPT MATERIALS

Bancroft Transcripts, Andrew Eliot, Jonathan Mayhew, Thomas Hollis, Correspondence 1761-1776. New York Public Library.

Bancroft Transcripts of Samuel and William S. Johnson letters.

Gerard Beekman Letter Book, New York Historical Society; valuable for intercolonial business and commerce.

Dirck Brinckerhoff Papers 1765-1768, Tomlinson collection. (N. Y. P. L.)

Chalmers Papers. (N. Y. P. L.)

Colden Scientific Correspondence. (N. Y. H. S.)

Thomas Dering, Journal, Boston, N. E., Customs office, N. Y.; for business.

Devoe's Index to Incidents in Newspapers to 1800 (N. Y. H. S.)

James Duane Papers (N. Y. H. S.) : indispensable for study of land speculation in New York; other interesting matter for politics, social relations, etc.

Record Book of James Emott, attorney and notary public, New York City, 1766-68. (N. Y. P. L.)

Forman Papers (N. Y. H. S.) : business relations between New York and New Jersey.

Gates Papers (N. Y. P. L.) : New York and Philadelphia relations.

Samuel Johnson Papers (Columbia University) ; academic and general cultural relations.

J. T. Kempe Papers (N. Y. H. S.) : legal relations, New York and Philadelphia.

Myers Collection; prominent civilians and officers in the colonial period. (N. Y. P. L.)

Joseph Reed Papers (N. Y. H. S.) : valuable for intercolonial references to land deals, politics, post office, etc.

Rutherford Papers (N. Y. H. S.) : real estate matter; other materials also included.

Schuyler Papers (N. Y. P. L.) ; miscellaneous matter.

Stirling Papers (N. Y. H. S.) ; for business and social affairs.
John Van Cortlandt Ledger, 1770-1792. (N. Y. P. L.)
John Van Cortlandt Letter Book, 1762-1769.
John and Stephen Von Cortlandt Letter Book, 1771-1792.
all three valuable for intercolonial business.
Wm. Walton's Book of Insurances (N. Y. Chamber of Commerce Library).
Wendell Family Papers (N. Y. P. L.) : New York and Massachusetts relations in land deals, etc.
H. C. Westervelt (N. Y. P. L.) : Collections of many items in New York colonial history.

NEWSPAPERS AND OTHER CONTEMPORARY PERIODICALS

Boston Evening Post, 1735-1775.
Boston Gazette and Country Journal, 1719-1798; originally "Boston Gazette"; it had other names in its long history.
New York Gazette and Weekly Mercury, 1768-1783.
New York Gazette or Weekly Post-Boy, 1747-1773.
New York Journal, 1766-1776.
Pennsylvania Journal or Weekly Advertiser, 1742-1793.
Pennsylvania Packet, 1771-1790; (1773, known as "Dunlap's Pennsylvania Packet" or the General Advertiser).
Hutchin's Improved; Being an Almanack ... for 1775 ... By John N. Hutchin's Philom, New York.
Poor Roger, 1758. The American Country Almanack, for ... 1758 ... by Roger More, Philodespot ... New York.
Rivington's New Almanack ... for 1774 ... by Copernicus Philomath, New York.
Willam Livingston, *The Independent Reflector* (N. Y., 1752-1753).
The American Magazine, Philadelphia, 1769.
The American Magazine and Historical Chronicle, Boston, 1743-1746.
The New American Magazine, Woodbridge, N. J., 1758-1760.
The Pennsylvania Magazine or American Monthly Museum, Philadelphia, 1775-1776.

PRINTED SOURCE MATERIAL

C. M. Andrews, *Guide to the Materials for American History to 1783 in the Public Record Office of Great Britain* (Carnegie Inst. of Washington, 1912-1914).

C. M. Andrews and F. G. Davenport, *Guide to the Manuscript Materials for the History of the United States to 1783, in the British Museum in minor London Archives, and in the libraries of Oxford and Cambridge* (Carnegie Inst. of Washington, Publica. no. 90).

Boston Record Commissioner's Report (Boston, 1881-1901) includes what I have cited as Town Records and Selectmen's Minutes.

Colden Letter Books, 1760-1775 (N. Y. H. S., 1876-1877), vols. 1-2.

Colden Papers (N. Y. H. S., 1917-1923), vols. 1-7. Indispensable for nearly all phases of colonial cultural life.

The Colonial Laws of New York, from the Year 1664 to the Revolution, Including the Acts of the Colonial Legislatures from 1691 to 1775 Inclusive (Albany, 1894), 5 vols.

Documents Relative to the Colonial History of the State of New York (Albany, 1853-1887), vols. 1-15.

Extracts from American newspapers, Relating to New Jersey (Paterson, N. J., 1894-1906), William Nelson, ed., vols. 1-8, ser. 2, vols. 1-3; Documents relating to the colonial history of the state of New Jersey, xi, xii, xix, xxiv, xxv-xxvii, ser. 2, vols. 1-3; cited as New Jersey Archives.

Benjamin Franklin, *Calendar of Papers* (Phila., printed for the American Philosophical Society 1906-08), 6 vols.

Illinois State Historical Library Collections (Springfield, 1903-   ).

Acts and Resolves, Public and Private, of Massachusetts Bay (Boston, 1867-1912), 21 vols.

New Hampshire State Papers Series (Concord, 1867-1915), vols. 1-33.

Pennsylvania Archives (1 ser.), vols. 1-12, 2nd ser., vols. 1-19; 3rd ser., vols. 1-30; 4th ser., vols. 1-12; 5th ser., vols. 1-8; 6th ser., vols. 1-15; 7th ser., vols. 1-5 (Phila., 1852-1856); (Harrisburg, 1874-1914).

Statutes at Large of Pennsylvania from 1682-1809 (Harrisburg, 1896-1911), vols. 2-18).

PUBLICATIONS OF HISTORICAL SOCIETIES AND PERIODICALS IN WHICH SOURCE MATERIAL IS FREQUENTLY INCLUDED

American Antiquarian Society Proceedings (new series, Worcester, 1880-   ).

American Historical Association, Annual Report (Washington, 1889-   ).

American Historical Association, Papers (N. Y., 1885-1891), vols. 1-5.

American Historical Review (N. Y., 1895-   ).

American Jewish Historical Society Publications (Baltimore, 1893-   ).

Colonial Society of Massachusetts, Transactions, 1892-   ; *Collections,* 1907-   .

Connecticut Historical Society Collections (Hartford, 1860-   ), vols. 1-   .

Essex Institute Historical Collections (Salem, 1859-1914), vols. 1-50.

Historical Society of Pennsylvania, Memoirs (Phila., 1826-1895), vols. 1-14.

Journal of Negro History, C. G. Woodson, ed., Jan., 1916-   .

Massachusetts Historical Society Proceedings, vols. I- , 1791-   ;
    Collections, vols. I- , 1792-
New England Historical and Genealogical Register (1847-   ), vols. I- .
New Hampshire Historical Society Collections (Concord, 1824-1915),
    vols. I-II.
New Haven Colony Historical Society Papers (1865-   ).
New Jersey Historical Society Proceedings (1845-   ), vols. I- ; *Col-
    lections* (1847-   ), vols. I- .
New York Genealogical and Biographical Record (1870-   ), vols. I- .
New York Historical Society Collections, vols. I-5, 1809-1830; 2nd ser.,
    vols. I-4, 1811-59; vols. I- , 1868-   .
New York Historical Society, Quarterly Bulletin, vols. I- , April,
    1917- .
New York Public Library Bulletin, Jan., 1897-
New York State Historical Association Proceedings (1901-1919), vols.
    1-17; after 1920, proceedings appear in association's quarterly journal.
Pennsylvania Magazine of History and Biography, vols. I- , 1877-   .
Rhode Island Historical Society Collections, 1827-   .
Southern History Association Publications (Washington, 1897-1907),
    vols. I-II.
Vermont Historical Society Collections (Montpelier, 1870-71), vols. I, 2.

BUSINESS AND BUSINESS MEN; COMMUNICATIONS

PRIMARY SOURCES

Thomas Balch, *Letters and Papers Relating Chiefly to the Provincial
    History of Pennsylvania (Shippen Papers),* (Phila., 1885); im-
    portant for social contacts also.
C. H. McIlwain, ed., *An Abridgement of the Indian Affairs . . . in the
    Colony of New York, from the Year 1678 to the Year 1751 by
    Peter Wraxall (Harvard Hist. Studies,* vol. xxi).
J. A. Stevens, Jr., ed., *Colonial Records of the New York Chamber of
    Commerce 1768-1784* (N. Y., 1867); valuable also for biographies
    of the members.
I. N. P. Stokes, ed., *The Iconography of Manhattan Island* (N. Y.,
    1915-1926), 5 vols. In volume 4 are the extracts from contem-
    porary sources which I used to illustrate all phases of colonial life.

SECONDARY AUTHORITIES

J. T. Adams, *Provincial Society (A History of American Life,* vol.
    iii, A. M. Schlesinger and D. R. Fox, eds., N. Y., 1927); valuable
    for all phases of colonial life except politics.
C. W. Alvord, *The Mississippi Valley in British Politics* (Cleveland,
    1917), 2 vols.

C. M. Andrews, *Colonial Folkways; A Chronicle* (*The Chronicles of America Series,* Allen Johnson, ed., vol. 9, New Haven, 1919).

J. L. Bishop, *A History of American Manufactures from 1608-1860* (Phila., 1866), 3 vols.

A. E. Brown, *John Hancock His Book* (Boston, 1898).

V. S. Clark, *History of Manufactures in the United States 1607-1860* Wash., 1916, Carnegie Inst. of Wash. Publica. 215b).

A. H. Cole, *The American Wool Manufacture* (Cambridge, 1926), 2 vols.

J. R. Commons and associates, *History of Labour in the United States* (N. Y., 1918), 2 vols.

S. A. Drake, *Old Boston Taverns and Tavern Clubs* (Boston, 1917).

A. M. Earle, *Home Life in Colonial Days* (N. Y., 1899).

——, *Stage Coach and Tavern Days* (N. Y., 1899).

M. A. Hanna, *The Trade of the Delaware Before the Revolution* (*Smith College Studies in History,* J. S. Bassett and S. B. Fay, eds., vol. ii, no. 4, Northampton, Mass., 1917).

B. E. Hazard, *The Organization of the Boot and Shoe Industry in Massachusetts Before 1875* (*Harvard Economic Studies,* vol. xxiii, Cambridge, 1921).

The Historical Magazine, and Notes and Queries concerning the Antiquities, History and Biography of America (1857-1875); various places and editors.

Henry A. Homes, *A Notice of Peter Hasenclever* (Albany Institute, 1874).

G. W. W. Houghton, *Coaches in Colonial New York* (N. Y. H. S., 1890).

Edward McCrady, *The History of South Carolina Under the Royal Government 1719-1776* (N. Y., 1899).

J. B. Pearse, *A Concise History of the Iron Manufacture of the American Colonies up to the Revolution, and of Pennsylvania Until the Present Time* (Phila., 1876).

W. E. Rich, *History of the United States Post Office to the Year 1820* (*Harvard Economic Studies,* vol. xxvii, Cambridge, 1924).

A. M. Schlesinger, *The Colonial Merchants and the American Revolution, 1763-1776* (*Col. Studies in Hist., Economics and Public Law*).

William Smith, *The History of the Post Office in British North America 1639-1870* (Cambridge, 1920).

Ralph Straus, *Carriages and Coaches; their History and Their Evolution* (London, 1912).

W. S. Tower, *A History of the American Whale Fishery* (*Publica. of Univ. of Penn., Series in Pol. Economy and Public Law,* no. 20, Phila., 1907).

Albert T. Volwiler, *George Croghan and the Westward Movement 1741-1782* (Cleveland, 1926).

L. H. Weeks, *A History of Paper Manufacturing in the United States 1690-1916* (N. Y., 1916).

M. A. Willard, *Roads of England in the Eighteenth Century* (Columbia Univ. MS. thesis).

Richardson Wright, *Hawkers and Walkers in Early America* (Phila., 1927).

SOCIAL CONTACTS

PRIMARY SOURCES

Thomas Balch, *Willing Letters and Papers* (Phila., 1922).

F. B. Dexter, ed., *The Literary Diary of Ezra Stiles* (N. Y., 1901), 3 vols. I used vol. I, important for many phases of colonial life.

A. B. Hart, ed., *Dr. Alexander Hamilton's Itinerarium 1744* (St. Louis, 1907); a trip through the colonies, amusing, and has valuable information on travel, cultural conditions, etc.

W. J. Mills, ed., William Paterson, *Glimpses of Colonial Society and Life at Princeton* (Phila., 1903); correspondence with fellow students.

The Works of John Woolman (Phila., 1800).

SECONDARY AUTHORITIES

Americana (N. Y., 1906-   ), vols. 1- .

W. R. Bagnall, *The Textile Industries of the United States* (Cambridge, 1893), used for references to philanthropic activities.

W. H. Bailey and O. O. Jones, *History of the Marine Society of Newburyport, Massachusetts* (Newburyport, 1906).

N. S. Barratt and J. F. Sachse, *Freemasonry in Pennsylvania 1727-1907* (Phila., 1907-1909), 2 vols.

W. H. Bayles, *Old Taverns of New York* (N. Y., 1915).

Charitable Irish Society of Boston (Boston, 1876).

J. D. Crimmins, *St. Patrick's Day; Its Celebration in New York and Other American Places, 1732-1845* (N. Y., 1902).

F. B. Culver, *Blooded Horses of Colonial Days; Classic Horse Matches in America Before the Revolution* (Baltimore, 1922).

J. S. Davis, *Essays in the Earlier History of American Corporations* (*Harvard Economic Studies,* vol. xvi, Cambridge, 1917), 2 vols.; used for philanthropic material.

A. M. Earle, *Colonial Days in Old New York* (N. Y., 1896).

R. H. Fox, *Dr. John Fothergill and his Friends: Chapters in Eighteenth Century Life* (London, 1919); for medical relations also, between Europe and America.

Harper's New Monthly Magazine, for articles on old New York.

W. C. Heffner, *History of Poor Relief Legislation in Pennsylvania 1682-1913* (Cleona, Pa., 1913).

C. A. Herrick, *White Servitude in Pennsylvania* (Phila., 1926).

M. M. Johnson, *The Beginnings of Freemasonry in America* (N. Y., 1924).

J. W. Jordan, *Colonial Families of Philadelphia* (N. Y., 1911), 2 vols.

C. P. Keith, *The Provincial Councillors of Pennsylvania ... and Descendants* (Phila., 1883).

W. W. Kemp, *The Support of Schools in Colonial New York by the Society for the Propagation of the Gospel in Foreign Parts* (*Contrib. to Educ., Teachers College, Columbia University*, no. 56, N. Y., 1913).

T. C. Knauff, *A History of the Society of the Sons of St. George ... at Philadelphia* (Phila., 1923).

O. H. Lang, *History of Freemasonry in the State of New York* (N. Y., 1922).

M. S. Locke, *Anti-slavery in America 1619-1808* (*Radcliffe College monographs*, no. 11, Boston, 1901).

The Marine Society of the City of New York, in the State of New York (N. Y., 1925).

G. A. Morrison, *History of Saint Andrew's Society of the State of New York* (N. Y., 1906).

W. B. Norris, *Annapolis; its Colonial and Naval Story* (N. Y., 1925).

G. C. D. Odell, *Annals of the New York Stage* (N. Y., 1927), vols. 1-2; includes all types of entertainments with many original extracts.

W. S. Pelletreau and J. H. Brown, *American Families of Historic Lineage* (N. Y., 1913), 2 vols.

A. F. Ross, *The History of Lotteries in New York* (N. Y., 1906?).

J. F. Sachse, *Benjamin Franklin as a Freemason* (Phila., 1906), original material.

——, *Old Masonic Lodges of Pennsylvania* (Phila., 1912-1913), vols. 1-2.

Theodore Sedgwick, *Memoir of the Life of W. Livingston* (N. Y., 1833).

G. O. Seilhamer, *History of the American Theatre* (Phila., 1888-91), 3 vols. I used vol. 1, which has many extracts from contemporary newspapers.

W. T. Shore, *John Woolman, His Life and Our Times* (London, 1913).

Esther Singleton, *Social New York under the Georges* (N. Y., 1902).

O. G. Sonneck, *Early Concert Life in America* (Leipzig, 1907).

——, *Early Opera in America* (N. Y., 1915).

S. V. Talcott, *Genealogical Notes of New York and New England Families* (Albany, 1883).

Roberts Vaux, *Memoirs of Anthony Benezet* (Phila., 1817).

J. W. Wallace, *A Century of Beneficence, 1769-1869. Historical Sketch of the Corporation for the Relief of the Widows and Children of Clergymen in the Communion of the Protestant Episcopal Church ... in Pennsylvania* (Phila., 1870).

G. K. Ward, *Andrew Warde and his Descendants, 1597-1910* (N. Y., 1910-11).

John Wentworth, *The Wentworth Genealogy, English and American* (Boston, 1878), 3 vols.

RELIGIOUS RELATIONS

PRIMARY SOURCES IN COLLECTIONS AND ELSEWHERE

American Catholic Historical Society Researches, 1884-   .
Bulletin of Friends' Historical Society of Philadelphia, 1906-   , vols. 1-   .
Ecclesiastical Records of the State of New York (Albany, 1901-1916), vols. 1-7.
German-American Annals, vols. 1-4, 1897-1902; vols. 1-17, n. s., 1903-1919.
Moravian Historical Society Transactions (Bethlehem, 1857-1923).
W. S. Perry, *Papers Relating to the History of the (Anglican) Church in Pennsylvania, 1680-1778* (Hartford, 1871).
Presbyterian Historical Society Journal, 1902-   , vols. 1-   .
United States Catholic Historical Magazine (N. Y., 1887-1893), vols. 1-4.

SECONDARY AUTHORITIES

J. T. Adams, *Revolutionary New England, 1691-1776* (Boston, 1923).
N. S. Barratt, *Outline of the History of Old St. Paul's Church, Philadelphia* (Phila., 1917).
E. R. Beadle, *The Old and the New 1743-1876. The Second Presbyterian Church of Philadelphia* (Phila., 1876).
David Benedict, *General History of the Baptist Denomination in America, and Other Parts of the World* (Boston, 1813), 2 vols.
The Bi-centennial Celebration of the Founding of the First Baptist Church of Philadelphia (Phila., 1899).
James Bowden, *History of the Society of Friends in America* (London, 1850-54), 2 vols.
J. M. Buckley, *History of Methodism in the United States* (N. Y., 1897), 2 vols.
A. L. Cross, *The Anglican Episcopate and the American Colonies* (*Harv. Hist. Studies,* vol. ix).
C. P. Daly, *The Settlement of the Jews in North America* (N. Y., 1893).
Morgan Dix, *A History of the Parish of Trinity Church in New York* (N. Y., 1898-1906), 4 vols.
Benjamin Dorr, *An Historical Account of Christ Church, Philadelphia* (N. Y., 1841).
A. B. Faust, *The German Element in the United States* (Boston, 1909), 2 vols.
J. I. Good, *History of the Reformed Church in the United States, 1725-1792* (Reading, Pa., 1899).
Peter Guilday, *The Life and Times of John Carroll, Archbishop of Baltimore, 1735-1815* (N. Y., 1922), 2 vols.

Harvard Studies and Notes, vol. v.

H. A. Hill, *History of the Old South Church (Third Church), Boston, 1669-1884* (Boston, 1890), 2 vols.

H. A. Hill and G. F. Bigelow, *An Historical Catalogue (1669-1882) of the Old South Church (Third Church)* (Boston, 1883).

E. F. Humphrey, *Nationalism and Religion in America, 1774-1789* (Boston, 1924).

C. H. Maxson, *The Great Awakening in the Middle Colonies* (Chicago, 1920).

New England Methodist Historical Society Transactions, Nos. 1, 2 (Boston 1859, 1861).

E. S. Ninde, *The Story of the American Hymn* (N. Y., 1921).

William Parkinson, *Jubilee; a Sermon containing a History of the Origin of the First Baptist Church in the City of New York* (N. Y., 1813).

Princeton Theological Review, vols. 1- , 1903- .

Abraham Ritter, *History of the Moravian Church in Philadelphia* (Phila., 1857).

H. P. Rosenbach, *The Jews in Philadelphia Prior to 1800* (Phila., 1883).

S. E. Seaman, *Annals of New York Methodism* (N. Y., 1892).

J. G. Shea, *Catholic Churches of New York City* (N. Y., 1878).

W. B. Sprague, *Annals of the American Pulpit* (N. Y., 1857-69), vols. 1-6, 8-9.

Abel Stevens, *History of the Religious Movement of the Eighteenth Century called Methodism* (N. Y., 1858-1861), 3 vols.

H. E. Stocker, *A History of the Moravian Church in New York City* (N. Y., 1922).

Joseph Tracy, *The Great Awakening* (Boston, 1842).

J. B. Wakeley, *Lost Chapters Recovered from the Early History of American Methodism* (N. Y., 1858).

N. E. Wood, *The History of the First Baptist Church of Boston (1665-1899)*, (Boston, 1899).

Printers and Printing

primary sources

The Essays, Humor and Poems of Nathaniel Ames, Father and Son, of Dedham, Massachusetts, from their Almanacks, 1726-1775, with Notes and Comments by Sam. Briggs (Cleveland, 1891).

P. L. Ford, *The Journals of Hugh Gaine, Printer* (N. Y., 1902), 2 vols.

H. A. Morrison, *Preliminary Check-list of American Almanacs, 1639-1800* (Wash., 1907).

William Nelson, *Check-list of the Issues of the Press of New Jersey, 1723-1800* (Paterson, 1899).

Oswald Seidensticker, *The First Century of German Printing in America, 1728-1830* (Phila., 1893).

Isaiah Thomas, *The History of Printing in America* (Worcester, 1810), 2 vols; contains in part a contemporary record.

In the publications of various societies are important sources for this chapter; especially publications of the American Antiquarian Society.

SECONDARY AUTHORITIES

J. H. Benton, *John Baskerville, Type-founder and Printer, 1706-1775* (Boston, 1914).

Bibliographical Essays; a Tribute to Wilberforce Eames (Cambridge, 1924).

J. T. Buckingham, *Specimens of Newspaper Literature* (Boston, 1850), 2 vols.

C. F. Dapp, *The Evolution of an American Patriot, John Henry Miller* (Phila., 1924).

Philip Freneau, *The American Village, a Poem,* with introduction by H. L. Koopman, bibliographical data by V. H. Paltsits (Providence, 1906).

R. V. Halsey, *Forgotten Books of the American Nursery* (Boston, 1911).

F. W. Hamilton, "Type and Presses in America" (Chicago, 1918, *Typographical Technical Series for Apprentices,* pt. viii, no. 55).

C. F. Heartman, *Check-list of Printers in the United States to the Close of the War of Independence* (N. Y., 1915, *Heartman's Hist. Series,* no. 9).

C. R. Hildeburn, *Sketches of Printers and Printing in Colonial New York* (N. Y., 1895).

Frederic Hudson, *Journalism in the United States from 1690 to 1872* (N. Y., 1873).

J. M. Lee, *History of American Journalism* (Boston, 1923, rev. edn.).

S. N. D. North, *History and Present Condition of the Newspaper and Periodical Press of the United States* (Wash., 1884 in 10th census, vol. 8).

J. C. Oswald, *Benjamin Franklin, Printer* (N. Y., 1917).

Livingston Rutherford, *John Peter Zenger* (N. Y., 1904).

J. W. Wallace, *Address (on) 200th Birthday of Mr. William Bradford* (Albany, 1863).

——, *An Old Philadelphian, Col. William Bradford, Sketches of his Life* (Phila., 1884).

S. B. Weeks, *The Press of North Carolina in the Eighteenth Century* (Brooklyn, 1891).

L. C. Wroth, *A History of Printing in Colonial Maryland 1686-1776* (Baltimore, 1922).

SCHOOLS AND SCHOOL BOOKS

PRIMARY SOURCES

Catalogue of Officers and Graduates of Yale University, 1701-1924.
P. L. Ford, *The New England Primer. A History of Its Origin and Development* (N. Y., 1897).
Harvard Quinquennial Catalogue (Cambridge, 1925).
C. F. Heartman, *The New England Printer issued Prior to 1830* (N. J., 1922, Heartman's Hist. Series, no. 15).
Matricula of King's College, MS. in Col. Univ. Library.
Princeton University General Catalogue 1746-1906 (Princeton, 1908)
University of Pennsylvania, Matriculates of the College (Phila., 1894).
J. R. Williams, ed., Philip Vickers Fithian, *Journal and Letters, 1767-1774* (Princeton, 1900).

SECONDARY AUTHORITIES

S. D. Alexander, *Princeton College During the Eighteenth Century* (N. Y., 1872).
C. K. Bolton and A. C. Potter, *The Librarians of Harvard College, 1667-1877* (*Harvard Univ. Library Bibliog. Contribs.*, no. 52).
W. C. Bronson, *The History of Brown University, 1764-1914* (Providence, 1914).
V. L. Collins, *President Witherspoon* (Princeton, 1925), 2 vols.
W. H. S. Demarest, *A History of Rutgers College* (New Brunswick, N. J., 1924).
F. B. Dexter, *A Selection from the Miscellaneous Historical Papers of Fifty Years* (New Haven, 1918).
——, *Biographical Sketches of the Graduates of Yale College with Annals of the College History* (N. Y., 1885-1912), vols. 1-6.
G. M. Giger, *History of the Cliosophic Society from 1765 to 1865* (Princeton, 1865).
R. A. Guild, *Early History of Brown University, Including the Life, Times and Correspondence of President Manning* (Providence, 1897).
History of Columbia University, 1754-1904 (N. Y., 1904).
John McLean, *History of the College of New Jersey, 1746-1854* (Phila., 1877), 2 vols.
T. H. Montgomery, *A History of the University of Pennsylvania to 1770* (Phila., 1900).
D. J. Pratt, *Annals of Public Education in the State of New York from 1626 to 1746* (Albany, 1872).
Josiah Quincy, *History of Harvard University* (Boston, 1840), 2 vols.
R. F. Seybolt, *Source Studies in American Colonial Education; the Evening School in Colonial America* (*Univ. of Illinois, Bureau of Ed. Research, Bulletin, 24*).

——, *The Private School* (*Univ. of Illinois, Bureau of Ed. Research, Bulletin, 28*).

R. F. Seybolt, " The Evening School in Colonial N. Y. City " (*Fifteenth Annual Rep. of the Education Dep't., University of the State of New York, 1917-1918*).

H. W. Smith, *Life and Correspondence of the Rev. William Smith* (Phila., 1879), 2 vols.

L. F. Snow, *The College Curriculum in the United States* (N. Y., 1907, *Columbia Univ. Contribs. to Educa., Teachers College Series, no. 10*).

M. C. Tyler, *A History of American Literature* (N. Y., 1895, Agawam ed., 2 vols. in 1).

S. E. Weber, *The Charity School Movement in Colonial Pennsylvania* (Phila., 190?).

J. P. Wickersham, *History of Education in Pennsylvania* (Lancaster, 1886).

William and Mary College Historical Quarterly, 1892, vols. 1-27; 2nd ser., 1- .

D. W. Woods, *John Witherspoon* (N. Y., 1906).

Thomas Woody, *Early Quaker Education in Pennsylvania* (N. Y., 1920, *Teachers College Contribs. to Educa., no. 105*).

ARTS AND ARTISTS

PRIMARY SOURCES

W. L. Andrews, *Fragments of American History Illustrated solely by the Works of Engravers in the XVIIIth Century* (N. Y., 1898).

Maurice Brix, *List of Philadelphia Silversmiths and Allied Artificers, from 1682 to 1852* (Phila., 1852).

G. F. Dow, *The Arts & Crafts in New England, 1704-1775, gleanings from Boston Newspapers* (Topsfield, 1927).

William Kelby, *Notes on American Artists, 1754-1820, Copied from Advertisements appearing in the Newspapers of the Day* (N. Y., 1922).

Letters and Papers of John Singleton Copley and Henry Pelham, 1739-1776 (Boston, 1914, *Mass. Hist. Soc. Coll.*, vol. 71).

James Lyon, *Urania* (Phila., 1761).

F. J. Metcalf, comp., *American Psalmody; or Titles of Books, Containing Tunes Printed in America from 1721-1820* (N. Y., 1917, *Heartman's Hist. Series, no. 27*).

James Warrington, *Short Titles of Books Relating to, or Illustrating the History and the Practise of Psalmody in the United States, 1620-1820* (Phila., 1898).

SECONDARY AUTHORITIES

C. D. Allen, *A Classified List of Early American Book-plates and a Note as to the Prominent Engravers* (N. Y., 1894).

C. L. Avery, *American Silver of the XVII and XVIIII Centuries* (N. Y., 1920).

F. W. Bayley, *The Life and Works of John Singleton Copley* (Boston, 1915).

F. W. Bayley and C. E. Goodspeed, eds., *William Dunlap; a History of the Rise and Progress of the Arts of Design in the United States* (Boston, 1918), 3 vols.

E. S. Bolton, *Wax Portraits and Silhouettes* (Boston, 1914).

Theodore Bolton, *Early American Portrait Draughtsmen in Crayons* (N. Y., 1923).

Frank Cousins and P. M. Riley, *The Colonial Architecture of Philadelphia* (Boston, 1920).

R. R. Drummond, *Early German Music in Philadelphia* (N. Y., 1910, *Americana Germanica*, n. s., vol. 9).

W. A. Dyer, *Early American Craftsmen* (N. Y., 1915).

J. J. Foster, *Miniature Painters, British and Foreign with Some Account of Those who Practised in America in the Eighteenth Century* (N. Y., 1903), 2 vols.

C. F. Gettemy, *The True Story of Paul Revere* (Boston, 1905).

F. W. P. Greenwood, *A History of King's Chapel in Boston* (Boston, 1833) ; for architectural references.

G. E. Hastings, *The Life and Works of Francis Hopkinson* (Chicago, 1926).

George Hood, *A History of Music in New England with Biographical Sketches of Reformers and Psalmists* (Boston, 1846).

F. W. Hunter, *Stiegel Glass* (Boston, 1914).

Fiske Kimball, *Domestic Architecture of the American Colonies and of the Early Republic* (N. Y., 1922).

Fiske Kimball, *Thomas Jefferson Architect* (Boston, 1916).

The Massachusetts Magazine, devoted to Massachusetts history, genealogy, biography (Salem, 1908-1918), vols. I-II.

L. G. Myers, *Some Notes on American Pewterers* (N. Y., 1926).

W. C. Poland, *Robert Feke* (Providence, 1907).

J. T. Scharf and Thompson Westcott, *History of Philadelphia* (Phila., 1884), 3 vols.

O. G. Sonneck, *Francis Hopkinson and James Lyon* (Wash., 1905).

——, *Suum Cuique; Essays in Music* (N. Y., 1916).

John Spargo, *Early American Pottery and China* (N. Y., 1926).

D. M. Stauffer, *American Engravers upon Copper and Steel* (N. Y., 1907), 2 vols.

W. R. Ware, ed., *The Georgian Period; being Photographs and Measured Drawings of Colonial Work with Text* (N. Y., 1923), 6 vols.; text in vol. 1.

A. H. Wharton, *Heirlooms in Miniatures* (Phila., 1898).

PHYSIC AND PHYSICIANS

PRIMARY SOURCES

Samuel Bard, *An Inquiry into the Nature, Cause and Cure of the Angina Suffocativa* (N. Y., 1771).

The Medical Register of New York, New Jersey and Connecticut (N. Y., 1862-1895), vols. 1-32; for items on N. Y. medicine, taken from newspapers.

Peter Middleton, *A Medical Discourse or an Historical Inquiry ... delivered at Opening the Medical School in ... New York* (N. Y., 1769).

John Morgan, *A Discourse upon the Institution of Medical Schools in America* (Phila., 1765).

Benjamin Rush, *Medical Inquiries and Observations* (Phila., 1809, 3rd ed.), 4 vols.

SECONDARY AUTHORITIES

American Irish Historical Society Journal, vol. for 1916.

American Medical and Philosophical Register (N. Y., 1811-1814), vols. 1-4.

Annals of Medical History, vols. 1- , 1917- .

S. F. Batchelder, *Bits of Harvard History* (Cambridge, 1924).

J. B. Beck, *An Historical Sketch of the State of Medicine in the American Colonies* (Albany, 1850).

Bulletin of New York Academy of Medicine, ser. 2, vols. 1- , March, 1924- .

Joseph Carson, *A History of the Medical Department of the University of Pennsylvania from its Foundation in 1765* (Phila., 1869).

S. A. Green, *History of Medicine in Massachusetts* (Boston, 1881).

T. F. Harrington, *The Harvard Medical School 1782-1905* (N. Y., 1905), 3 vols.

F. P. Henry, ed., *Standard History of the Medical Profession in Philadelphia* (Chicago, 1897).

A. C. Jacobson, *The Medical Times*, May, 1916 (a reprint).

T. G. Morton and F. Woodbury, *The History of the Pennsylvania Hospital 1751-1895* (Phila., 1895).

G. W. Norris, *The Early History of Medicine in Philadelphia* (Phila., 1886).

F. R. Packard, *The History of Medicine in the United States* (Phila., 1901).

William Pepper, *The Medical Side of Benjamin Franklin* (Phila., 1911) ; contains mainly original material.

Gurdon W. Russell, *Early Medicine, and Early Medical Men in Connecticut* (*Proc. of Conn. Med. Soc.*, New Haven, 1892).

The Society of the New York Hospital (N. Y., 1921).

James Thacher, *American Medical Biography* (Boston, 1828), 2 vols.

J. M. Toner, *Contributions to the Annals of Medical Progress and Medical Education in the United States Before and During the War of Independence* (Wash., 1874).

Stephen Wickes, *History of Medicine in New Jersey and its Medical Men from the Settlement of the Province to 1800* (Newark, 1879).

SCIENCE AND CURIOSITY

PRIMARY SOURCES

American Philosophical Society Proceedings, vol. 1- , 1838- ; a volume covering proceedings 1744-1838 is bound with vol. 22.

B. Franklin, *Experiments and Observations on Electricity made at Philadelphia, added Letters and Papers on Philosophical Subjects* (London, 1769).

Asa Gray, *Selections from the Scientific Correspondence of Cadwallader Colden with Gronovius, Linnaeus, Collinson and Other Naturalists* (New Haven, 1843).

Transactions of the American Philosophical Society held at Philadelphia for Promoting Useful Knowledge, vol. 1, 1769-1771 ; vol. 2, 1786.

Colden Papers and Franklin, *Calendar of Papers*, are invaluable for this section.

SECONDARY AUTHORITIES

American Library Association Bulletin, vol. 1- , 1907- .

P. W. Bidwell and J. I. Falconer, *History of Agriculture in the Northern United States 1620-1860* (Carnegie Inst. of Wash., 1925).

H. T. Buckle, *The History of Civilization in England* (London, 1882 ed.), 3 vols.

Lyman Carrier, *The Beginnings of Agriculture in America* (N. Y., 1923).

H. W. Ducachet, *A Biographical Memoir of Samuel Bard* (Phila., 1821).

Samuel Miller, *A Brief Retrospect of the Eighteenth Century* (N. Y., 1803), 2 vols.

Simon Newcomb, *Discussions of Observations of the Transits of Venus in 1761 and 1765* (Wash., 1891, U. S. nautical almanac office, astronomical papers, vol. 2).

Pennsylvania University, *University Lectures Delivered by Members of the Faculty in the Free Public Lecture Course* (*1913-1921*).

H. N. Stevens, *Lewis Evans; His Map of the Middle British Colonies in America* (London, 1920, 2nd ed.).

*Two Lectures on Comets, also an Essay on Comets by A. Oliver, Jun.,
Esq., with Sketches of the Lives of Professor Winthrop and Mr.
Oliver* (Boston, 1811).

THE SECULARIZATION OF AMERICAN LIFE

PRIMARY SOURCES

F. B. Dexter, *Documentary History of Yale University* (New Haven,
1916).

——, ed., *Extracts from the Itineraries and Correspondence of Ezra
Stiles* (New Haven, 1916) ; generally useful.

Charles Evans, *American Bibliography* (Chicago, 1903-25), vols. 1-9;
useful for all phases of colonial culture.

Samuel Johnson, *Elementa Philosophica; Containing Chiefly Noetica, or
Things Relating to the Mind or Understanding; and Ethica, or
Things Relating to the Moral Behaviour* (Phila., 1752).

*Rhode Island Imprints; a List of Books, Pamphlets, Newspapers and
Broadsides Printed at Newport, Providence, Warren, Rhode Island,
between 1727-1800* (Providence, 1914).

Oscar Wegelin, comp., *Early American Plays, 1714-1830* (N. Y., 1905,
2nd ed.).

SECONDARY AUTHORITIES

G. M. Abbott, *A Short History of the Library Company of Philadelphia*
(Phila , 1913).

C. F. Adams, *Massachusetts, Its Historians and Its History* (Boston,
1893).

E. C. Cook, *Literary Influences in Colonial Newspapers 1704-1750* (N. Y.,
1912, *Columbia Univ., Studies in English and Comparative Literature*).

Columbia University Quarterly (1898-1919), vols. 1-21.

Dartmouth Alumni Magazine, vols. 1- , 1908- .

W. A. Duer, *The Life of William Alexander, Earl of Stirling* (N. Y.,
1847).

S. A. Eliot, *A Sketch of the History of Harvard College and of Its
Present State* (Boston, 1848).

A. B. Keep, *History of the New York Society Library* (N. Y., 1908).

The Library; a Quarterly Review of Bibliography and Library Lore,
Jan., 1889- , in several series.

E. P. Oberholtzer, *The Literary History of Philadelphia* (Phila., 1906).

V. L. Parrington, *Main Currents in American Thought* (N. Y., 1927),
2 vols.

Benjamin Pierce, *A History of Harvard University from its Foundation, in the Year 1636 to the Period of the American Revolution*
(Cambridge, 1833).

A. C. Potter, *The Library of Harvard University; Descriptive and Historical Notes* (*Harvard Univ. Library, Bibliog. Contrib.*, no. 55).

I. W. Riley, *American Philosophy. The Early Schools* (N. Y., 1907).

A. H. Smyth, *Philadelphia Magazines and Their Contributors, 1741-1850* (Phila., 1892).

Justin Winsor, ed., *The Memorial History of Boston* (Boston, 1880-81), 4 vols.

Yale Review, 1892-1911, vols. 1-19; n. s., vols. 1-   , 1911-

A NEW NATION IN EMBRYO

PRIMARY SOURCES

C. F. Adams, *The Works of John Adams* (Boston, 1850-56), 10 vols.

Copy of Moot Cases (N. Y. H. S.).

C. H. Firth, ed., *An American Garland; Being a Collection of Ballads Relating to America 1563-1759* (Oxford, 1915).

H. P. Johnston, ed., *The Correspondence and Public Papers of John Jay, First Chief-Justice of the United States* (N. Y., 1890-93), 4 vols.

C. H. Lincoln, ed., *The Correspondence of William Shirley* (N. Y., 1912), 2 vols.

Josiah Quincy, *Memoir of the Life of Josiah Quincy, Jun. of Massachusetts* (Boston, 1874) ; for journal and political correspondence.

A. H. Smyth, *The Writings of Benjamin Franklin* (N. Y., 1905-07), vols. 1-10.

SECONDARY AUTHORITIES

S. G. Arnold, *History of the State of Rhode Island and Providence Plantations* (N. Y., 1859-1860), 2 vols.

S. A. Ashe, *History of North Carolina* (Greensboro, N. C., 1908-25), 2 vols.

C. L. Becker, *The History of Political Parties in the Province of New York 1760-1776* (Bul. of Univ. of Wisconsin, Hist. Series vol. 2, no. 1).

F. M. Eastman, *Courts and Lawyers of Pennsylvania, a History 1623-1923* (N. Y., 1922), 3 vols.

Richard Frothingham, *The Rise of the Republic of the United States* (Boston, 1872).

L. H. Gipson, *Jared Ingersoll; a Study of American Loyalism in Relation to British Colonial Government* (New Haven, 1920, *Yale Hist. Pub., Miscellany* viii).

E. A. Jones, *American Members of the Inns of Court* (London, 1924).

E. Q. Keasbey, *The Courts and Lawyers of New Jersey 1661-1912* (N. Y., 1912), 3 vols.

B. A. Konkle, *George Bryan and the Constitution of Pennsylvania 1731-1791* (Phila., 1922).

G. P. Krapp, *The English Language in America* (N. Y., 1925), 2 vols.

J. H. Martin, *Martin's Bench and Bar of Philadelphia* (Phila., 1883).

John Sanderson, *Biography of the Signers to the Declaration of Independence* (Phila., 1823-27), vols. 1-9.

J. T. Scharf, *History of Delaware* (Phila., 1888), 2 vols.

C. J. Stillé, *The Life and Times of John Dickinson 1732-1808* (Phila., 1891).

M. C. Tyler, *The Literary History of the American Revolution 1763-1783* (N. Y., 1897, student's edn., 2 vols. in 1).

Wilkins Updike, *Memoirs of the Rhode Island Bar* (Boston, 1842).

Charles Warren, *A History of the American Bar* (Boston, 1911).

Emory Washburn, *Judicial History of Massachusetts, 1630-1775* (Boston, 1840).

INDEX

245